A Companion to Ricoeur's *Fallible Man*

Studies in the Thought of Paul Ricoeur

Series Editors:
Greg S. Johnson, Pacific Lutheran University/Oxford University (ELAC), and Dan R. Stiver, Hardin-Simmons University

Studies in the Thought of Paul Ricoeur, a series in conjunction with the *Society for Ricoeur Studies*, aims to generate research on Ricoeur, about whom interest is rapidly growing both nationally (United States and Canada) and internationally. Broadly construed, the series has three interrelated themes. First, we develop the historical connections to and in Ricoeur's thought. Second, we extend Ricoeur's dialogue with contemporary thinkers representing a variety of disciplines. Third, we utilize Ricoeur to address future prospects in philosophy and other fields that respond to emerging issues of importance. The series approaches these themes from the belief that Ricoeur's thought is not just suited to theoretical exchanges, but can and does matter for how we actually engage in the many dimensions that constitute lived existence.

Recent Titles in the Series
A Companion to Ricoeur's Fallible Man, Edited by Scott Davidson

Ricoeur's Hermeneutics of Religion: Rebirth of the Capable Self, by Brian Gregor

Ideology and Utopia in the Twenty-first Century: The Surplus of Meaning in Ricoeur's Dialectical Concept, Edited by Stephanie Arel and Dan R. Stiver

Ricoeur and the Third Discourse of the Person: From Philosophy and Neuroscience to Psychiatry and Theology, by Michael T. H. Wong

A Companion to Ricoeur's Freedom and Nature, Edited by Scott Davidson

Paul Ricoeur's Moral Anthropology: Singularity, Responsibility, and Justice, by Geoffrey Dierckxsens

Ricoeur's Personalist Republicanism: Personhood and Citizenship, by Dries Deweer

Paul Ricoeur's Hermeneutics and the Discourse of Mark 13: Appropriating the Apocalyptic, by Peter C. de Vries

Ricoeur, Culture, and Recognition: A Hermeneutic of Cultural Subjectivity, by Timo Helenius

Feminist Explorations of Paul Ricoeur's Philosophy, Edited by Annemie Halsema and Fernanda Henriques

Paul Ricoeur in the Age of Hermeneutical Reason: Poetics, Praxis, and Critique, Edited by Roger W. H. Savage

In Response to the Religious Other: Ricoeur and the Fragility of Interreligious Encounters, by Marianne Moyaert

Imagination and Postmodernity, by Patrick L. Bourgeois

A Companion to Ricoeur's *Fallible Man*

Edited by
Scott Davidson

LEXINGTON BOOKS
Lanham • Boulder • New York • London

Published by Lexington Books
An imprint of The Rowman & Littlefield Publishing Group, Inc.
4501 Forbes Boulevard, Suite 200, Lanham, Maryland 20706
www.rowman.com

6 Tinworth Street, London SE11 5AL, United Kingdom

Copyright © 2019 The Rowman & Littlefield Publishing Group, Inc.

Excerpts from Ricoeur, Paul, *Fallible Man*. Trans. Charles A. Kelbley. New York: Fordham University Press. 1986. Reprinted in English with permission.

Excerpts from Ricoeur, Paul, *Freedom and Nature*. Trans. Erazhim V. Kohak. Evanston: Northwestern University Press. 1966. Reprinted in English with permission.

All rights reserved. No part of this book may be reproduced in any form or by any electronic or mechanical means, including information storage and retrieval systems, without written permission from the publisher, except by a reviewer who may quote passages in a review.

British Library Cataloguing in Publication Information Available

Library of Congress Cataloging-in-Publication Data Available

ISBN: 978-1-4985-8711-2 (cloth)
ISBN: 978-1-4985-8713-6 (pbk)
ISBN: 978-1-4985-8712-9 (electronic)

Contents

Acknowledgments   vii

Introduction: The Kantian Architecture of Ricoeur's *Fallible Man*   ix
Scott Davidson

PART I: HISTORICAL INFLUENCES   1

1   Imagination and Religion: The Myth of Innocence in *Fallible Man*   3
    Daniel Frey

2   Karl Jaspers: The Clarification of Existence   19
    Jérôme Porée

3   Reflection, the Body, and Fallibility:
    The Mysterious Influence of Marcel in Ricoeur's *Fallible Man*   43
    Brian Gregor

4   The Limitation of the Ethical Vision of the World:
    The Influence of Jean Nabert   65
    Scott Davidson

PART II: THEMATIC AVENUES   83

5   The Imagination: From Ideation to Innocence   85
    Luz Ascárate

6   "Making Sense of (Moral) Things": *Fallible Man* in Relation
    to Enactivism   101
    Geoffrey Dierckxsens

7 The Self Is Embodied and Discursive: Tracing the
   Phenomenological Background of Ricoeur's Narrative Identity   125
   Annemie Halsema

8 From Fallibility to Fragility: How the Theory of Narrative
   Transformed the Notion of Character of *Fallible Man*   145
   Pol Vandevelde

9 The Quest of Recognizing One's Self   163
   Timo Helenius

10 Finitude, Culpability, and Suffering: The Question of Evil
   in Ricoeur   179
   Jean-Luc Amalric

Index   201

About the Contributors   209

Acknowledgments

I would like to thank Oklahoma City University for granting me a research sabbatical leave in the fall of 2018 to work on this volume. I have also benefited from the input of the students enrolled in my philosophy seminar class as I worked to develop an accessible overview of *Fallible Man*. I also thank Robert Wood at the University of Dallas for sharing his own very detailed diagram of *Fallible Man* which inspired me to develop the simplified diagram presented in the Introduction. Finally, I want to thank all of my new colleagues in the Philosophy Department at West Virginia University for their support and feedback on an earlier draft of the introduction to this book.

Introduction

The Kantian Architecture of Ricoeur's Fallible Man

Scott Davidson

Ricoeur's philosophy of the will is undoubtedly the crowning achievement of his early career, and in spite of new developments in his thinking, it continues to exert an influence through the rest of his intellectual itinerary. In 1950, Ricoeur published the first installment of his trilogy on the will, *Freedom and Nature*. The book's central thesis concerns the reciprocity between the voluntary and the involuntary. In addition to demonstrating this thesis, Ricoeur situated the book's contribution within a much broader vision of the philosophy of the will. The eidetics of the will developed in *Freedom and Nature* was announced as the first step in a project that would then move to an empirics of the bad will and culminate with a poetics of the will. As an eidetic of the will, the analyses of *Freedom and Nature* were carried under the methodological constraints of Husserl's eidetic method, which is to say that they bracketed all normative questions concerning the will and simply provided a value-neutral description of its essential features. Operating within these brackets, it is possible to describe the full range of human potential as "the undifferentiated keyboard upon which the guilty as well as the innocent man might play" (Ricoeur 1986: xli). But in order to bring normative considerations into play and to enter into the empirical realm of the will, Ricoeur observes that it is necessary to lift these brackets. This allows for an encounter with "the opaque and absurd" notion of the fault which only "remains a foreign body in the eidetics of man" (Ricoeur 1986: xlii).

Over the decade that separates *Freedom and Nature* from the proposed "empirics of the will," the project that Ricoeur initially envisioned underwent a major shift: the proposed "empirics of the will" resulted in two books rather than one. The second volume of his philosophy of the will—published in 1960 as *Finitude and Guilt*—included both *Fallible Man* and *Symbolism of Evil*. This change of plan reflects a significant evolution in Ricoeur's thinking concerning the topic of "the fault," whereby he comes to believe that a two-sided approach, which he calls a "concrete mythics," is necessary (Ricoeur 1986: xlii). This dual approach accounts for the division of labor between the two books that comprise *Finitude and Guilt.* While the task of *The Symbolism of Evil* is to approach the question of the fault from the perspective of the *actuality* of how evil is described in myths and symbols, the task of *Fallible Man* is to approach the fault from the perspective of the question of what makes it a *possibility.* Ricoeur explains:

> Just as the symbolics of evil represented an enlargement of the mythics proposed by *Freedom and Nature*, the theory of fallibility represents a broadening of the anthropological perspective of the first work, which was more closely centered on the structure of the will. . . . The duality of the voluntary and the involuntary is brought back into a much vaster dialectic dominated by the ideas of disproportion, the polarity within him of the finite and the infinite, and his activity of intermediation or mediation. Man's specific weakness and his essential fallibility are ultimately sought within this structure of mediation between the pole of his finitude and the pole of his infinitude. (Ricoeur 1986: xliv)

Setting aside the symbolics of evil for consideration in another context (see Davidson 2020), the above passage provides a helpful elucidation of the relation between *Freedom and Nature* and *Fallible Man.* The latter work extends the earlier dialectic between the voluntary and involuntary will and inscribes it within an even broader dialectic between the finite and the infinite. It is in the disproportion between these two poles that Ricoeur will locate the source of human fallibility. The source of error, in short, is to be found in our unsuccessful but necessary attempts to bridge the finite and the infinite. Insofar as *Fallible Man* seeks to establish the conditions of the possibility for human error, it bears a close resemblance to Kant's philosophy. Indeed, Ricoeur himself describes *Fallible Man* as his most Kantian book, and I suggest that this resemblance pertains not only to its style but also to the substance of Ricoeur's argument.

In his *Lectures on Logic*, Kant famously identifies the field of philosophy with the following four questions: 1. What can I know? 2. What should I do? 3. What may I hope? 4. What is man? According to Kant, metaphysics is the field that answers the first question, morality the second, and religion the third. Kant further suggests that these first three questions can be placed under the general heading of anthropology, insofar as together they contribute an answer to the fourth question, the anthropological question, What is man? (Kant 1992: 538 [25]). These four philosophical questions, I will show, provide valuable insight into the structure of *Fallible Man.* Kant's first three questions correspond with each of the three central chapters of *Fallible*

Man, and when considered together, they shed light on Ricoeur's answer to the anthropological question concerning the nature of the human being. The working hypothesis of *Fallible Man* is that to be human is to undergo an experience of disproportion in relation to oneself (Ricoeur 1986: 1), and this experience is articulated on three different registers in the three central chapters of *Fallible Man*.

Chapter 2, Transcendental Synthesis, responds to the question, "What can I know?" The structure of this chapter is modeled on Kant's account of knowledge in the *Critique of Pure Reason*. In the briefest terms, Kant's first critique famously asserts that "thoughts without intuitions are empty; intuitions without concepts are blind" (B75). This entails that our empirical judgments about the world must be formed through a synthesis that draws from two different sources: intuitions and concepts. So, in order to arrive at an empirical judgment, the sense data that we initially receive passively must be structured in such a manner that they can be brought into alignment with our concepts. Kant locates this power in the "imagination," whose role is to take up what is given and to organize it in terms of a schema. By making intuitions apprehensible for our concepts, this schematism provided by the imagination then allows us to make empirical judgments that determine or constitute the objects of our experience. For example, the sense experience of what is given simply as a "this" comes to be conceptually determined as an object, for instance, as a "desk."

Following this model, Ricoeur elaborates the Kantian distinction between intuitions and concepts in terms of a contrast between the finitude of perspective and the infinitude of the word (*verbe*). On the one hand, perceptual experience is always perspectival. I always see an object from a particular point of view, and in this respect, my point of view signifies a limitation of my experience to one particular perspective in space and time. But, at the same time, Ricoeur insists that perspective is not simply negative; my embodied point of view is also an opening onto the world. The finitude of perspective could thus be described as a narrow opening. On the other hand, in reference to the objects of my perception, my experience always points beyond my own finite perspective. The meaning of objects is not determined solely by my own perceptual point of view; it includes the other possible points of view toward it. This unity of all possible perspectives is what my words signify when I refer to the object. What, then, mediates between the finitude of seeing and the infinitude of saying? Borrowing from Kant, Ricoeur asserts that this mediation is accomplished by the work of the pure imagination. The imagination unifies my finite, actual perspective toward an object with the infinite number of potential perspectives toward it. Through this synthesis, I am able to constitute the meaning of the object.

Yet, along with this accomplishment, the transcendental synthesis reveals its own limitations. Echoing a common charge leveled against Kant's theory of knowledge, Ricoeur asserts that "this synthesis is consciousness but not self-consciousness" (Ricoeur 1986: 45). In other words, the theoretical synthesis provides knowledge of objects, and it may even allow us to know the self as an object. But it does not yet provide an account of self-consciousness which would establish the self in its relation to itself. This surplus of meaning, which exceeds the bounds of the transcendental synthesis, will be pursued in the transition that leads from the theoretical to the practical domain.

Chapter 3, Practical Synthesis, provides an answer to Kant's second question, "What should I do?" Here, as Ricoeur explains, the formal structure of the theoretical synthesis is extended to the practical domain of human action:

> All the aspects of "practical" finitude that can be understood on the basis of the transcendental notion of perspective may be summed up in the notion of character. All the aspects of "practical" infinitude that can be understood on the basis of the transcendental notion of meaning may be summed up in the notion of happiness. The "practical" mediation that extends the mediation of the transcendental imagination, projected into the object, is the constitution of the person by means of "respect." (Ricoeur 1986: 50)

Accordingly, the three stages in the analysis of the practical synthesis will be character, happiness, and respect for persons.[1] In the first two stages of the practical synthesis, Ricoeur establishes an original disproportion between the finitude of character and the infinitude of happiness. On the one hand, Ricoeur's analysis of character follows the pattern of the "narrow openness" of perceptual perspective that was glimpsed on the theoretical level but is now extended to the context of human action. Accordingly, the finitude of character signifies "the limited openness of our field of motivation taken as a whole" (Ricoeur 1986: 60); my character signifies a zero point, a particular orientation, from which I am able to carry out actions in the world. But just as the finite perspective of perception points beyond itself toward an ideal meaning, so too my particular motives and actions point beyond themselves toward happiness as an ideal that exceeds them. Ricoeur follows Aristotle in observing that the happiness of a whole life is not itself a finite end that can be achieved, instead the infinitude of happiness signifies that it remains an ideal or a horizon that we can pursue but not complete. The question then becomes, can there be a synthesis of these two extremes?

The practical synthesis is accomplished through the mediation of the concept of the person, or more precisely, of the person's humanity. The key idea here is that a person is at once a finite being who offers a unique perspective on the world and a human being who shares humanity with all other beings.

Just as the pure imagination mediates between understanding and sensibility on the theoretical plane, Ricoeur looks to the moral feeling of respect as a way to synthesize the singularity of the person with the universal humanity of the person. Of course, it is common knowledge that respect occupies an entirely unique position in Kant's ethics. Respect is the only feeling that is not pathological; for Kant, it is the only moral feeling, precisely because it does not result from desire but from reason's discovery of the moral law. Just as respect provides a middle term between the realm of intelligibility and the realm of sensibility in Kant's ethics, Ricoeur utilizes it in much the same way to carry out the practical synthesis of the person. The proper role of respect for persons, accordingly, would be to provide a schema that combines the finitude of my character as a unique individual with the infinitude of the good life for human beings in general. In so doing, it would place some boundaries on an individual's actual life plans but also concretize the ideal of the good life in such a way that it personalizes the vision of the good life. This practical synthesis ultimately answers to a rational demand for totality or completeness of the practical self. However, Ricoeur concludes the chapter by arguing that the practical synthesis still provides only an abstract form of self-consciousness—an idealized relation to oneself. It does not yet establish a concrete or personal self-relation, and this limitation is what motivates the transition from the practical to the affective domain in the subsequent chapter.

Chapter 4, Affective Fragility, provides an indirect answer to Kant's third question, "What may I hope?" To be clear, it does not yet delve into the topic of hope to the same extent as Ricoeur's later work, instead its task is more preparatory in nature. It seeks to carry the mythic accounts of the feeling of disproportion, which are the topic of the first chapter, up to the level of reason. Engaging with traditional treatises on the passions, a major focus of Ricoeur's philosophy of feeling is to show that the passions are not negative by definition. To be sure, we often encounter the passions in their "fallen" condition as vices, but it is also possible to trace them back to a more primordial, innocent state where they are the expression of fundamental "quests of the heart" that orient the aspirations of all human beings. Drawing from Kant's anthropology of the passions, Ricoeur identifies three of these basic quests [*Suchen*]: the passion to possess [*Habsucht*] which manifests itself objectively in economic life, the pursuit of power [*Herrsucht*] which characterizes political life, and the search for esteem [*Ehrsucht*] which manifests itself in the social realm. Each of these passions has a legitimate role in giving value to a human life, but each is also capable of falling into misuse, as expressed in the vices of greed, tyranny, and vanity.

The transition from the practical to the affective domain involves a shift of focus from the realm of actions to the human strivings from which they arise. Accordingly, the finitude of character now becomes the finitude of vital desire (*epithumia*), while the infinitude of happiness as an ideal becomes the infinitude of the spiritual or intellectual aspiration (*eros*) (Ricoeur 1986: 92).[2] Vital desires terminate in pleasure or the cessation of pain, whereas spiritual love aspires more broadly toward happiness. As a result, the self can find itself under the sway of two different affective projects: "the organic life that reaches its term in the instantaneous perfection of pleasure and that of the spiritual life that aspires to totality, to the perfection of happiness" (Ricoeur 1986: 132). Again, the question becomes whether there might exist some kind of third term which allows these two affective poles to be mediated, and here Ricoeur draws from Plato's notion of the heart (*thumos*), which falls under the sway of both reason and desire.

The struggle of the heart can be dramatized by posing the following questions concerning the passions, "When will I have enough? When will my authority be sufficiently established? When will I be sufficiently appreciated? Where do we find in all this that "enough," that 'sufficiently'?" (Ricoeur 1978: 33). In wrestling with questions such as these, the heart attempts to mediate between the competing demands of the vital and the spiritual desires; it seeks to integrate them into human aspirations and to embody these aspirations in institutions. But such mediations are always precarious and easily undone by either side. Just as the heart can fall prey to the pull of instinct, likewise Ricoeur observes that this mediation can be undone from the side of the great passions of spiritual desire: "only a being who wants the all and who schematizes it in the objects of human desire is able to make a mistake, that is, to take his object for the absolute, to forget the symbolic character of the bond between happiness and an object of desire: forgetting this makes the symbol an idol; the impassioned life becomes a passionate existence" (Ricoeur 1986: 131). This is why the work of mediation is most fragile within the affective realm of the heart. The heart is fundamentally conflicted; it is not only torn by conflicting desires but also challenges the work of mediation through its own restlessness. From the vantage point of affective life, the self is conflicted (Ricoeur 1986: 132). The result of a philosophy of feeling, accordingly, is not a higher synthesis but an unresolved conflict within oneself. And this means that if the hope for reconciliation is achievable, it always remains fragile.

Together, the three central chapters of *Fallible Man* point the way toward Ricoeur's answer to Kant's fourth question, "What is man?" Indeed, in his 1995 "Intellectual Autobiography," Ricoeur describes *Fallible Man* precisely as the development of an ontology of human finitude. Although this ontology is developed explicitly in dialogue with Kant, it also provides an indirect response to Heidegger, and more precisely, to Heidegger's reading of Kant. In *Kant and the Main Problem of Metaphysics*, Heidegger also examines Kant's four questions, but he reverses their direction. Whereas the first three questions flow into the fourth for Kant, Heidegger reads the fourth question as the truly fundamental one, such that an answer to it will reveal the answers to the first three questions. According to Heidegger, the being of the human being is defined in terms of its temporality, and so it is human temporality, or finitude, which prepares an answer to the other three questions.

But Heidegger's mistake, according to Ricoeur's view, consists of taking the short route to the meaning of human being, as exemplified by his direct answer to the fourth question without proceeding through the other three. We have seen that the chapters of *Fallible Man*, by contrast, follow a more circuitous path that proceeds through the first three questions in order to prepare the way for an answer to the fourth. Yet, *Fallible Man* does not only differ with Heidegger in terms of its methodology. Ricoeur casts doubt on whether a philosophical anthropology should be centered on the concept of finitude, instead we have seen that he develops this through the triad finitude–infinitude–mediation (cf. Ricoeur 1978: 21). Ricoeur offers an ontology of disproportion according to which a human being is defined precisely by the disproportion of the finite and the infinite. This disproportion can be understood in terms of the notion of the fault which Ricoeur borrows from Jean Nabert. This concept should be taken in a couple of senses. In its geological sense, the word "fault" refers to a "fissure" or a "break" that divides something in two. In this sense, it signifies the way in which the self is divided or out of synch with itself. Just like a crack that weakens the structural integrity of the soil, the disproportion of the finite and the infinite with oneself is the source of the frailty or fragility of the human being. This frailty is identified on each level of human existence studied in *Fallible Man*: on the theoretical level of the pure imagination, on the practical level of moral respect, and lastly on the affective level of feeling. In addition, the word "fault" also has a moral connotation, as when we speak of the commission of a mistake or some form of misconduct. In this sense, to be "at fault" is to be in the wrong. Accordingly, these two senses of the fault establish the condition of the possibility of human fallibility; it is because there is a fault line in the human being which divides the self from itself that it is possible, in turn, for the human to commit a fault and to do evil. Ricoeur's analysis of human fallibility, in this way, paves the way for the passage from the neutrality of *Freedom and Nature* and into the historical reality of evil that will be taken up in *The Symbolism of Evil*.

OUTLINE OF CHAPTERS

The first part of this book provides useful context for readers of *Fallible Man* through an examination of some of the key figures who influence the book's argument: Rousseau, Karl Jaspers, Gabriel Marcel, and Jean Nabert. The French philosopher of religion, Daniel Frey, has made many significant

Table I.1 An Outline of the Structure of *Fallible Man*

Realm	Finite	Mediation	Infinite
Knowing: What can I know?			Idea of the world
Chapter 2: Transcendental Synthesis	Perspective (appearing) • Kantian sensibility	Consciousness as synthesis of the object • Kant's schemas of transcendental imagination	Language (verbal meaning) • Kant's categories of understanding
Willing: What should I do?			Idea of humanity
Chapter 3: Practical Synthesis	Character • Affective perspective • Practical perspective • Total field of motivation	Respect for persons • Person as an end in itself • Person as a task • Respect as a synthesis of reason and sensibility	Human happiness • As demand of reason • As object of desire • As excess of meaning
Feeling: What may I hope?			Idea of love for the world
Chapter 4: Affective Fragility	*Epithumia:* Vital desires • Having [*Habsucht*] • Power [*Herrsucht*] • Esteem [*Ersucht*]	*Thumos:* Heart • Economics—property • Politics—citizenship • Social—recognition	*Eros:* Spiritual quests • Being oneself • Being in community • Being with others
Being: What is Man?			Kant's category of quality
Conclusion: The Concept of Fallibility	Negation: Existential difference perspective character vital feeling	Limitation: Mediation as fallibility A fragile mediation of the finite and the infinite	Reality: Originary Affirmation The verb The ideal of human happiness Eros or the happy heart

contributions to Ricoeur scholarship in France. His chapter "Imagination and Religion: The Myth of Innocence in *Fallible Man*" situates Ricoeur's imagination of innocence in relation to Rousseau. According to Ricœur, when Rousseau secularized the Christian theme of the fall and identified evil with the entrance into sociability and history, he in fact rediscovered the intention of the Genesis myth, which is to indicate the point of passage from the state of innocence to that of civilization. Rousseau and Ricœur thus share the same idea: despite the entrance into history and society, which is precisely a fall, the natural human goodness nonetheless remains indispensable and present at the heart of social being. Ricœur credits Rousseau with a schema which superimposes an original goodness over evil. Frey emphasizes that this is possible through the power of the imagination: while the philosophical imagination gives rise to a conception of originary goodness through the fallen (*Fallible Man*), the mythico-poetic imagination offers a figure of the original innocence as an innocence regained (*The Symbolism of Evil*). And finally, the utopian imagination invites within the heart of history the courage of concrete action—a central theme that was developed by Ricoeur later. Despite their different modalities, these three aspects of the imagination share the ability to liberate the essential from its empirical realizations: the original is thus the indication of an understanding of the factual, of the historical, and of what is still to come.

One of the leading experts on Ricoeur's early work, Jérôme Porée, situates the argument of *Fallible Man* within the context of Ricoeur's earlier engagement with the work of Karl Jaspers. In his chapter, "Karl Jaspers: The Clarification of Existence," Porée ponders the significance of Ricoeur's observation that "I owe to Karl Jaspers for having sheltered my admiration for German thought from the madness of the environment and from the 'terror of History.'" Porée notes that it is not Jaspers alone who occupied Ricoeur's thoughts during his captivity under the Nazi occupation. Heidegger was also reread "with great care" but yet did not surmount the influence of Jaspers. Porée wonders: How then can one explain why Jaspers soon ceased to be his privileged interlocutor? Was it Jaspers's lack of rigor? A notion of existence that was too psychological? A conception of the relation between existence and transcendence that was too theological? The lack of a true method of deciphering transcendence? Perhaps all of these at the same time? Moreover, the regrets expressed by Ricoeur at the end of the 1980s only heighten the perplexity in their claim to a fidelity that is stronger than all the ruptures with Jaspers. It is in this sense that Porée receives his invitation, issued at the time of the re-publication of the French translation of *Philosophy*, to "reread Jaspers after Heidegger." By carrying out this re-reading, Porée's chapter follows the order of the last two parts of Jaspers's work, devoted respectively to the "clarification of existence" and to the "ciphers" of transcendence. This allows him to discern both what Ricœur retains from his reading of Jaspers and what he elaborates differently. Jaspers's key lesson for a reading of *Fallible Man* is that the hope for reconciliation always triumphs over the reality of disproportion and discord.

In "Reflection, the Body, and Fallibility," Brian Gregor explores the work of another one of Ricoeur's early mentors, Gabriel Marcel. Despite the lack of explicit references to Marcel in *Fallible Man*, Gregor shows that Marcel's work is both an impetus for Ricoeur's account of philosophical reflection, showing that the self-positing act of reflection is always already rooted in concrete existence, as well as a tacit target of his own view, with regard to Marcel's critique of objectivity as well as his related distinction between problem and mystery. While Ricoeur is sympathetic to Marcel's critique of objectifying thinking, he is also determined to give objectivity and primary reflection their due. This is why *Fallible Man* draws from Kant and Husserl more than Marcel. Like Marcel, Ricoeur roots philosophy in concrete existence and a participation in being. But instead of taking a shortcut to this destination, he insists on the detour through more objective modes of reflection. Drawing from this point, Gregor concludes that *Fallible Man* puts forward a view that does not pose the alternative of either objectivity or existence; instead he espouses a view which includes objectivity and existence.

Scott Davidson's chapter, "The Limitation of an Ethical Vision of the World," examines the influence of Jean Nabert, to whom *Fallible Man* is dedicated. While Nabert's work is not widely known in the English-speaking world, his influence becomes evident at first on a methodological plane when the task of *Fallible Man* is defined in relation to its predecessor, *Freedom and Nature*. The preceding work bracketed and set aside any evaluative questions that might concern the morality of the will; its focus was restricted to providing a value-neutral description of the will. But with *Fallible Man*, Ricoeur announces the removal of those brackets so that he can engage in a reflection on the experience of "the fault," a concept that is borrowed directly from Nabert. Nabert's influence turns out to be substantive as well as methodological. Through his reflection on the fault, Ricoeur is able to account for the human possibility to err [*posse peccare*] and thus to show how evil can be traced back to human wrongdoing. But Nabert's conception of the fault also helps him to delineate the limitations of the so-called "ethical vision of the world." In addition to the evil that can be traced back to some form of wrongdoing, Nabert's philosophy thematizes an ontological conception of the fault that escapes rationalization and recovery. In short, the fault reveals that a full account of evil requires consideration not only of wrongdoing but also of the suffering of evil as undeserved and unjustifiable.

The second division of this project is entitled "Thematic Avenues," and it is comprised of six chapters that work together to explore an interlocking set of themes opened up by *Fallible Man*. While Husserlian phenomenology may be less evident in the second volume of his *Philosophy of the Will*, Luz Ascárate's "The Imagination: From Ideation to Innocence" shows that it remains a decisive resource on the way to Ricoeur's hermeneutics, specifically in the anthropology of fallibility developed in *Fallible Man*. Ricoeur's reinterpretation of the Kantian concept of the imagination and his concept of innocence are made possible by Husserlian phenomenology. The importance of this claim is twofold. First, it strengthens the overall unity of Ricoeur's theory of the imagination through his career. Second, it situates Ricoeur's philosophy of the imagination within the context of the history of philosophy, in the sense that it provides new access to the realm of the possible which is concealed by modern ontology. This access to the realm of possibilities demonstrates that the phenomenological notion of imaginative variations plays a central role in the overall argument of the *Fallible Man*: despite the actual failings of actual human beings, it establishes innocence as a fundamental human possibility.

Geoffrey Dierckxsens's chapter "Making Sense of (Moral) Things" examines similarities and differences between Ricoeur's work and enactivism. The first part establishes a connection between Ricoeur's concept of imagination in *Fallible Man* and the enactivist approach to the imagination, based on the notion of enactive simulation, or the idea that we use imagination for re-enacting past experiences. Ricoeur's account of the imagination, he argues, should be understood ontologically, as a way of expressing being, of making sense of life's experiences, which also functions as a motivating factor for acting and for making sense of present situations. In this sense, Ricoeur is close to the enactivist account. Yet, the second part shows that where Ricoeur differs from enactivism pertains to the moral significance of the imagination. We use the moral imagination to re-enact experiences and place them in a larger perspective, in order to make moral decisions, and to understand the values of communities, among other possible examples. Even though this aspect of Ricoeur's thought goes beyond anything that has been developed by enactivism thus far, Dierckxsens suggests that Ricoeur's account of the moral imagination can be instructive to future developments in enactivism.

In "The Self is Embodied and Discursive," Annemie Halsema situates Ricoeur's account of the self within the context of contemporary debates concerning the narrative self. Some critics argue that narrative identity only captures one aspect of the self: the reflexive side which is articulated in language. They argue that this aspect of selfhood needs to be complemented by an experiential subjectivity that is prelinguistic. Halsema returns to *Fallible Man* in search of an answer to the question of whether the latter aspect of the self can be located there. In this way, she proposes to read Ricoeur's account of the self in reverse, starting from the account of narrative identity in *Oneself as Another* (1990) and going back to *Fallible Man* (1960). In *Fallible Man*, she shows that Ricoeur provides a notion of the self that is not merely linguistic and narrative. Taking into account the relationship between body, language, and self in *Fallible Man*, Ricoeur describes a self that is at once embodied and discursive; in fact, the phenomenal and linguistic aspects of the self are so deeply intertwined that they can no longer be distinguished.

Pol Vandevelde's chapter "From Fallibility to Fragility" examines the notion of character in *Fallible Man* and wonders how this notion is transformed into that of a "narrative character" in Ricoeur's later works, such that "life" comes to be spoken of as being "in search of narratives" (1991b) and "the narrative category of character" comes to "contribute . . . to the discussion of personal identity" (1992: 143; 1960a:170). Tracing the transformation that takes place from Ricoeur's early work *Fallible Man* to later works such as *Oneself as Another*, Vandevelde shows that the later work resorbs the tensions that Ricoeur is only able to name in *Fallible Man*—in terms of what he calls the "disproportion" between the finitude of human beings (as manifested by their character) and their aspiration to infinity or "happiness." Narrative identity is able to find concordance within the discordance of a human life. Moreover, Vandevelde adds that narrative character marks a radical shift with regard to the notion of character: by giving precedence to the question of who narrates over the question of what an individual is, precedence is given to ethics over ontology.

In "The Quest of Recognizing One's Self," Timo Helenius emphasizes the connection between the fallible self and the notion of a capable self described in Ricoeur's later work, suggesting that human disproportion should be understood as "a power to fail" (Ricoeur 1986: 145). In contrast with interpretations that would distinguish between Ricoeur's early and late anthropology (i.e., between "being fallible" and "being capable"), Helenius argues for the continuity of Ricoeur's anthropology of a being who is "capable of falling." The reciprocity between being fallen and being capable, according to his view, is Ricoeur's thesis from the very beginning. This means that it is only in contrast with one's limits and incapacities that the understanding of being capable, or the "I can," can be formulated. Helenius then employs this as a framework to illuminate Ricoeur's account of recognition. The search for recognition, accordingly, takes place within a cultural context—which includes the various orders of recognition—where other people help us to become aware of our capacities as well as our failures.

Jean-Luc Amalric, who currently serves as editor of the journal Ricoeur *Studies*, closes the book with his chapter "Finitude, Culpability, and Suffering." Amalric reflects on the meaning of the opposition between *Finitude and Guilt,* which to recall is the title of the volume that includes *Fallible Man* and *The Symbolism of Evil*. In contrast with a dominant philosophical tradition that reduces evil to finitude in order to be able to integrate it into the rationality of its discourse, Ricoeur's volume conveys the irreducible difference between finitude and guilt. The chapter begins with an examination of the close connection between the question of evil and the question of Ricoeur's methodology. In addition to a consideration of the methodological "epoche" of the fault and transcendence implemented in *Freedom and Nature* and *Fallible Man*, Amalric goes on to examine Ricoeur's treatment of the question of suffering. His examination of the complex set of relationships between finitude, guilt, and suffering enables him to sketch an account of the evolution of Ricoeur's thinking on evil. As is well known, Ricoeur himself characterized this evolution by emphasizing how he had come to pay increasing attention to the question of evil and suffering in relation to the issue of moral evil and guilt. But the whole problem, then, is to know exactly what the distinction between finitude and guilt comes to mean in this later context. Amalric suggests that the question of evil accompanies the whole trajectory of Ricoeur's work and that the epoche of guilt continues to function throughout. Its function, he suggests, is to keep the question of evil within the horizon of wisdom, by preventing it from enclosing itself in a purely theoretical or systematic framework of knowledge.

CONCLUSION

Up to this point, the overview of *Fallible Man* has discussed the core chapters but has not yet touched on the opening and closing parts of the book. To understand the full message of *Fallible Man*, it is important to note that the book begins and ends with the topic of pathos or feeling. Chapter 1, The *Pathétique* of Misery, starts with a particular type of pathos—the pathos of misery—that precedes and motivates philosophical reflection. Here Ricoeur draws from the resources of "myth" rather than reason, borrowing first from various uses of myth in Platonic philosophy as well as the famous paragraph 72 on the experience of disproportion in Pascal's *Pensées*. Between the ideas of the infinitely large and that of the infinitely small, Pascal locates the human being in the middle, in between these two polar opposites. But for Ricoeur this middle ground does not simply locate the human being somewhere in the middle of the great chain of being, instead his *pathétique* aims to internalize this intermediate state and identify it with the activity of mediating between the finite and infinite aspects of the human. As such, the experience of disproportion signifies the feeling of undergoing this inner conflict between two incommensurate and irreconcilable extremes.

So why then does *Fallible Man* begin with pathos? If Ricoeur begins with what he calls "pathos of misery" (*pathétique de misère*), his starting point is consistent with a point that he continually reaffirms throughout his career. That is, philosophy does not begin on its own or as a self-contained discoursed; it is always motivated initially by something else, that is, by nonphilosophical or pre-philosophical experiences that prompt reflection. This is precisely what the first chapter, the so-called *pathétique*, indicates. The experience of fallibility neither begin with philosophy nor does it need to be discovered by philosophers, instead it originates in ordinary human experience, with the undergoing of something or with suffering in the broad sense of the term. This pathos is expressed in many different types of nonphilosophical discourse spanning different cultures and historical periods. Philosophical reflection, for Ricoeur, begins from the pathos of a nonphilosophical experience; its role is then to carry this experience to the level of reflection and to make it intelligible.

And why, then, does the book also end with feeling, or, pathos? Here Ricoeur wants to resist the Hegelian temptation of a totalizing dialectic that would resolve the tensions of pathos on the level of reason. The role of pathos at the end of the book is thus to resist the integration or enclosure of the polarity of the finite and the infinite into a higher unity. Although the task of integration or mediation is necessary, the fragility of pathos ensures that it remains incomplete and takes the form of what might be called a "broken" or "open" dialectic. Within such a dialectic, each mediation remains unstable and capable of being undone. This means that the work of mediation can be conducive to a better understanding of oneself, but it does not ever fully overcome the initial experience of disproportion. As a result, the task of self-understanding or self-development never arrives at completion; it remains an infinite task.

Ultimately, the significance of this reflection that begins and ends in feeling is to leave a door open to what exceeds the ethical vision of the world. The ethical vision satisfies the human longing to believe that everything happens for a reason. Accordingly, it traces all forms of evil back to some prior cause, often to some form of wrongdoing or error. Although this rational process can help to render evil intelligible, the key point is that wrongdoing does not account for the full scope of the experience of evil. In addition to the wrong that we do, there is also the wrong that we suffer, sometimes unjustifiably. This too is part of the experience of human limitation. The pathos of suffering unjustified evil—in the form of undeserved suffering or unjust suffering—resists our efforts to synthesize it, to integrate it into our experience, and to render it intelligible. In response to such experiences of evil, we find ourselves undone and at a loss for words. To paraphrase Ricoeur, whereas evildoing gives much to talk about, the suffering of evil gives much to be silent about.[3]

NOTES

1. Taken together, they are an interesting precursor to the "little ethics" that is developed several decades later in *Oneself as Another*. There Ricoeur describes the "ethical aim" in terms of the "desire for the good life with and for others under just institutions." The parallel consists of the fact that there too Ricoeur begins with character and then proceeds to the good life by passing through the Kantian idea of persons.

2. Although Ricoeur defines this contrast by using the Greek terms *epithumia* and *eros*, this contrast could easily be called into question in the sense that e*pithumia* commonly refers to a type of striving or desire that is quite close to his construal of *eros* here. One possible alternative, which might better support his point, would be between the Greek term for appetite (*orexis*) and desire (*epithumia*) in the broader sense of a quest.

3. See Jean-Luc Amalric's commentary on this passage in Chapter 10 of this volume.

REFERENCES

Davidson, Scott. 2020. *A Companion to Ricoeur's The Symbolism of Evil*. Ed. Scott Davidson. Lexington Books.

Heidegger, Martin. 1997. *Kant and the Main Problem of Metaphysics*. Trans. Richard Taft. Bloomington: Indiana University Press.

Kant, Immanuel. 1992. *Lectures on Logic*. Trans. J. Michael Young. Cambridge: Cambridge University Press.

Kant, Immanuel. 2006. *Anthropology from a Pragmatic Point of View*. Ed. Robert B. Louden. Cambridge: Cambridge University Press.

Plato. 2004. *The Republic*. Trans. C.D.C. Reeve. Indianapolis: Hackett.

Reagan, Charles E. and David Stewart, eds. 1978. *The Philosophy of Paul Ricoeur: An Anthology of His Work*. Boston: Beacon Press.

Ricoeur, Paul. 1966. *Freedom and Nature*. Trans. Erazhim V. Kohak. Evanston: Northwestern University Press.

Ricoeur, Paul. 1967. *The Symbolism of Evil*. Trans. Emerson Buchanan. Boston: Beacon Press.

Ricoeur, Paul. 1986. *Fallible Man*. Trans. Charles A. Kelbley. New York: Fordham University Press.

Ricoeur, Paul. 1992. *Oneself as Another*. Trans. Kathleen Blamey. Chicago: The University of Chicago Press.

Rousseau, Jean-Jacques. 2011. Discourse on the Origin of Inequality. In *The Basic Political Writings*. Trans. Donald A. Cress. Indianapolis: Hackett, 29–120.

Part I

HISTORICAL INFLUENCES

Chapter 1

Imagination and Religion
The Myth of Innocence in Fallible Man

Daniel Frey

THE REORIENTATION OF THE INITIAL PROJECT OF THE PHILOSOPHY OF THE WILL

We know that the development of *The Philosophy of the Will* did not go as Ricoeur had planned. The *Philosophy of the Will*, as Ricoeur conceived it in his 1948 thesis, was originally supposed to connect the eidetic of the will to an empirical study of the passions and the fault, which finally would have been followed up by a "concrete *mythics*" emerging from a poetics of the will (Ricoeur 1966: 25–26). Such a long-term project takes time, so it is not surprising that the second volume, comprising two books, appears ten years after its announcement. What is even more surprising is that, along the way, the project was radically revised and modified. In fact, we can recall that in the actual development of his *Philosophy of the Will*, Ricoeur would extend the pure description implemented in the first volume to the first book of the second volume, *Fallible Man*, while the empirics of the passions will be replaced by a hermeneutics of the fault dedicated to the interpretation of the symbols of evil, constituting the second book of the second volume, *The Symbolism of Evil*. This latter book, however, gives up—without explicitly stating it—the prospect of a poetics of the will in relation to what Ricoeur called "Transcendence." In fact, Ricoeur is silent about this enigmatic "revolution at the very center of my self" that was announced in his thesis, which would have allowed him to no longer restrict the opening to transcendence as an alienation, as an abandonment of one's fundamental freedom (Ricoeur 1966: 32).

The "Foreword" to *Fallible Man* opens quite naturally with this change of perspective. Ricoeur acknowledges that the reasons for making a detour through a *"concrete mythics"* (Ricoeur 1986a: xlii; original emphasis) has appeared in the meantime, along with the complications caused by this detour, such that "methodological questions" (Ricoeur 1986a: xlIii) have dominated the development of the book, according to its author. It is worthwhile to stop there, in order to understand the link between myth and imagination mentioned in the title of this chapter.

A DETOUR ANNOUNCED BY THE DECIPHERING OF MYTHS

The first reason for the detour is that it appeared to Ricoeur that the passions and the fault do not lend themselves to any description, even empirical, insofar as their "encoded" language is already the language of myths (Ricoeur 1986a: xlii). Although he does not indicate it, but as can be seen in reading the 1947 books that are devoted to Karl Jaspers, it is indeed with Jaspers that Ricoeur found this conception of philosophy as *deciphering* nonphilosophical myths that are an inexhaustible resource of thought. The following excerpt from the book on Jaspers and Marcel attests to this:

> [For Jaspers] the theory of ciphers marks the stage entrance of *myth* in the philosophy of existence. When Jaspers asserts that faith is not an imperfect knowledge, the faith of which he is dreaming is not oriented towards dogma as in G. Marcel, but towards *myth*. Myth is not a provisional approximation of knowledge, but the ultimate resource by which the philosopher can still speak about transcendence. Philosophy becomes a universal myth where art, religions and philosophies regain their truth as a cipher. (Ricoeur 1948: 46–47)

Ricoeur therefore abandoned the empirical study that he had initially projected, and forced himself to justify the introduction of a "mythics into philosophical reflection" (Ricoeur 1986a: xlii)—without, however, mentioning hermeneutics[1]—because the myths of evil cannot be constituted for philosophy as raw data, as is the case with the history of religions. In the 1953 essay to which he refers his readers in a footnote, the philosopher thus sought to prepare a welcome ground for the "myths of the fall, chaos, exile, and divine blindness," which consists in reconstructing "the universe of discourse" from which these myths are drawn:

> It then appeared that myths could only be understood as secondary elaborations of a more fundamental language that I call the language of confession; it is this language of confession that speaks to the philosopher of the fault and evil; for this language of confession is remarkable in that it is through and through *symbolic*; it does not speak of stain, sin, and guilt in direct and proper terms, but in indirect and figurative terms; to understand this language

of confession is to implement an exegesis of the symbol that calls for rules of deciphering, that is to say, a hermeneutic. (Ricoeur 1986a: xlii; original emphasis; tr. mod.)

The study to which the philosopher refers his reader, entitled "Tragic Guilt and Biblical Guilt," actually constituted a test beyond *Finitude and Guilt*. It is actually an essay of comparative mythology, where the narrative of guilt in Greek tragedy[2] is confronted with its figuration in the biblical myth of origins recorded in Genesis (see Ricoeur 1953/4). It is worthwhile to dwell on this point, because Ricoeur applies the concept of the "phenomenological reduction" to the Biblical and Greek religious symbols:

> The application of the comparative method to Greek myths and Hebraic myths is conditioned by the *neutralization* of the act of faith that could eventually be reattached to these myths but a redeeming act that concerns *me*, which concerns *us*; the election of Israel, the Creed of the Christian Church concerning the second Adam undergo a sort of *phenomenological reduction* by which the transforming intention that goes from the pagan myth to the Hebrew myth is retained, but without the historian taking part; the myth retained in its structure and in its intention thus becomes a meaningful cultural *phenomenon*. This methodological artifice—because it is an artifice, like all the sciences practice when developing their "object"—henceforth allows a homogeneous comparison of myths in terms of a single phenomenology. (Ricoeur 1994: 299)

The phenomenological reduction evoked here seems to be synonymous with the suspension of assent, an *epoche* in the Husserlian sense of the word. By affirming that the prerequisite for the comparative study of myths is the suspension of the act of faith, whereby the subject could reconnect the myth to an act of salvation—whether the latter derives from the Christian faith or the Dionysian pagan religion—Ricoeur formalizes a methodological rule that is essential to the hermeneutics of symbolic language that he is undertaking. It should also be noted that if *the act of faith* is suspended, *belief* is lived through but yet "in a neutralized mode": far from being inconsequential, to us, this distinction seems to express the whole difference between the scientific attitude, concerning which Ricoeur says elsewhere that it "proceeds from a certain 'reduction' of our total relation to the world; only one aspect of the world is retained: its quantitative and measurable aspect" (Ricoeur 1952)[3] and the phenomenological attitude. Indeed, if it is enough to suspend all faith in the reality evoked by religious myths in order to study them scientifically, it is necessary, in order to propose a phenomenological analysis of them,[4] to be open to the religious intention expressed by the symbols and narratives that employ them. Ricoeur explicitly says this on the first page of the introduction to *The Symbolism of Evil* (entitled "The Phenomenology of Confession"), when he calls for "a repetition in imagination and sympathy" of the confession that the religious consciousness makes of evil:

> If the "re-enactment" [*répétition*] of the *confession* of human evil by the religious consciousness does not take place in philosophy, this *confession* nevertheless belongs already within its sphere of interest, for this confession is a *word*, a word that man pronounces about himself; every word can and must be recovered in the element of philosophical discourse. We will soon say what the philosophical site, if you will, of this "repetition" is, which is already no longer a religious lived experience and which is not yet philosophy. (Ricoeur 1967: 4; original emphasis; tr. mod.)

If it is conceivable that the phenomenological repetition of the confession is no longer religion, why is it not yet philosophy? Because all that comes from philosophy is a conceptual approach to evil which asks, what is "the human place of evil, its entry point into human reality"? (Ricoeur 1986a: xliii; tr. mod.)

AN ANTHROPOLOGY OF FALLIBILITY: THE ETHICAL VISION OF THE WORLD

This search for a conceptual approach is the reason why the detour through a hermeneutic of the symbols of evil is itself preceded by an "outline of a philosophical anthropology" (Ricoeur 1986a: xliii):

> This study focuses on the theme of fallibility, that is, the constitutional weakness that makes evil possible; through the concept of fallibility, philosophical anthropology comes to encounter the symbolism of evil, just as the symbolism of evil brings myths to philosophical discourse; through the concept of fallibility, the doctrine of the human approaches the threshold of intelligibility where it is comprehensible that through man evil has been able to "enter the world"; beyond this threshold begins the enigma of an emergence concerning which there is nothing but indirect and encrypted discourse. Just as the symbolics of evil represented an extension of the mythic that the *Freedom and Nature* proposed, the theory of fallibility represents an expansion of the anthropological perspective of the first work which was more narrowly focused on the structure of the will. (Ricoeur 1986a: xliii; tr. mod.)[5]

The above excerpt offers the second of the reasons why Ricoeur amended his initial project. Before arriving at an interpretation of the symbols of evil, it was still necessary to move from the polarity of the voluntary and the involuntary to the broader polarity of finitude and infinitude, which in fact opens the study of *Fallible Man*, and that Ricoeur, again, had tested in a number of previous studies that are cited in footnotes.[6] It is indeed the function of a "reflexive thought" to constitute a concept of fallibility designating "the possibility of evil" (Ricoeur 1986a: xliv), before the mythical language about its entrance into the world is interpreted. Ricoeur already signals to his reader that the hermeneutics of the symbols of evil is not "homogeneous" with such a reflexive philosophy, insofar as it will require the invention of "rules of transposition [. . .] into a new type of philosophical discourse," which will be done in the conclusion to *Finitude and Guilt* "The Symbol gives rise to Thought"—which is in the eyes of the author "the pivotal point of the whole work" (Ricoeur 1986a: xliv). Thus a hiatus exists, on the level of method, between a pure reflection and a philosophical hermeneutic, since it will be a question of "both respecting the specificity of the symbolic world of expressions and of thinking not 'behind' but 'starting from' the symbol," that is to say, of preparing for the empirics of the servile will anticipated by his thesis (Ricoeur 1986a: xliv; see also xlv).

This is where the philosopher announces—his experience, however, should have led him to be more cautious!—a "third part, which will be published in a later volume [. . .] entirely devoted to this thinking that starts from the symbol" (Ricoeur 1986a: xliv). In this announcement painted in broad brush strokes, it is clear that this third volume would have been more directly devoted to "empirics of the servile will," which would engage psychoanalysis as well as criminal law, political philosophy—and in a general manner, the social sciences (Ricoeur 1986a: xliv; tr. mod.). This announcement, once again, was a bit too risky since there would not be a third volume devoted to thinking starting from the symbol of the servile will, no more than there was a third volume offering a "concrete mythics" back to back with a poetics of the will. However, there was a deeper engagement than initially foreseen with the question of psychoanalysis, which led to *Freud and Philosophy* (1965), as well as a mixture of hermeneutical tests of great importance collected in *The Conflict of Interpretations* (1969), which do offer segments of a poetics of will, as we will try to show.

Let's return to the hiatus mentioned earlier, in order to say that the pure reflection implemented in the first part of *Finitude and Guilt* is paradoxical in that it moves toward a philosophical interpretation of the symbols of evil by using the only resource that is available to the philosopher, that of the "ethical vision of the world," but a resource which cannot suffice however. This is why Ricoeur does not hesitate to disorient his reader by stating that to designate the stakes of *Fallible Man*, he could have "chosen for the subtitle of this book: *The Grandeur and Limits of an Ethical Vision of the World*" (Ricoeur 1986a: xlvi; original emphasis). This involves going all the way through to a mutual understanding of evil and freedom; the grandeur of pure reflection is precisely to "try to understand evil through freedom"[7] by leaving behind any speculation about other sources of evil than human freedom. Ricoeur stands firm on this point: *"the humanity of the human is, in any case, the space of manifestation of evil"* (Ricoeur 1986a: xlvi; emphasis added).[8]

It is important to be aware of the specificity of this vigorous entry into the matter: here the first word is up to philosophy, in this case, to ethics. The affirmation of freedom therefore has a primacy over religious discourses that have denounced human guilt since time immemorial.[9] The philosopher is the one who, invariably, honors the background of goodness of human freedom which is more fundamental than its deviance, and who at the same time relentlessly calls humans to responsibility. The philosopher is a moralist for whom there is only one conceivable freedom: a "freedom that recognizes itself as *responsible*, that vows to take evil as *evil committed* and confesses that it depends on freedom for evil not to be" (Ricoeur 1986: xlvii; emphasis added). This entryway into the question of evil through human freedom is already recognized by Ricoeur to be at work in Kant's "Essay on Radical Evil," where "through formalism, evil tends to be reduced to a maxim of the free will" (Ricoeur 1986a: xlvii).[10] Note that Ricoeur writes "tends to be reduced": in the ethical approach to evil initiated by Ricoeur in the wake of Kant, "it is very possible indeed that the human is not the radical origin of evil, that he is not the absolute villain." But immediately afterward, Ricoeur clarifies: "Even if evil were contemporaneous with the radical origin of things, it would remain the case that it is manifest in the way it *affects* human existence" (Ricoeur 1986a: xlvi; original emphasis).

So this is the indelible grandeur of the ethical vision of the entrance of evil into the world. But Ricoeur also has as a project, as we have seen in the introduction of *Freedom and Nature*, of accounting for the unavailable nature of freedom, servile freedom. He has not forgotten it, and reiterates in the preface of *Fallible Man* that "the enigma of the servile will," the enigma of a *"free will that binds itself and finds itself always already bound*, is the ultimate theme that the symbol gives to be thought" (Ricoeur 1986a: xlv; original emphasis). In the debt that he intends to honor with regard to Jean Nabert,[11] Ricoeur has found an additional reason to arrive at a philosophical reflection on the servile will. Indeed, Ricoeur asserts that he has drawn a meditation from the reflexive philosopher that is the reverse of the one he draws from Kant. This Nabertian meditation never ceases to "broaden and deepen the doctrine of freedom under the sting of the evil which, however, it has taken back into itself," to the point that with Nabert, one may understand that "in an ethical vision, it is not only true that freedom is the reason for evil, but the confession of evil is also the condition of the consciousness of freedom" (Ricoeur 1986a: xlvii and xlix). It is particularly in a "difficulty" with Nabert's *Essay On Evil* that Ricoeur sees the link with the theme of the servile will:

If Evil is [as Nabert maintains] "the unjustifiable," can it be fully reiterated in the confession that freedom makes of it? This difficulty is one that I encounter in another way, in the *symbolics of evil*. The main enigma of this symbolics is that the world of myths is already itself a broken world; the myth of the fall which is the matrix of all subsequent speculations concerning the origin of evil in human freedom [. . .] leaves outside itself the rich mythics of chaos, of tragic blindness, and of the exiled soul; even if the philosopher wagers on the superiority of the myth of the fall because of its affinity with the confession that freedom makes of its responsibility, even if this wager allows all the other myths to be regrouped with the myth of the fall as their center of reference, it remains that [. . .] the exegesis of the myth of the fall directly leads to the appearance of this tension between two meanings: on the one side, evil enters into the world insofar as the human posits it, but it is only posited because the human *cedes* to the adversary's investment. The limit of an ethical vision of evil and of the world is already signified in this ambiguous structure of the myth of the fall: by positing evil, freedom is in the grip of an other. (Ricoeur 1986a: xlix; original emphasis)

The link between the difficulty evoked by Ricoeur and the theme of the servile will is not easy to discover. One indication would be the discreet critique of Nabert in this excerpt, which could be made explicit by a more candid one that Ricoeur proposes at the end of a glowing book review entitled "*L'Essai sur le Mal* de Jean Nabert."[12] There he regretted Nabert's tendency to identify evil and finitude, insofar as the fact of being finite and having to choose ultimately seems for him to be the equivalent of evil itself (Ricoeur 1992: 248). Despite his approval of the book as a whole, Ricoeur reaffirms, after *L'Essai de Nabert*, "that it is a task of the philosophy of evil to distinguish between evil and finitude" (Ricoeur 1992: 248). He reiterates all the values he grants—along with Nabert himself, and also with Kant—to the assertion of a fundamental difference between the original affirmation, good in itself, by which the subject posits itself in being, and the preference of this same subject for itself to the exclusion of any other. In other words, the affirmation of a freedom that may or may not do evil is in principle different from a passivity experienced in doing it: everything happens as if, in freely choosing to do evil, I was actually only giving in to it. It is precisely the lesson of the symbolism of evil that Ricoeur anticipates at the end of his foreword, as usual. The broken character of the mythical field evoked here is due to the fact that the affinity of the biblical myth of the fall with the discourse of ethics (evil is the fruit of freedom) does not prevent other myths from depicting a form of exteriority of evil toward the human. The real development of the symbolic will show that this exteriority originates in the symbol of the stain, which was not completely eliminated from the biblical symbol of guilt (or from the Genesis narrative).

Here we have arrived at the center of our proposal: our hypothesis is that the exercise of pure reflection implemented in *Fallible Man* is based in part on the power of the representation of innocence in the biblical myth of origins.

PURE REFLECTION ON THE ORIGINARY: THE POWER OF THE IMAGINATION

Fallible Man, as has been noted, is situated on the threshold of a hermeneutic of myths and symbols of evil. But the introduction of the mythical in the philosophical reflection announced by Ricoeur's Foreword begins long before *The Symbolism of Evil*. Already with *Fallible Man*, the central theme of the mythical, *the imagination of innocence,* appears at the core of the analyses derived from pure reflection. Here is a particularly striking example, which occurs in the analysis of affectivity:

> With the affective closure, we recover the feeling of the original difference between myself and every other; feeling good or bad is feeling my singularity as inexpressible and incommunicable; just as one's place cannot be shared, the affective situation in which I find myself and feel myself cannot be exchanged. *It is here that egoism, as a vice, finds its opportunity: out of difference, it makes a preference.* But the preference for oneself, inherent in all inclinations, is what the Stoics called an attachment to oneself, an original tendency to want good for oneself, a love of one's own constitution, that I would readily call a love of oneself as a point of view. (Ricoeur 1986a: 55; emphasis added)

Ricoeur asserts the point forcefully: if I can come to give myself preference over the whole world, it is first because I am constitutively carried by a desire to be which, in itself, is good. In particular, I am a being who is naturally led toward self-love. Our hypothesis is that the place of the *myth* (and thus of the imagination) is inscribed in these analyses deriving from pure reflection, insofar as these analyses are all pointing toward the state of innocence through its constant betrayal in our fallen being.

The Innocent Nature of Man: Ricoeur in the Footsteps of Rousseau

Of course, Kant already evoked, as the first "original provision to the good in human nature," "the physical and simply mechanical self-love" by which the human being emerges from animality (Kant AK VI, 26). But Kant himself owed this idea to Rousseau who, first and much more strongly, had issued a plea for a morally neutral "love of self," because it is the expression of a natural will for self-preservation.¹³ If Ricoeur, like Rousseau, does not hesitate to speak about self-love rather than attachment, like the Stoics, it is because he represents the self-love of the human being as the trace of a lost innocence that the mythical narrative of Genesis lets us imagine.¹⁴ Ricoeur also tends to identify this state of innocence with the affirmation of an original goodness of the human being. Rousseau, as we know, affirmed the natural goodness of man even though he never ceased to denounce the wickedness of human society. In an important 1952 essay devoted to the "revival of non-philosophy through philosophy,"¹⁵ Ricoeur comments on the book *The Philosophy of Existence of Jean-Jacques Rousseau* (1952) by his friend Pierre Burgelin. It presents what he considers to be "Rousseau's stroke of genius, which coincides with the wound of his life and perhaps with the crack of his psyche":

> To have identified guilt and socialization. This stroke of genius began the modern philosophy of history. Philosophy is no longer meta-physics but meta-history: it is necessary to pierce through the fact of sociality up to what is beyond our history, up to this *natural goodness* which is both *our innocence* and *our nature*. [. . .] The rich and informed power of innocence and the wickedness of the limited achievements of history do not belong on the same level; they are like an *overlaying* [*surimpression*]. (Ricoeur 1994: 169)

By secularizing the biblical myth of the fall and by identifying evil as the entrance into sociability and history, Rousseau regains the intention of the myth, which is to indicate the point of passage from the state of innocence to that of civilization, since it is clearly stated that after the fall work (with all its painfulness) will form the daily life of humans (*Genesis* 3, 17–19). Natural human goodness remains nonetheless; it is unavailable but yet present at the heart of social being. Here Ricoeur finds the opportunity to credit Rousseau with a schema, that of "overlaying," which is in reality his own, since it was already present in his thesis:

> The fault is understood as a lost innocence, as a paradise lost. The objection is therefore right to deny us any direct description of innocence. Yet it is not the lost paradise of innocence that we are claiming to describe, but the structures that are the fundamental possibilities offered both to innocence and the fault as the common keyboard of a human nature on which mythical innocence and empirical guilt play in such different ways. (Ricoeur 1966: 26; tr. mod.)

When he develops this schema of overlaying ten years later, in *The Symbolism of Evil*, Ricoeur pays homage to Rousseau, in close proximity to Kant:

> This is what Rousseau brilliantly understood: the human is "naturally good," but we know the human under the regime of civilization—that is to say, of

history—only as "depraved." Above all, that is what Kant understood with admirable rigor in his *Essay on Radical Evil*: the human is "destined" to the good and "prone" to evil. This paradox of "destination" and "inclination" concentrates the entire meaning of the symbol of the fall. (Ricoeur 1967: 252; original emphasis; tr. mod.)

The proximity between Rousseau and Kant should not, however, give rise to an identification between them, insofar as the notion of *respect* for the person, which forms the synthesis of character and happiness in Kant (see Ricoeur 1986: 69 ff.), is based in the final instance on an ethical dualism "where the duality of good and evil is already constituted and where man has already chosen the side of evil" (Ricoeur 1986: 75). In short, one finds in Kant a "pessimistic anthropology dominated by the theory of radical evil," while pure reflection on fallibility requires another anthropology than one which is already situated "in the circle of fallenness" (Ricoeur 1986: 75; tr. mod.). It is a question of seizing the possibility of failing and not the actuality of evil:

> We have no other access to the origin than through the fallen; in return, if the fallen does not give an indication of that from which it has fallen, no philosophy of the original is possible and one cannot even say that man is fallen; for the very idea of fallenness involves a reference to the loss of some innocence that we understand enough to name it and to designate the present condition present as a gap [écart], a loss, or a fall. (Ricoeur 1986a: 76)

In an analysis resulting from pure reflection, the right to represent innocence through fallenness is undeniable from the methodological point of view, as one can see in the above passage. Yet, it is clear that this research itself already bears the imprint of a philosophical reading of the myth of Genesis. In other words, Ricoeur implements in pure reflection a form of philosophical imagination which is conceptual in nature and which assumes (without directly justifying) a particular reading of the biblical myth that conceives innocence as what endures through and in spite of the fall—hence the schema, so fecund, of the "overlaying" of original goodness and historical wickedness. From the point of view of what religion gives philosophy to think, the *power of the imagination* is held there, in the call that is sent to the philosopher by the myth of origins to conceive an intrinsic goodness of all human acts, which is always denatured and betrayed. Ricoeurian anthropology of *Fallible Man*, in particular, is directed toward the original mode of human being, while highlighting the mistakes and deviances which, from a pragmatic point of view, characterize the practical modalities of its being. In this regard, Rousseau's influence seems to outweigh the considerable influence of Kant: with the latter, who is also heavily influenced by Rousseau,[16]

Ricoeur pays the utmost attention to the disfigured aspect of the human passions, but with the former, he constantly intends this original goodness which Rousseau denotes as "natural goodness."

From Fallen Figures of Self-feeling to the Restoration of the Original

The central passions studied by Kant's practical anthropology, relating to possession [*Habsucht*], domination [*Herrschsucht*], and honor [*Ehrsucht*] (see Ricoeur 1986a: 111), will provide a place for Ricoeur's masterful study of having, power and valuing, before they become disfigured. Under the heading of "affective fragility," the philosopher proposes a "philosophy of feeling," in which the feeling of the self can be understood starting from appropriation (having is necessary to be a subject), the effort of civilization against nature (power is at first only a differentiation of functions for this purpose) and the desire for recognition that each one addresses to others (value aiming first toward the esteemed character of the self as a human being, as an end in itself). In studying these specific forms of the desire to be human, Ricoeur's intention is clearly aimed toward the original state of these constituent modalities of the affective being as having, power and worth,[17] all the while also seeing in them the opportunities to fall:

> Kant places himself immediately in front of the *fallen* figures of human affectivity; the *Sucht* of each of these passions expresses the modality of aberration, of delirium, under which they enter into history; an anthropology elaborated from a practical point of view is undoubtedly justified in doing so [. . .] But a philosophical anthropology must be more demanding; it must proceed to the restoration of the original that is at the root of the fallen; just as Aristotle describes the perfection of pleasure beyond all forms of "intemperance," we must recover, behind this triple *Sucht,* an authentic *Suchen* [. . .] the quest of humanity [. . .] constitutive of human praxis and the human self; we must proceed in this way, because even if we only *empirically know* these fundamental quests under their disfigured and hideous face, in the form of greed, the passions of power and vanity, we *understand* these passions *in their essence* only as perversions . . .; it must even be said that what we understand, first of all, is the primordial modalities of human desire and constituents with regard to the humanity of the human; and then we understand the "passions" only as a gap [écart], deviation, fallenness, from these original quests. This understanding of the original first and the fallen second, starting from and through the original[18], undoubtedly requires a kind of imagination of innocence, the imagination of a "reign" where the quests of having, power and worth would not be what they actually are; but this imagination is not a fantastic dream; it is an "imaginative variation," to speak like Husserl, which manifests the essence, breaking the prestige of the fact. (Ricoeur 1986a: 111–12; original emphasis)

In this passage, the expression "restoration of the original" refers to the description of the original modality of human affectivity, made possible by an imaginative variation of a phenomenological nature. At the same time, as is often the case with Ricoeur, there is a term of biblical provenance, suggesting a community of insight between the philosophical and the biblical imaginations: "The imagination of a 'reign,'" understood as the reign of God that the evangelical parables evoke in many ways ("The Kingdom of God is similar to"). The theme of power will also bring Ricoeur to clarify this biblical allusion, since he will write a little later about: "the utopia of a Kingdom of God, a City of God, an empire of minds, or a kingdom of ends, implies an imagination of a non-violent power. This imagination releases the essence, and this essence regulates all efforts to actually transform power through the education of freedom" (Ricoeur 1986a: 120; trans. mod.).

For Ricoeur, imagination is already in power: *the philosophical imagination* allows us to conceive the original through the fallen, *the mythico-poetic imagination* offers a figuration of original innocence as innocence regained; *the utopian imagination* invites within history the courage for concrete action—and, of course, the theme of utopia will be the subject of important developments later on. Distinguished by their modalities, these three aspects of imagination are rejoined in their ability to liberate the essence of its empirical achievements: the original is thus the indication of an understanding of the factual and historical, depending on whether it is envisioned as what fundamentally is, what is originally, or what is yet to come.

In every way, the origin is what grounds essences but factual reality does not know. It is absent from actual human history since human history always already moves within the empirical realm of the passions. Only the mythical narrative can figure it, in its naivety—since it is prior to the invention of history—which lets it believe in the possibility of designating the tipping point where the *origin* becomes *the beginning* of history, the passage from innocent humanity to real and present humanity. Based on original freedom, without which human responsibility would be nothing but a meaningless word, ethics comes too late when it comes to observing the passage to the deviant act by which one passes from fallibility to the fault. It has already been accomplished, everywhere and always, because the human cannot cope with its emotional fragility. This leads to the painful worries about having enough, being powerful enough, and being recognized enough.[19] Worry [*l'inquiétude*] is indeed the mode of expression of self-feeling: "It is noteworthy," observes Ricoeur, "that the self is never assured [*assuré*]" (Ricoeur 1986a: 126; tr. mod.), that it is relentless in the quest for what would justify its existence through *domination over the other*. This is indeed a quest for *being,* in someone whose fragility is constitutive of his or her personhood; but this quest is a pathos, for this great fragility only knows—in order to be—how to give precedence to its own desire to be over any other consideration.

Ricoeur returns, in conclusion, to this relation between the philosophical and mythical imaginations which appears to be the representative of his relation to religion in this volume, even if it is dedicated to pure philosophy. And this definitively places it on the threshold of *The Symbolism of Evil*:

> Innocence would be fallibility without fault, and this fallibility would be only fragility, only weakness, but not fallenness. It does not matter that I can represent innocence only by way of myth, as a state realized "elsewhere" and "long ago" in places and times that have no place in the geography and history of rational man. The essence of the myth of innocence is to give a symbol of the original which trans-pires (*trans-parait*) in fallenness and is denounced as fallenness; my innocence is my original constitution, projected into a fantastical story. This imagination is nothing scandalous for philosophy; the imagination is an indispensable way of investigating the possible; [. . .] One could say, in the style of Husserlian eidetics, that innocence is the imaginative variation that makes the essence of the original constitution stand out, by letting it appear *on* another existential modality; [. . .] I must understand together and as an overlaying [*surimpresssion*] the original destination of "goodness" and its historical manifestation in wickedness [*méchanceté*]; however original wickedness may be, goodness is even more original. That is why, as we will see, a myth of the fall is only possible in the context of a myth of creation and innocence. If we had understood this, we would not have wondered if "the image of God" can be lost, as if, in becoming wicked, man ceased to be human; nor would we have accused Rousseau of inconsistency when he professed, with obstinacy, the natural goodness of man *and* his historical and cultural perversity. (Ricoeur 1986a: 145; original emphasis)

This text is representative of Ricoeur's style in the 1950–1960s: long sentences in a row, separated only by semicolons—Ricoeur was fond of them—which invite a quick reading, in one breath, as if each sentence could not make sense without the following one, which nevertheless has another, complementary perspective. In the end, and in one gesture, the opposites connect—here goodness and wickedness, the mythical fable and the eidetic—not by taste or the way of the dialectic but because, *actually*, the original is the index for understanding the fallen, and innocence for wickedness. Philosophy only knows this when it listens to the mythical *logos* which it always knew but without ever knowing it, that is to say, without thematizing its own discourse. This is perhaps the lesson that will have to be expected from *The Symbolism of Evil*: to aim toward a *reflexive* state of human knowledge, in this case to reach a philosophical awareness of the passage from the original to the fallen, from fallibility to evil. When Ricoeur announces that the next volume will focus on the "continuous transition of vertigo" that seems to lead from the freedom of the human will to the bad will, when he expresses an "ultimate paradox" that "evil only proceeds from this weakness because it is posited" (Ricoeur 1986a: 146: original emphasis), he shows the tenor of this philosophical hermeneutics that meditates on pre-philosophical discourse, the paradoxical nature of the lessons it draws from a *logos* which, because it is formed out of symbols woven together by a narrative, tends to be chronologized in the form of a canvas governed by the narrative logic of a before and an after that the philosopher has learned—thanks to the myth, but below it—to read as "an overlapping."

Translated by Scott Davidson

NOTES

1. The word will appear only at the end of volume, under the title of a "*philosophical* hermeneutic" (Ricoeur 1967: 353; original emphasis).

2. Many elements of the tragic part are found in the first part of "The Wicked God and the "Tragic" Vision of Existence," in *The Symbolism of Evil,* 211–231. In the same year, Ricoeur also published another essay on the tragic alone, through this time a reading of Gerhard Nebel, Henri Gouhier and Karl Jaspers. See "Sur le tragique," in Ricoeur 1994: 187–209.

3. Ricoeur, "L'homme de science et l'homme de foi," *Le Semeur,* 1952, 16.

4. It should be noted here that phenomenology and hermeneutics are already linked, the second being a specification of the first, which seems to foreshadow the important thesis set forth in *From Text to Action,* according to which "*Phenomenology remains the unsurpassable presupposition of hermeneutics.* On the other hand, phenomenology cannot constitute itself without a *hermeneutical presupposition*" ("Phenomenology and Hermeneutics," in *From Text to Action,* 26; Ricoeur's emphasis).

5. Ricoeur 1986: xliii (tr. mod.). The quoted expression most likely refers to the Apostle Paul in *Romans* 5.1: "Wherefore, just as by one man [Adam] *sin entered the world*, and by sin death [. . .]" (emphasis added).

6. This is "Negativity and the Originary Affirmation (1956)," the study entitled "Feeling (1959)," "The Unity of the Voluntary and the Involuntary as a Limit Idea (1951)," and "Methods and Tasks of a Phenomenology of the Will (1952)." See Ricoeur 1986a: xliii, note 4 and note 5. The first was included in *History and Truth,* while the others appear later in *À l'école de la phénoménologie.*

7. Ricoeur 1986a: xlvi.

8. The comparison with Kant is eloquent, who wrote in the "Essay on Radical Evil" that opens *Religion within the Limits of Reason Alone*: "A penchant for evil can only be attached to the moral faculty of the arbitrator." There is nothing morally wrong (that is, likely to be imputed) outside of what is our own *action* [AK Vi3]" (Kant's emphasis).

9. Recall again the remarkable *incipit* of *Religion within the Limits of the Reason Alone*: "that the world is bad, is a complaint as old as history and even the oldest poetry, as ancient as the oldest of all poems, I mean the religion of priests" (Kant, *Religion within the Limits of Reason Alone,* 29).

10. Kant's *Religion within the Limits of the Reason Alone* opens in effect with a first part entitled "From the immanence of the bad principle to the good, or on the radical evil in human nature" [AK VI, 19]. Previously published in 1792 under the title "On Radical Evil" in the *Berlinische Monatsschrift*.

11. To whom *Fallible Man* is also dedicated.

12. "*L'essai sur le mal* de Jean Nabert" was published in *Esprit* in 1957, two years after the publication of Nabert's book. It is reprinted in Ricoeur 1992: 237–262.

13. Jean-Jacques Rousseau, *Discours sur l'origine et les fondements de l'inégalité parmi les hommes* (1754), in *Œuvres complètes* III. *Du Contrat social—Écrits politiques*, B. Gagnebin et M. Reymond dir., Paris, Gallimard, 1964, p. 109–237, at 126.

14. In this sense, Ricoeur does not hesitate later to write, at the time around *Oneself as Another*: "This is the profound reason why the command in Leviticus dares to state: "You will love thy neighbor as yourself" [*Leviticus*, 19, 18]. There is absolutely nothing shocking in this 'as yourself': I will say that we are in search of a right to the love ourselves; this is the first ethical impulse" ("L'éthique, la morale, la règle," *Autres Temps*, no. 24 (1989–90), 55).

15. Ricoeur 1952: 760–775. The text is reprinted with a somewhat unfortunate title as: "Philosophie et prophétisme I (1952)" in Ricoeur 1994: 153–172, cited at 153.

16. See the thesis of J. Ferrari, *Les sources françaises de la philosophie de Kant*, Université de Paris IV, 1976, 1981, whose third part is devoted to "Kant lecteur de Rousseau," pp. 171–253. See also D. Frey, "La culture, *fin dernière* de la nature. Kant critique de Rousseau," in G. Vincent (dir.), *La Partition des cultures. Droits culturels et Droits de l'Homme* (Strasbourg: Presses Universitaires de Strasbourg, 2008): 69–97.

17. Ricoeur places this study under the sign of the *thumos* (a term taken from book IV of Plato's *Republic*; see also Ricoeur 1986: 7 ff.), locating the affective fragility of the human, torn between the vital and the spiritual (ee Ricoeur 1986: 106 ff).

18. The attentive reader will have spotted a tension between this passage and the previous one, which affirmed the possibility of seizing the original not through oneself but through the fallen. Ricoeur's conclusion will remove this apparent contradiction: "In short, it is always '*through*' the fallen that the original appears [. . .] But in return, this reference to the original constitutes evil as a fault. I can only think evil as evil 'starting from' that from which it falls. The 'through' is thus reciprocal with a 'starting from'; and it is this 'starting from' which permits it to be to said that fallibility is the *condition* of evil, while evil is the revelation of fallibility" (Ricoeur 1986: 144; original emphasis).

19. "When would I have enough? When will my authority be established? When will I be appreciated enough, recognized?" (Ricoeur 1986: 126).

REFERENCES

Ricoeur, Paul. 1948. *Gabriel Marcel et Karl Jaspers*. Paris: Editions du Temps Présent.

Ricoeur, Paul. 1952. Aux frontières de la philosophie. *Esprit* 20, no. 11: 760–775.

Ricoeur, Paul. 1953/4. Culpabilité Tragique et Culpabilité biblique. *Revue d'histoire et de philosophie religieuses de la Faculté de théologie protestante de l'université de Strasbourg*, no. 33: 285–307.
Ricoeur, Paul. 1966. *Freedom and Nature*. Trans. Erazhim V. Kohak. Evanston: Northwestern University Press.
Ricoeur, Paul. 1967. *The Symbolism of Evil*. Trans. Emerson Buchanan. Boston: Beacon Press.
Ricoeur, Paul. 1986a. *Fallible Man*. Trans. Charles A. Kelbley. New York: Fordham University Press.
Ricoeur, Paul. 1986b. *À l'école de la phénoménologie*. Paris: Vrin.
Ricoeur, Paul. 1991. *From Text to Action: Essays in Hermeneutics, II*. Trans. Kathleen Blamey and John B. Thompson. Evanston: Northwestern University Press.
Ricoeur, Paul. 1992. *Lectures 2*. Paris: Seuil: 237–262.
Ricoeur, Paul. 1994. Sur le tragique. In *Lectures 3*. Paris: Seuil: 187–209.
Rousseau, Jean-Jacques. 1964. *Discours sur l'origine et les fondements de l'inégalité parmi les hommes (1754)*. In *Œuvres complètes* III. *Du Contrat social—Écrits politiques*. Eds. B. Gagnebin et M. Reymond. Paris: Gallimard, 110–240.

Chapter 2

Karl Jaspers
The Clarification of Existence
Jérôme Porée

"I am indebted to Karl Jaspers for having placed my admiration for German thinking outside of the reach of our surroundings and of the 'terror of history'" (Ricoeur 1995: 9). With these words Paul Ricoeur expresses his debt to Karl Jaspers, who "directed and inspired" his thought during his captivity in the camps of Pomerania after the phony war. Not that Jaspers was the only source of inspiration for Ricoeur during that period. He also took up a "careful reading of Heidegger" (Ricoeur 1995: 10). Nonetheless, he considers Jaspers to have a greater influence on his thinking, because philosophy, for Jaspers, is not only of general value, but contains the truth "with which we live" (Jaspers 1989: xviii).[1] His philosophy seeks to lead readers to make free and responsible decisions through a rigorous clarification of their motives. Ricoeur's first book is thus devoted to Jaspers's philosophy, which he published just after the war, together with Mikel Dufrenne, his companion during his years of captivity (Ricoeur and Dufrenne 1947). In his second book which was published the following year, Ricoeur combines Jaspers's thought with that of Gabriel Marcel, both of whom were important influences on the development of his own thought.[2]

However, from the start Ricoeur was careful not to confound philosophy and religion. Convinced that human understanding implies the understanding of human boundaries, he did not want to renounce philosophy too rapidly. Neither was it his intention to develop an impossible "religious philosophy." Marcel seems more eager than Jaspers to go in such a direction. While developing philosophical problems, he more easily reaches the threshold of "mystery." Contrary to Marcel, however, the principal concern of Jaspers was to connect reason and existence. Pulled out of a dogmatic slumber by both Kierkegaard's and Nietzsche's critiques of reason in the name of existence, he did not want to sacrifice either reason or existence. A series of conferences in 1935, entitled *"Vernunft und Existenz,"* powerfully affirm this: reason without existence is empty, but existence without reason is blind.³ Freed from the illusion of "an immobile realm of truth," reason would have the task, as announced in the second volume of his *Philosophie*, "of clarifying existence." In this way, it was a question of pushing back the point where reflection falls into silence. This can only happen at the price of the "paradox" a keyword of a new "philosophical logic" which aims to surmount the contradictions of a "divisive understanding" that is opposed to the thought of existence and the relation that unites it to transcendence.⁴ But, the paradox was a bridging of the gap between existence and transcendence. A "philosophy of the paradox" was more of a philosophy, in this sense, than a "philosophy of mystery."

Ricoeur's notion of transcendence in his philosophy of the will was inspired mostly by Jaspers. In the third volume of his *Philosophie*, Jaspers modestly designates an absent God, whose ciphers [*chiffres*] are visible in nature, history and the human being. This understanding of transcendence is opposed to the conception developed in Heidegger's *Being and Time*. Indeed, for Heidegger "transcendence" is only another name for finitude. Transcendence is fundamentally a part of existence for Heidegger and expresses the structure of the project and vocation in the world. There is thus no other transcendence than a worldly transcendence deployed within existence as its unsurpassable "horizon."⁵ The "secret" of this transcendence is time, and our dreams of eternity exist within the same finite existence as our anxiety about nothingness. For Heidegger, this analysis of human existence equals the destruction of metaphysics, whose ambition was to transcend the world itself. Part of this ambition is the desire to abolish time and to escape the truth of existence. The Heideggerian analysis of being-in-the-world breaks with this desire. It is well known, this analysis culminates in an ontology of being-toward-death. For Jaspers, on the contrary, even though existence is essentially finite, it faces transcendence as its other. Finitude originally contains a lack, which it takes up by opening itself to what it is not. This involves a transcendence which Descartes describes as the idea of the infinite, and this discovery permits the finite "I" to understand its own insufficiency. Without this transcendence, existence is nothing but a "demonic challenge" (Jaspers 2003: 190). Thus the "illumination of existence" calls for an illumination of transcendence, according to Jaspers, whose road leads "beyond-the-world." This does not imply forgetting the critique of the metaphysics of modernity, driven by "prophecy" and "science" (Jaspers 1989: 634). Jaspers's metaphysics does not have the intention to thematize "transcendence in itself," but rather "the existential relations with transcendence" (Jaspers 1989: 637). Everything happens as if existence were "an encoded scripture of transcendence," which is decipherable in principle (Jaspers 1989: 637).

To the question of whether transcendence is only the "transcendence of finitude" (in other words, whether finitude is the general characteristic of human reality), Ricoeur answers negatively at the beginning of the 1960s, just as he did at the beginning of the 1940s.[6] Between finitude and transcendence, there is not identity, but "polarity." This polarity obligates us to speak "of infinitude as much as of human finitude,"[7] and invites us to search within finitude "indications" of infinitude (Ricoeur 1948: 23). Jaspers was right to develop, against Heidegger, a "philosophy of two origins" [*philosophie à deux foyers*] (Ricoeur and Dufrenne 1947: 363 ff.) and to bear witness to the contradictions that disturb existence and that reflect both the "law of the day" and the "passion of the night."[8] The only possible ontology is a paradoxical one in the style of Descartes's *Third Meditation* or—and perhaps this comparison is better because this paradoxical ontology[31] is detected in feeling rather than reason—in the style of Pascal's fragments on the "disproportion of man" (Ricoeur 1965: 22).[9] In such an ontology, the description of finitude overlaps with the deciphering of transcendence (ibid.). And they both contribute to clarifying what Jaspers calls the "choice" of existence. Ricoeur, in turn, refuses to reduce this choice to the desperate "resolution" of an existence to its own mortality. This leads to a deepening of Ricoeur's "active sympathy" into a "loving struggle," to use an expression borrowed from Jaspers's *Philosophy*, which describes communication in its highest form (Ricoeur and Dufrenne 1947: 15).

How can we explain then the fact that Jaspers later ceased to be Ricoeur's privileged interlocutor? How can we explain the fact that this privilege shifted to someone whose thought did not inspire the same sympathy and who, later, was criticized for having developed a philosophy poorly equipped for moral and political decision-making? (ibid.) Was it due to Jaspers's lack of rigor,[10] or an overly psychological notion of existence,[11] or an overly theological conception of the relation between existence and transcendence[12] or the lack of a true method for deciphering transcendence in Jaspers's philosophy?[13] Perhaps it was all of this together. Nonetheless, whatever the reasons might be, the regrets that Ricoeur expresses at the end of the 1990s only make these questions more puzzling.[14] They demonstrate a fidelity to Jaspers that is stronger than any of these ruptures. It is in this regard that we should understand Ricoeur's suggestion, which he expressed on the occasion of the publication of a new edition of *Philosophy*, "to read Jaspers after Heidegger" (Ricoeur 1991: 156). In developing this re-reading, I will follow the order of the two final parts of Jaspers's work, which are devoted respectively to the illumination of existence and the reading of the ciphers of transcendence. This will allow us to see more clearly what Ricoeur retained from his reading of Jaspers as well as what he rejects or reworks. This is not to say that the first part of Jaspers's work, "Orientation in the World," is insignificant. It shows the role in Jaspers's philosophy of existence for rationality and scientific objectivity. Nonetheless, it is the second and third parts that take up the ethical stakes of an investigation that reconnects the fundamental freedom of existence and that discovers this freedom itself as an other.

Freedom, however, is only the first of three features that characterize existence; the two others are communication and historicity. Not surprisingly, they reflect the entire drama that constitutes existence and, even less surprising, they are at odds with objective understanding and can only be expressed as paradoxes: freedom implies necessity, communication implies solitude, and historicity unites time and eternity. It manifests existence as a "situated unconditionality" (Jaspers 1989: 421). These paradoxes express a "shattered human condition" (Jaspers 1989: 458). Insofar as they are crucial for Ricoeur's philosophical anthropology, each of them deserves a close analysis.

FREEDOM

Freedom has the "first"[15] but also the final word within the illumination of existence" (Jaspers 1989: 402). Communication and historicity, both in their own way, presuppose freedom. Certainly, there is no proof of freedom. Yet, that does not mean it does not exist, only that it is not an object or a property of an object. Rather, freedom begins where objective knowledge ends, in particular with the knowledge that we have of ourselves. Kant's thought echoes here. Human beings are more than what they know about themselves (Jaspers 1951: 84). We also experience this freedom when making decisions. Deciding implies the frightening certainty of relying completely on oneself (Jaspers 1989: 407). In vain we search to escape this certainty by imputing others with decisions or by searching the causes of our actions in the course of our experience. Yet, escape presupposes anxiety (ibid.). Bad faith, which results from this anxiety, does not calm down existence, which "trembles" in front of its possibilities (Jaspers 1989: 457). Thus, the "crisis" introduced by the moment of decision is never completely eliminated (Jaspers 1989: 407). Here the influence of Kierkegaard is superimposed on Kant.

This comes down to speaking about decision, in line with Kant, as an "unconditional act," or to use Kierkegaard's metaphor of the "leap." The notion of choice is only suitable for Jaspers, if one does not restrict it to a struggle between motivations, obtained through a calculation ensuring the agent of right action (Jaspers 1989: 405). It rather resembles, in this respect, an arbitrary decision (Jaspers 1989: 406). Nevertheless, this resemblance should not deceive us. It only holds with respect to objective theories of decision, against which the traditional conception of the free will is too weak. The anguishing decision of existence is not an arbitrary choice, in truth. If one is speaking about an "existential choice," the sense of the word "choice" breaks from a psychology of the free will (Jaspers 1989: 405). "I am myself the freedom of this choice" (Jaspers 1989: 406).

The freedom Jaspers describes is not by definition "a tool ready to use" (Jaspers 1989: 406). Saying that we are free amounts to saying "that we do not possess freedom by ourselves" (Jaspers 1951: 85) but rather that we receive freedom "as a gift" (Jaspers 1951: 85; cf. 1989: 405). For that reason there exists a "paradox in being oneself" (Jaspers 1989: 300): to be oneself does not mean being completely independent. Freedom, by which I choose myself, is not itself chosen. I am responsible for myself, but I come to myself, despite myself and without knowing how exactly. In sum, ipseity is not fundamentally a fixed state, but a reception of oneself by oneself. Reflection, by which oneself endeavors to truly be oneself, should not create an illusion. This effort begins before every reflection, and it does not annul, even afterward, the passivity of this originally coming to oneself.[16] The self's freedom is continually a given freedom. The pitfall of reflection is precisely to forget, as a result of freedom, the gift that founds freedom. It thereby abolishes the difference between free decision and free creation. Freedom in the traditional sense of the *causa sui* claims to escape every limitation. It becomes a "phantom" of "absolute freedom" (Jaspers 1989: 415) which precisely differs from human freedom. This kind of absolute freedom only knows and wants itself (ibid). As a totality without outside, it cuts itself off from its roots and loses itself in the unreal (Jaspers 1989: 294; tr. mod.). The freedom of existence is completely different. If it is truth that I make myself in freedom, it is also true that I did not make it. "Original freedom" does not mean that it is its own origin. Rather, it always stands behind freedom and nothing is an absolute beginning.

Yet, the paradox expressed in the language of the gift will also be expressed in the paradox of necessity. I cannot want not to want; I cannot choose not to choose. In relation to its origin, freedom becomes a destiny here. This paradox does not only concern freedom in general, it emerges with every particular choice. Our destiny is not only that we are free, but also that we are in a world that preexists us. In this world only decision finds a foothold. Although it limits freedom, the same world also makes freedom possible. The same goes for our past choices: when we let them go, we also depart from ourselves. It is the weight that weighs on decision that gives it its reality. The choice of being oneself does not amount to "being another person in another world" (Jaspers 1989: 406). On the contrary, it is choosing to "maintain" oneself *as oneself* in the world. This is what Jaspers understands as fidelity. Fidelity would not have any for a substantial self, nor for a consciousness entirely delivered over to changing states and circumstances. Thus, through the past that binds it, through the gift that founds it and through the world in which it determines itself, "existential freedom" implies an "existential necessity" (Ricoeur and Dufrenne 1947: 147). This necessity is different from the causality of the will of the empirical subject. It is not the absolute necessity of nature either, nor that of character (Jaspers 1989: 292). Instead, it is a necessity intrinsic to freedom itself.[17]

Concretely, the voluntary act attests to this unity of freedom and necessity. It would be a mistake indeed to simply oppose the voluntary to "involuntary" desires, sentiments, or drives. Such an opposition would only consider two options: either mastering them or surrendering to them. Moreover, this opposition corresponds empirically to psychopathological phenomena that reinforce one another (Jaspers 1989: 386).[18] For example, the feeling of powerlessness that certain psychoses cause is reinforced when the patient tries to control his states and representations intellectually (Jaspers 2000: 121). And experience demonstrates that, in a more general sense, "straightforward and immediate willing" does not accomplish much, when its "psychological background" is not clarified (Jaspers 1989: 386). Violently opposed to the vital rhythms of the body and to the profound forces of desire, straightforward and immediate willing is but a sterile will, surrounded by emptiness and with only its own motives as goal. The truthful will, on the other hand, finds its origins in the involuntary, even if it is opposed to the involuntary. Paradoxically, opposition goes hand in hand here with unity. This unity gives the will its force. The truthful will is thus more than just "a challenge of a formal ego" or the "narrow demand of an individual that pretends to have enough with itself" (Jaspers 1989: 395).

Yet, how can the will escape the suffocation of mastery and the illusion of independence? The response to this question is always the same for Jaspers: consent to the involuntary. However, one should not confuse two different types of consent. The first is the empirical subject's adaption to the demands of the situation. This is untruthful consent. The second, truthful consent amounts to the existential decision that is the acceptance of *being-in-situation* and that welcomes that which appeared strange before. While untruthful consent is self-evident, truthful consent is more difficult and implies tensions and conflicts. It implies battling against carefree lived existence, as well as against its opposite, that is, against experiences that push us to revolt or despair. Its initial motive is nevertheless always the same: "I did not create myself," "my beginning is not *the* beginning," "I did not choose my parents" (Jaspers 1989: 432). My birth precedes me and appears to be the fruit of another will. Yet, these different phrases that express the same motive raise the question whether it is still possible here to speak of a decision. Is this reciprocity of the voluntary and the involuntary not simply the absolutely involuntary of life, in the category of suffering and death? And what about the actions that I have accomplished but that I simply could not avoided in my situation?

However, at this point the paradox again reverses: "I accept the origin of my being, which is nevertheless prior to any of my acts" (Jaspers 1989: 417). I accept the choice of my parents and recognize myself as being "co-responsible" (Jaspers 1989: 432). "I accept all that, as far as I am aware, I could not have avoided" (Jaspers 1989: 417). Life and death, suffering and fault, my character, my history, the inevitable failure of all my struggles against myself: all this enters the realm of freedom, a liberty whose unconditional character can only be maintained in a mode of "as if."[19] Everything passes indeed "as if I had chosen myself the way I am before time, and in a way that I recognized as my own this factually ever unaccomplished choice, by assuming my acts." Everything passes "as if I feel my consciousness after all [. . .] to be the origin of [. . .] the circumstances of my situation (Jasper 1989: 417; cf. 292). The paradox, formulated in this sense, is one of an "a situated unconditionality." It will be stand at the core of the determination of existence as "historicity." Yet, this paradox is first of all a hypothesis which Jaspers formulates unsurprisingly in terms that recall Kant's position on radical evil and original sin. Indeed, guilt presupposes freedom. Evil would not exist without a human being capable of doing evil. Yet "even though I am a free being, I struggle not to become guilty. In fact, I am already culpable of the fact of my freedom" (Jaspers 1989: 417). Pleading innocence would only amount to denying freedom itself.

Is the capable human being necessarily a *culpable* human being? Is fallibility, understood as the possibility to do wrong, different from the fault, that is to say, the action that realizes this possibility? Does an anthropology of existence have to consider existence as the "undifferentiated keyboard" which is played by both innocent and culpable human beings? (Ricoeur 1986: xli). Moreover, does not the decision that makes the human culpable result from the contingency of choice and anteriority of innocence? If we have followed Jaspers up to this point, it was in order to arrive at the point where Ricoeur seems to depart from Jaspers's philosophy.[20] This distance, however, is introduced within the greatest proximity. It is this close affinity that I will first discuss.

It is tempting, at this point, to turn immediately to Ricoeur's *Freedom and Nature* where he states that "to will is not to create" (Ricoeur 1965: 486). These words conclude a work that posits the "reciprocity of the voluntary and involuntary" and then recognizes the existence of an "absolute involuntary" which is attested in character, the unconsciousness and life, and closes with a wisdom whose ultimate form is a "consent to the involuntary." "An only human freedom," according to the phrase that summarizes the orientation of *Freedom and Nature*, is a freedom united with necessity. More essentially, it is a freedom united with the freedom of another. Stoicism is thus taken as an "imperfect consent": it risks becoming "a kind of detachment and scorn through which the soul withdraws into its own circularity" (Ricoeur 1965: 470). The phenomenology of birth, which Ricoeur sketches in the final pages of *Freedom and Nature* moves away from this risk: to be born is to be engendered; to consent to one's own birth is thus to accept that one does not create oneself. The goal of this consent is not to reduce life to an impersonal structure, but a happy dependence that constitutes for each person filiation. If filiation is then prolonged by education, one will be convinced that one receives freedom, just like one receives life.[21] Commencing existence is to continue the work of another. It is thus more of a question of the power to "welcome" than a power of position (Ricoeur 1965: 34). However, Jaspers also denounces, as we have seen, the illusion of independence. In spite of certain heroic traits that contradict with Ricoeur's focus on "affective fragility," freedom is thus for him too a capacity to welcome. He puts the accent on the gift, which is a formal determination of being oneself. A given freedom is therefore a freedom open to what it is not or a freedom that looks for truth elsewhere than in itself. This freedom is a self-cause but also finds its aim in itself, but to the extent that it has been received from an other, it can only find it in another. Hence the following phrase: "I receive myself as a gift," implies an other (Jaspers 1989: 300). I am truly myself if I "I give myself endlessly again to the other" in communication (Jaspers 1989: 326; cf. Jaspers 2003: 227). The gift, thus understood, does not have any moral or religious content. It is only formal. Yet, this form marks the transition from existential freedom to what Jaspers calls "existential communication."[22]

COMMUNICATION

Communication is, for Jaspers, not only the "universal condition of being human" (Jaspers 2003: 208) but also makes us the singular beings that we are (Jaspers 2003: 205). What is at stake in communication is the "origin of being oneself" (Jaspers 1989: 305). Indeed, one is that communication goes from "understanding to understanding," but the other is that communication goes from "existence to existence" (Jaspers 1951: 27). If the former is an impersonal and general procedure of validating concepts and propositions in a universal consciousness, the latter is a singular relation between persons that mutually recognize each other (Jaspers 1989: 310).

I can thus see the collapse of all the things that surround me: "but what remains is the humans who are with me" and I share with them that which is for me, as it is for all of them, truthful being (Jaspers 1989: 356). Communication, as an original determination of existence, explains why unconditional freedom is not an absolute freedom. Freedom is relative to other freedoms[23]: "it is only truly freedom within an existence shared with other existences"

(Jaspers 1989: 43). Together, different freedoms are what they are and together they can reach what everyone wants to reach (Jaspers 1989: 310). The paradox that the philosophy existence must face is that of a being who is by itself but who can only effectively be through an other (Jaspers 1989: 305).[24] The freedom of existence implies a solitude that is not solipsism and that is only possible by means of communication. In order to clarify this, it is helpful to take a closer look at existential communication.

Existential communication is irreducible, as I have argued, to the communication from understanding to understanding—or what can provisionally be called rational communication. Yet, existential communication is equally irreducible to "empirical communication," that is to say communication conditioned by the situation in which human beings, as being-there [*Dasein*], are vitally interested. These distinctions on the level of communication mirror Jaspers's distinction in the sphere of ipseity between existence, general consciousness, and empirical consciousness.

Empirical communication demands nothing more than abandoning oneself to the traditions and customs governing the life of a particular community. It demands each person to act, believe, and think what everyone does, believes, and thinks, respectively. By exchanging goals, opinions, and ideas, the individual may have a clear mind, but "one's self-consciousness remains hidden" (Jaspers 1989: 306). Confused with the collective consciousness of society, it is more of an unconsciousness. Not being truly a self, the individual cannot enter into a relation with another self. The community is thus the enemy of communication. It operates as a process of disappropriation and closure.

Rational communication, on the contrary, tells a different story. Through rational communication the self becomes self-conscious and open to universal goals. The laws of communication should therefore not be confused with those of the community to which one belongs. Rather, communication shows itself capable, through the act of reason, of breaking the circle of habits and conventions of communal life. This is made possible when argumentation has surpassed the level of negotiation and has reached the level of discussion and true dialogue (Jaspers 2003: 212–13). That which communication perceives as true can be understood as such by everyone. This aim is essentially different from those pursued by the "encumbered individual" (Jaspers 1989: 307). This ultimate goal presents itself as a call that invites us to open oneself and to break with those on whom one depends empirically. Here, under the influence of Kant, a sharp dividing line can be drawn between understanding and reason. Reason goes beyond what stops the understanding—where everything appears in terms of determinate objects—by projecting before consciousness the idea of a whole that cannot be known but conveys a boundless will to communicate. The Platonic dialogues, in their incompleteness, also attest to this pursuit, are an example of this.

Indeed, the essence of "true communication" is to support "an unlimited exchange of questions and responses" (Jaspers 1989: 318). However, the reference to Plato should not mislead: it should not lead to the belief that one can already find in Plato a notion of communication that associates reason with existence, and which would be the expression, in this sense, of what Jaspers understands as true communication. "Dialectical argumentation" only expresses "the dialectical structure of cognitive thought" (Jaspers 1989: 354), which can belong to anyone and which does not imply the birth of true communication. This is the price of the claim to universality, but it remains an abstract universality. "Valid for all" differs from the singularity of every single being. Everyone "understands the same thing" but in this understanding only forms "an impersonal community" (Jaspers 1989: 306–07). Communication is thus without substance, it is an indifferent *medium* of a truth found outside of this communication and in which no one can recognize oneself.[25] A truth "originally tied to communication" would be completely different. On the one hand, it would not exist outside of effective communication (Jaspers 2003: 234). On the other hand, it would permit everybody to find oneself in it. One should therefore take the following formula literally: "the truth begins with two." Truth thus implies a communication between irreplaceable persons (Jaspers 2003: 226) who are called not only to open themselves internally to one another but also to take the relation that unites them as an absolute relation (Jaspers 1989: 313). This is existential communication and mutual promotion of freedoms. This communication finds its goal within itself. There is thus no *hiatus* between being oneself and being true, nor is there one, consequently, between uniqueness and similarity, between singularity and universality, between solitude and belonging to a community of "all humans" (Jaspers 1989: 314). Jaspers elaborates at great length this paradox of "communication within solitude" (ibid.). He expresses it in terms of a "polarity" within "possible existence" itself, which thus appears to have a double origin. Jaspers's complete formulation of this paradox goes as follows: "communication establishes itself each time between two beings [. . .] who approach each other starting from their own solitude. Yet they only know this solitude because they communicate with each other" (Jaspers 1989: 313).[26]

The following phrases are significant: "each time" and "between two beings." The first phrase invites us to consider communication as an event. The second one suggests that communication is always "the secret of two persons" (Jaspers 1989: 317). Yet, both of these formulas can also be easily superimposed. If communication is an event, then it can only be a relation between two persons. In this respect, Jaspers distances himself from both Husserl and Heidegger. It is remarkable that Husserl only discusses the topic of communication in a few unpublished texts. In fact, his theory of intersubjectivity in *Cartesian Meditations* is not a theory of communication. In their book, Ricoeur and Dufrenne insist on this point: if the other is implied in the life of the *ego cogito*, it is foremost to guarantee the objectivity of the *cogitatum*. It is not as "a concrete presence with which I can interact" (Ricoeur and Dufrenne 1947: 154). Jaspers's issue is not a transcendental problem; it is a problem of fact and not of principle. But it is not an ontological problem either, at least if one means by the latter a theory of the structures of human reality. The notion of an event must be distinguished from that of a structure. The "each time" of existential communication concerns a relation that takes the form of an encounter. Jaspers thus does not adopt Heidegger's theory of *Mitsein*. The relation with the other does not presuppose, for him, an openness to a world that would stand "in the background." Rather, the world opens itself time and again starting from the relation with the other. Otherwise, nothing would be able to break its totality. Everything would submit to the kingdom of the "one." In this anonymous world, "others" would only count insofar as they play a role or are a number. The world also commences with two, one could say. It is not the case that the communication of existence would only have a private aspect. It extends to anybody who chooses to find oneself there. But this existence is not a totality either. On the contrary, it is based on the "original fact" of the plurality of existences. Moreover, existence presupposes that each one, each time, recognizes each one for him or herself. This recognition is, as I mentioned earlier, the condition without which there would be no true communication. For Jaspers, communication is not possible with the I or the other alone. Without doubt, communication is a "need" for the I (Jaspers 1989: 310). This need results from "the suffering that the lack of communication provokes" (Jaspers 1951: 28). Yet, the other is not a means for my own ends. On the contrary, "I cannot be free, if the other is not free" (Jaspers 1989: 310). So, in order to be entirely oneself, it is up to me to allow the other to be himself or herself. Recognition not only demands of the I "a sacrifice of internal solidity" and the "risk" of being questioned by the other in one's own being (Jaspers 1989: 326). Recognition also calls to liberate the other with regard to him or herself. The "reciprocity" of recognition is thus not a give and take. Reciprocity is constituted by a solicitude without calculation or compensation, rather than by an exchange of interests. For this reason, it has an unconditional character and opens an authentic "solidarity" that is opposed to the struggle of life in society as in nature, as well as to solitude and suffering. This solidarity results from mutual solicitude.[27] It consists of each one promoting, as much as possible, the freedom of the other (Jaspers 1989: 317).

The topics just discussed accentuate the moral tone of Jaspers's account of existential communication but do not conflict with its epistemological aspects, either. Indeed, what would the common search for truth be, without the mutual promotion of freedoms that struggle with one another in order to keep communication open? What is more, this openness resists a totalization of the truth in a knowledge would regard the plurality of existences from above. Struggle, for Jaspers, does not belong completely to the sphere of vital interests, but it does not belong to a science of the structures of consciousness either. The truth of this struggle is not the "opposition of self-consciousnesses" that clash either to dominate or to serve and then gets resolved on a higher level, as Hegel understands it in the *Phenomenology of Spirit*.[28]

After all, this kind of thinking is that of a self-consciousness in general (ibid.). It is not a thinking of the singular person, nor does the singular person only play a mediating role attributed by speculative philosophy. Instead, for those who freely unite their solitudes, there is neither a surpassing nor a reconciliation in the perspective opened by what Jaspers understands as transcendence. Can we call this understanding dialectical, given that it describes transformations that result from uniting other existences with that of oneself (which implies that "we are neither I, nor the other of substances [. . .] that would exist before communication")? (Jaspers 1989: 320). If we can call Jaspers's thought a dialectic without *Aufhebung*, this is because the plurality of existences is insurmountable and their struggle never resolved.

Communication itself is thus insufficient for Jaspers. This is not only the case for empirical and rational communication, but also for existential communication. Indeed, existential communication does not surpass empirical (particular) communication and rational (universal) communication through a dialectical movement. Nor is it possible to establish oneself immediately on the level of existential communication. Existential communication can only be achieved within a situation in which empirical communication is accomplished in the horizon opened by rational communication. Both empirical and rational communications are thus conditions, or better, necessary "mediations" for the development of existential communication. Neither society, with its customs and positive laws, nor reason, its ideas and formal rules, become meaningless for the human being who decides to enter into a relation of existential communication with other humans. But from one level to the other, there is no progression, only a succession of "leaps" that introduce a "tension" between them. The only privilege of existential communication is that it carries this tension to the highest level of irresolution.

The insufficiency of existential communication is not purely negative. On the one hand, we can recognize and assume this insufficiency. On the other hand, it turns communication itself into an infinite task. The desire for a communication "open for everyone" presupposes the narrowness of communication accessible only to some. The desire for "unlimited" communication does not overlook the illusions, distortions, and violence which often block philosophical discussion from its true goals. However, one then arrives at the paradox of communication, understood as the always incomplete search for an accord between existences. This incompleteness does not conflict with the idea of "a final achievement that overcomes communication" and would have no more need for accord. This achievement is itself "the manifestation of a depth which cannot be filled, except by transcendence" where everything is "presence" and where all communication must be conceived "as if it were silenced" (Jaspers 2003: 245–46). This is the reason that "ultimate communication is silence" (Jaspers 2003: 249). If truth begins with two, it ends where duality becomes unity. However, what counts as true within transcendence is an illusion in the world and in history. Authentic communication is thus ultimately "torn apart." It knows that it cannot become what it desires. The immediacy of love thus does not dispense of the mediations that always imply the actual combat of existences. These mediations are the sources of a double polarity for the existence open to transcendence: the first relates existence to reason and the second relates existence to situatedness. Given that these polarities keep communication indefinitely distant from its goal, they cannot be ignored without abstraction or peril.

Ricoeur is sensitive to this double polarity when reading Jaspers. And he remains faithful to it, while criticizing other approaches to communication. In particular, he offers parallel objections against the formalism of a communication without context—which is illustrated, for example, by discourse ethics and the Rawlsian fiction of the "veil of ignorance"—and against the prophetism of a communication without context and rules, examples of which can be found in Marcel, and, in another sense, Levinas.

Ricoeur's second objection is formulated in his early works, that is, in his comparative study of Marcel and Jaspers. This objection marks clearly Ricoeur's preference for Jaspers's philosophy over that of Marcel. The principal concern of Marcel is indeed to distinguish between two categories: the existential category of the second person "you" and the objective category of third person "him/her/it." In authentic communication, we address ourselves always to the "you." Yet under the pressure of circumstances or of the collectivity and the institutions regulating it, we treat the "you" as "he/she/it." We thereby disconnect the person from his/her personality. This type of treatment has an impact. Indeed, as Marcel writes "when the "you" disappears, the "I" becomes *it* for itself."[29] The "we" of interpersonal communication loses itself then in the impersonal "one." And this "one" prevails in opinion, democracy, science, and industrial civilization. Ricoeur objects that this type of thinking lacks a positive reflection on society, law, and institutions (Ricoeur 1948: 170), as well as a consideration of existence and transcendence "in the real context of the present" (Ricoeur 1948: 170). He particularly remarks, with regard to the spirit of democracy, that it is "a historical force that incarnates similitude of humanity before the law rather than impersonal knowledge," which is proper to science and technology.

Ricoeur's reflection is thus broadened to the role of the third party, which is only rarely the source of depersonalization that Marcel envisions in this form of communication. Instead, Ricoeur's reflection enriches Marcel's thought by pointing out something that would not exist without the third, namely, justice. The role of justice in Ricoeur's later work is well known. In his "little ethics" in *Oneself as Another*, the accent is first placed on "solicitude," to which according to Levinas, we are called by the other in the "face to face" of an "interpersonal relation": "the other is also the other than 'you'; [. . .] justice goes beyond the face-to-face relation." Yet rather than taking away something from solicitude, justice adds to it "to the extent that justice concerns humanity as such" (Ricoeur 1992: 189 and 202). In both cases, the bottom-line is the same; the impersonal third person "he/she/it" should be conceived as a *medium* of personal relationships (Ricoeur 1992: 177). This conception belongs precisely to Jaspers. His attention to real "situations of communication" leads him to envision the economic order, the legal order, the political order and cultural order as where a "certain humanization of relations between individuals" is pursued, in spite of the obstacles and threats they may face. Without this humanization, these individuals would not be full persons (Ricoeur 1948: 197). This is particularly apparent in his theory of the State. Although existence certainly transcends and is authorized to contest it, it nonetheless receives part of its dignity from the state (Ricoeur 1948: 199).

More generally, Ricoeur has two convictions that result from his interpretation of Jaspers's theory of communication, and without exaggeration one can say that they remain present throughout his entire work and sum up its spirit. The first is that "there is never a direct route from myself to myself" (Ricoeur 1948: 200). The second conviction is that the task of philosophy is "to protect the different levels of humanity and to recognize their positivity as well as their ultimate destitution," with regard to the relation that unites them with transcendence (Ricoeur 1948: 177). Love may well be the distant source of communication and may silently determine its end. Yet, love does not authorize communication to proceed immediately toward this goal. Before death, one has to live in this world, and in order to live in this world, one has to accept the mediations that turn a possible existence into a real existence. Due to the various languages we speak, these mediations remain always imperfect and can never abolish the tragedy of our existence through a higher logic.

HISTORICITY AND LIMIT SITUATIONS

Jaspers's notion of "historicity" reflects this concern for mediations and their inevitable imperfections. This notion without doubt finds its counterpart in

Ricoeur's later work, with the concept of "the historical condition," understood as an "insurmountable mode of being" in which we exist (Ricoeur 2004: 284). The existential accent of this phrase echoes Jaspers's theme of historicity. By introducing this theme, Jaspers has two intentions. First, he aims to include historical knowledge within the hermeneutics of existence, but to qualify its claims to be scientific. The second intention of Jaspers's idea of historicity is to reveal a tension, proper to existence, between the "burden of history" and that which is given as "ahistorical" or even "supra-historical" (Ricoeur 2004: 292 ff.). This second line of the analysis proceeds through a discussion of Heidegger's ontology of being-in the-world and, more specifically, of Heidegger's reduction of being-in-the-world to being-toward-death. In spite of the methodological difference marked by a preference for "hermeneutics" over "illumination" in the first line of the analysis, this second line shows the deep affinities between the two thinkers.[30] Yet in order to grasp fully the meaning of Jaspers's hermeneutics, one should note the continuity between the theme of historicity and the meaning implied by his notion of "limit situations."

Historicity is, like freedom or communication, a defining feature of existence. Yet, while existence confirms its unconditional character in freedom and communication, historicity is the reminder—at the heart of this affirmation—of everything that conditions it. That which is conditioned for Jaspers refers first of all to the "unity of existence and empirical reality" (Jaspers 1989: 360). It is thus the existential fact of being in the world, or the fact of *Existenz* being *Dasein* as well.[31] Historicity understood in this sense equals situatedness and the "resistance" that it offers to the vocation of existence. Within it, all the polarities come together that lead it to the breaking point and that it must assume in order to truly be itself.

"To assume" is the keyword here. While situatedness is undergone and appears as a destiny to empirical consciousness, it is up to existence to "appropriate" it and "face" situatedness.[32] Historicity, understood as the unity of existence and empirical reality, can also be defined then as a "unity of freedom and necessity" (Jaspers 1989: 362). It is, so to speak, the conversion of destiny into freedom. We have seen earlier this paradox: although I am "free by origin," I cannot "begin from nowhere"; all my actions presuppose my "belonging" to a world that I did not create myself (Jaspers 1989: 433). Situatedness is "already there" and signifies that there is always something "already decided" for me (Jaspers 1989: 362–63). Yet, like a bird that would like to take away the resistance of the air, I have no right to complain. Situatedness keeps me from falling into nothingness, even though it limits my freedom as well (Ibid.). The emphasis here is placed on the dialectic between belonging and appropriation, and on its positive function in the constitution of responsibility and the orientation of decision. Or to put it in Gadamer's terms, historicity itself has the structure of communication. The fundamental attitude of the existence which assumes its situatedness consists in recognizing that others have existed before oneself and in "allowing these others to question oneself" (Jaspers 1989: 379). Better still, it consist in transferring to the future, by incorporating it into decision, the meaning of this questioning and thus to ask oneself: "Can you want what you are doing to be realized in the world? Can you want a world where this is possible? Can you assume such a world for eternity?" (Ibid.).

Yet, this final question gives rise to a novel paradox and tension within the analysis of historicity. As a "unity of existence and of empirical reality" and "unity of liberty and of necessity," historicity is also a "unity of time and eternity" (Jaspers 1989: 363). Fidelity is the best example of this paradox, given that it has the power to surmount the empirical succession of events and to animate that which has passed away. Fidelity certainly presupposes the temporality of existence, but it assumes this temporality in view of a meaning that it does not exhaust. And what holds true for fidelity holds even more true for the decision that founds and sums up the wish to remain oneself in all circumstances. The instant of decision is not equal to the other moments of time. It does not disappear in the "passing" of time, where all events intertwine, before getting mixed up and finally disappearing. This is what Kierkegaard calls the encounter of the temporal and the eternal, where time becomes the manifestation of eternity. All we can say about it is "that it resides elsewhere than where it appears temporally" (Jaspers 1989: 365). The ultimate paradox of historicity is therefore this: "existence is conquered by decisions that are made over course of time," but these decisions simultaneously "determine what is eternal" (Jaspers 1989: 364–65). This paradox is, as we have seen, the paradox of an existence open to transcendence. The more our finitude of being-in-the-world imposes itself upon us, the more we are conscious of a being that is different from our own being and from the being of the world (Jaspers 1989: 361).[33] And just as the ultimate sense of communication is noncommunicable, the ultimate sense of historicity is beyond the world and its history. The "appropriation" of situatedness is this not only one of accepting traits that constitute finitude, but also of assuming traits that point to the "beyond." Yet, how is this appropriation possible?

Jaspers's description of "limit situations" provides an answer to this question. The word "limit" signifies "there is something else, but, at the same time, this something else is not accessible to empirical consciousness" (Jaspers 1989: 423). This means that the simple fact of belonging to a certain situation does not have any consequences. In this state of belonging we are only preoccupied with calculating our best interests in the situation. We are fully and only in situatedness, being-in-the-world. But it so happens that we are incapable of maintaining ourselves simply in the context situation. The ground thus seems to crumble under our feet (Jaspers 1989: 458). Belonging to the world is no longer self-evident. The world instead appears "uncertain" and "problematic." Our plans and calculations are consequently insufficient. Everything points to the impossibility of continuing to exist in this way. We become conscious, by our failures, of the inevitable failure of our existence in the world. Not that this would lead us necessarily to despair. Yet, we are called in question to such a radical extent that we can no longer ignore the truth of our being: "situatedness becomes a limit situation when awakening subjectivity to existence by shaking its empirical life" and by depriving it of the rest it was searching for (Jaspers 1989: 43). Historicity, in its antinomic structure, has this general significance (Jaspers 1989: 458).[34] Yet, this is even more so the case for death, suffering, the culpability that accompanies our actions like a shadow and from which not even the beautiful soul can find refuge, as well as for the endless struggle for life and dignity. These are, for Jaspers, the principal limit situations.[35]

The role Jaspers grants to these limit situations distantly resembles Husserl's idea of the phenomenological *epoche*.[36] However, the experience that enables limit situations is not simply an experience of consciousness, and even less so a methodology that evokes an experience in the mind of a disinterested spectator.[37] Rather, limit situations are more close to what Heidegger terms *Angst*: they "break" with the regular course of experiences and place existence in front of itself.[38] They reveal to existence the finitude of its being-in-the-world. Yet, whereas Heidegger's *Angst* calls for death to be the unique sense of finitude, limit situations, according to Jaspers, grant multiple meanings to finitude. And whereas finitude, understood exclusively from the perspective of mortality, leads us to take the world as the ultimate horizon of existence, limit situations invite us to project ourselves beyond this horizon. This is why "authentic" existence,[39] that is, existence called by this confrontation with itself to decision and responsibility, cannot be reduced to an existence courageous and resolute toward its own death.[40] There exist multiple limit situations, and therefore also multiple senses of finitude and ultimately multiples ways of relating finitude with transcendence.

In both of his works on Jaspers, Ricoeur focuses at length on this multiplicity. For Heidegger "the human being jumps into the world to decease there, and only death is an authentic resolution [. . .], freedom is freedom toward death. For Jaspers, on the contrary, death does not have this privilege [. . .], it is only one of the limit situations and not systematically linked to the three others." This is the reason that if "for Heidegger Jaspers's thought will always lack clarity," "for Jaspers Heidegger's philosophy will always lack faith and hope" (Ricoeur and Dufrenne 1947: 366–67). Does the lucidity of *Angst*, however, only stand for the "desperate courage" that implies for Heidegger, in line with the Stoics, the individual's "resolution" in the solitary confrontation with his/her own death? The greatest *Angst* is not that of ceasing to be; instead it is to give way to this *Angst* itself and to let oneself fall into the pitfalls of a world in which life, poorly lived, would be like a second death. The Kierkegaardian conception of *Angst* is much richer, in this respect, than the Heideggerian one (Ricoeur and Dufrenne 1947: 186). This is also the case for Jaspers's notion of *Angst*, who distinguishes "existential *Angst*" from "vital *Angst*" (Jaspers 1989: 440). It follows that death cannot simply be taken as the ultimate truth of existence.

Another question is whether the only authentic death is death in the first person. Jaspers's analysis of the first of the four limit situations can convince that the answer to this question is negative. First of all, it is important to note that, in limit situations, there is no death in the general sense of the word.[41] Death is either my death or the death of my neighbor. And, "the death of my neighbor [. . .] is the most profound rupture in phenomenal life." It entails an "existential shock" that reveals, by way of contrast, the truth of communication and the place of the other in ourselves (Jaspers 1989: 437). Ricoeur, commenting on this text, affirms this: "the greatest solitude" is the solitude resulting from the death of a parent or a friend (Ricoeur 1948: 205). And, we know that Ricoeur does not change his opinion on this issue throughout his writings. What he writes in *Freedom and Nature*, "the decisive encounter with death, is the 'death' of being loved" (Jaspers 1989: 432) is repeated fifty years later in *Memory, History, Forgetting* in arguing for "the multiple senses of death" where it is "the death of the other"—further expanded to the death "of all others"—which determines through reflection "my relation to my own death" (Ricoeur 2004: 360). The suffering of loss and the suffering of the culpability of the murderer are authentic experiences of finitude, no less than the anxiety of nothingness.[42]

THE SENSE OF TRANSCENDENCE

Yet limit situations do not only manifest the finitude of our being-in-the-world, by marking our being-in-the world with the stamp of failure, these situations also invite us to detect the ciphers of transcendence. Historically speaking, this was the domain of speculative metaphysics, but it becomes a matter of concrete realizing their meaning. One should therefore distinguish between speculative or "formal" metaphysics and the "existential relations with transcendence." These two directions are also opened by limit-situations, to the extent that they are devoted to a consciousness that is "absolute" not in the sense of a knowledge that it does not possess, but in the sense of actions that it is urged to do and that should be understood as "absolute actions."[43] These actions allow the sense of transcendence to "enter into empirical reality." These actions are thus a paradoxical operation: they first aim to depart from the world (Jaspers 1989: 495), in order to receive inspiration and then return to the world. Insofar they depend on our freedom; these actions can follow opposite directions. For example, suicide and fidelity in spite of all betrayals are two extremes along this arc of possibilities offered to our decision. But only the second option—fidelity—expresses a correct deciphering of transcendence. Indeed: "It would be a mistake to absolutize freedom in order to make it a transcendent being." "When we truly decide [. . .] we are conscious of not owing our own being to ourselves" (Jaspers 1951: 85–86). Consequently, one might assert, in spite of the possible suspicion one might have that these phrases are intended to distinguish between ontology and theology: existence is transcendence. Suicide sanctions this mistake, that is, it results from a mistaken inversion of the sense of transcendence. The role of metaphysics, as Jaspers understands it, is to be a remedy for this possible inversion. Through an appropriate reading of the ciphers of transcendence, it arouses the attitudes and actions that render existence effectively possible.

However, we face two problems here. These problems express the primary "perplexities" that Ricoeur has with regard to Jaspers's philosophy. The first problem concerns the method of reading the ciphers of transcendence. Indeed, one has to admit that this method is essentially lacking. The circular relation that unites the "elucidation" of existence and "deciphering" of transcendence demonstrates this lack more precisely. The illumination of existence is deprived of the intuitive method that Husserl established through the phenomenological reduction. The "absolute consciousness," which emerges from the initial shock of limit situations, should not mislead us: these situations remain in themselves "opaque" and deprived of sense. They place existence in front of an enigma and do not provide the means to find its solution. How could one not be tempted then to superimpose, ever the circle of this illumination and this deciphering, the hermeneutical circle of understanding and interpretation? One can hypothesize that it is because Ricoeur had examined, by reading Jaspers, the "possibility of an existential philosophy" (Ricoeur 1948: 235 ff.), that Ricoeur moved, less than a decade later, along the path of a hermeneutic phenomenology, which he would never abandon. When it comes to the interpretation of transcendence, this hypothesis is further supported by the development in his later work of a theory of imagination, a theory of symbols, and a theory of language. Jaspers's metaphysics identifies this project but is only able to offer a preliminary sketch.[44] If the world in its entirety is "the manuscript of an Other," then there must be the means to translate this manuscript into the language of the people that inhabit this world.

For Ricoeur, the problem of Jaspers's philosophy of existence is essentially the possibility of a philosophy that is "completely torn apart." Indeed, all of Jaspers's philosophy ultimately closes in on "failure" as the "ultimate key" to transcendence. This failure is a failure of reconciliation which animates an existence divided by suffering and by the fault. The "antinomies of being-oneself" are thus destined to endure as long as we live in this world. They do not give hope in this world for remission or redemption. Yet, are we not condemned again either to "flee" into other worlds or the "hopeless courage" from which Jaspers's entire philosophy sought to protect existence? This is no longer simply a question of method. What is at stake, instead, is a concrete metaphysics—or, to put it differently, a metaphysics of action—which ought to open a connection between existence and transcendence. For this connection to succeed, it is necessary for transcendence to be more than a "limit idea"; it would have to be more than the almost eclipsed trace of an absent God. Yet, more than the question of determining whether transcendence should be located in metaphysics or religion,[45] it is the nature of the actions that embody transcendence that lead Ricoeur to distance himself from Jaspers's philosophy. A single thread, in this regard, connects Ricoeur's first work to his last published works. What is expressed throughout, with respect to the concepts of the gift[46] and of pardon (see Ricoeur 2004) in his later writings, as well as the idea of "lived reconciliation" in his first work is the following (Ricoeur and Dufrenne 1947: 382ff.): whether it is a matter of suffering or of the fault, and without negating the seriousness of their impact on existence, for Ricoeur reconciliation always has the last word (Ricoeur and Dufrenne 1947: 388).

Translated by Geoffrey Dierckxsens

NOTES

1. Translator's note: due to significant discrepancies between the French and English translations of Jaspers's work, we will translate directly from the French translation and refer to the French edition throughout.

2. Ricoeur, *Gabriel Marcel et Karl Jaspers* (Paris: Ed. du Temps Présent, 1948). It is Marcel who introduced Ricoeur to Jaspers's work, sometime before the war, through an article he published in *Recherches*.

3. Karl Jaspers, "La Raison et l'existence," in *Karl Jaspers: Nietzsche et le christianisme*, trad. J. Hersch et R. Givord (Paris: Bayard, 2003): 111–313. Reason turns to violence and becomes the plaything of "instincts" and the prey of "mundane powers" (131).

4. Jaspers's conception of reason puts him in opposition to both positivism and idealism. This leads him to distinguish reason from a "divisive understanding" (of which science shows at the same time its power and its limits) and from the "impersonal divinity" of the systematic philosophies (where it creates the illusion of absolute truth). This made Jaspers what Ricoeur calls, borrowing an expression from Eric Weil, a post-Hegelian Kantian

5. Martin Heidegger, *Being and Time*, § 69. The secret of transcendence is nothing other than existence and temporality here and now.

6. This is Ricoeur's position in *Freedom and Nature*, which is the same as in his 1947 book on Jaspers.

7. Since "the human being is no less destined to unlimited rationality, to totality and bliss, than to be limited to a perspective, delivered to death and riveted to desire" (ibid., pp. 23–24).

8. The Heideggerian analytic of being-in-the-world remains unaware of these contradictions. It prejudges both the meaning of transcendence (which is arbitrarily reduced to finitude) and the meaning of finitude (which is arbitrarily reduced to mortality).

9. See also Ricoeur 1986:12. Ricoeur ultimately speaks in the same sense of "an ontology of disproportion."

10. Already in the Preface of their analysis, Ricoeur and Dufrenne speak about the "extraordinarily confusing plan" of Jaspers's *Philosophy* (1947: 16).

11. Caused by Heidegger's distinction between "existential" and "existentiell."

12. One imagines here the blows struck by the "Heideggerian" critique of onto-theology.

13. In other words, it is the absence of hermeneutics.

14. In 1986 in "Éclairer l'existence" in *Lectures 1* (Paris: Seuil, 1991): 156. Also see Ricoeur 1995.

15. Note that this is not the case in Jaspers's work itself, which opens, surprisingly, with the notion of communication. However, in Ricoeur's and Dufrenne's interpretation, freedom is prior to communication. They thus put the order of argumentation in accord with the order of reality.

16. However great an effort one exercises to be oneself, "it comes to oneself as a gift" (Jaspers 1989: 300). The same goes for responsibility: as far as I am free, "I am responsible for myself" "and yet I receive myself only as a gift."

17. This without doubt reflects the dialectic of personal identity that Jaspers seems to defend on several occasions (Jaspers 1989: 292, 294, etc.), but he does not develop it.

18. For these phenomena, see *Psychopathologie Générale* (Paris: Bibliothèque des introuvables, 2000): ch. I, section I, § 4: "Les instincts et la volonté."

19. Sartre would forget this and surrender more easily than Jaspers to decisionism.

20. I will come back to this difference concerning transcendence between Ricoeur and Jaspers. *Freedom and Nature* already confirms that "the salvation of freedom by transcendence" unites with a certain "imagination of innocence."

21. What birth is literally to life, education is to freedom (Ricoeur 1965: 442).

22. When we are truly free, so we read in l'*Introduction à la philosophie*, "we understand that we are not free only by ourselves" (Jaspers 1951: 86).

23. For this reason, existence has nothing to learn from a "philosophy of autarchy," founded on "the desperate resolution of being-oneself" (Jaspers 1989: 310). "The human being can search for the road that leads to truth in a non-fanatic unconditional state, in a resoluteness that remains open" (Jaspers 2003: 203).

24. "If we understand it in its existential sense, [the phrase: 'I exist only by communicating with the other'] leads to a paradox: being-oneself is for itself, yet without being for oneself or without being alone with oneself, which it truly is."

25. In philosophy itself, discussion is only an "instrument of true communication" and always runs the risk to reduce this communication to an intellectual game (Jaspers 1989: 343).

26. I cannot become myself without entering into communication, and I cannot enter into communication without being myself.

27. Ricoeur's distinction between "true" and "false" reciprocity (the former called "mutuality") in *The Course of Recognition* is well known. But this distinction is not explicit in Jaspers's thought.

28. Hegel, *Phénoménologie de l'Esprit*, B, IV, b.

29. Gabriel Marcel's *Journal métaphysique* is cited by Ricoeur, *Gabriel Marcel et Karl Jaspers*, 170.

30. I will return later to this difference in method.

31. *Existenz* surely means "more" than *Dasein*. Yet, *Existenz* can only assume this "more" as *Dasein*. Without this, *Existenz* would be a mere escape into the non-reality of "other-worlds." The concept of historicity thus allows to gap a bridge between both of these senses of existence, without completely effacing their opposition or without the possibility of completely including one within the other.

32. However, one should be careful not to minimize the role of historical knowledge in this appropriation. This knowledge does not only concern "empirical history," that is to say the objective succession of events, which the historicity of existence presupposes, even though they seem to be opposed to each other. Yet, historicity designates precisely the relation that unites existence and empirical reality. Historicity cannot ignore its condition. To put it differently, for Jaspers historical explanation has to be included in the understanding of historicity (see, for example, Jaspers 1989: 358). For this reason, Jaspers also expresses his gratitude toward Ricoeur and Dufrenne for having recognized in their book the importance of historical knowledge, while others often criticized Jaspers for "being hostile to science and slipping into romanticism." It is well known that Ricoeur makes a great effort in his epistemology of history to overcome the duality between explanation and understanding and to include the former into the latter. In doing so, he found without doubt inspiration in Jaspers's thought.

33. "Transcendence only reveals itself to me as not belonging to the world, only when I am and do something unconditionally within empirical reality."

34. "What we call antinomies are irreconcilable relations [. . .], contradictions that cannot be resolved, but that only become more profound when one thinks them clearly, oppositions that do not constitute a whole and subsist as irretrievable ruptures."

35. This is not to say that there are no other limit situations than the ones mentioned here. Nonetheless, it is possible preliminarily to place limit situations into two categories. Death and suffering should be understood within the first category: these experiences impose themselves on us without us being there. The second category, in which culpability and struggle should be placed, is constraints on our personhood and initiatives.

36. See in *Ideas I* and in texts of the same period, where "*epoche*" is understood in relation to "the positing of the world."

37. More precisely, Jaspers analyzes existential experience in three moments which correspond with three successive "leaps" connected to these different modalities of being oneself. The first is that of the empirical consciousness searching for

the security of a general truth, which transforms every situation into an object. The second moment reverses this direction of the first moment: consciousness thinks itself as being-in-situation; it abandons the "tranquil station of knowing" for the inquietude of finitude. However, thinking finitude is not yet the same as existing in finitude. Therefore, a third change is necessary—a third leap which alone is decisive because it leads philosophy to real life.

38. There is similar terminology here in Jaspers's *Philosophie* (458), Heidegger's *Being and Time* (§ 54) and Ricoeur.

39. This term "authenticity" is common to both Jaspers and Heidegger.

40. Authentic existence does not escape the world and ignores one's own death. Authentic existence does not have another place than the world, nor does it have another certitude than death. Yet the world must be lost as the limited horizon of our mortal life in order to be regained as the unlimited space where we attest, by our actions, to the hopes and aspirations that transcend mortal existence.

41. This sense corresponds with what Heidegger calls, in § 51 of *Being and Time*, the inauthenticity of the "one dies."

42. The death of the other bridges a gap, in this sense, between the first and the other two of Jaspers' limit situations.

43. The titles of Book II, Chapters 8 and 9, respectively, of Jaspers's *Philosophie*.

44. See Jaspers, *Philosophie*, Book III, Chapter 4.

45. This question invites us to consider whether Ricoeur is closer to Marcel than to Jaspers.

46. See Ricoeur 2005.

REFERENCES

Hegel, G.W.F. 1977. *Phenomenology of Spirit*, trans. A.V. Miller. Oxford: Oxford University Press.

Heidegger, Martin. 2010. *Being and Time: A Revised Edition of the Stambaugh Translation*, trans. Joan Stambaugh and Dennis J. Schmidt. Albany: SUNY Press.

Jaspers, Karl. 2003. "La Raison et l'existence." In *Karl Jaspers: Nietzsche et le christianisme*, trad. J. Hersch et R. Givord. Paris: Bayard: 111–313.

Jaspers, Karl. 2000. *Psychopathologie Générale*. Paris: Bibliothèque des introuvables.

Jaspers, Karl. 1989. *Philosophie*, trad. J. Hersch. Paris, Berlin, Heidelberg: Springer-Verlag.

Jaspers, Karl. 1951. *Introduction à la philosophie*. Paris: Plon.

Ricoeur, Paul. 2005. *The Course of Recognition*, trans. David Pellauer. Havard: Harvard University Press.

Ricoeur, Paul. 2004. *Memory, History, Forgetting*, trans. Kathleen Blamey and David Pellauer. Chicago: The University of Chicago Press.

Ricoeur, Paul. 1995. "Intellectual Autobiography." In *The Philosophy of Paul Ricoeur*, ed. L.E. Hahn. Chicago: Open Court.

Ricoeur, Paul. 1992. *Oneself as Another*, trans. Kathleen Blamey. Chicago: The University of Chicago Press.

Ricoeur, Paul. 1986. *Fallible Man*, trans. Charles A. Kelbley. New York: Fordham University Press.

Ricoeur, Paul. 1965. *Freedom and Nature*, trans. Erazim V. Kohak. Evanston: Northwestern University Press.

Ricoeur, Paul. 1948. *Gabriel Marcel et Karl Jaspers*. Paris: Editions du Temps Présent.

Ricoeur, Paul and Mikel Dufrenne. 1947. *Karl Jaspers et la philosophie de l'existence*. Paris: Seuil.

Chapter 3

Reflection, the Body, and Fallibility
The Mysterious Influence of Marcel in Ricoeur's Fallible Man

Brian Gregor

The name of Gabriel Marcel never appears in Ricoeur's *Fallible Man,* but his influence is present throughout. The book, which is the second in Ricoeur's trilogy on the *Philosophy of the Will,* presupposes the fundamental anthropological insights developed in the first volume, *Freedom and Nature.* That earlier book was dedicated to Marcel, and for good reason: his insights are central to Ricoeur's conception of and reflections on the lived body—the embodied *I can.* It is therefore a bit surprising that Ricoeur never mentions Marcel anywhere in *Fallible Man.* Nevertheless, Marcel continues to play a role in the book, as an unspoken influence and interlocutor in Ricoeur's efforts to analyze the mystery of fallibility.

Marcel was a key influence on Ricoeur, both personally and intellectually, but he is not as widely studied as he once was or should be. Marcel's philosophy of existence was an impetus in Ricoeur's rethinking of philosophical reflection, showing that the self-positing act of reflection is always already rooted in concrete existence. Ricoeur also learned from Marcel's challenge to objectivity, which is an abstraction from concrete existence. This opposition of objectivity and existence is the basis for Marcel's distinction between problem and mystery, and his attendant distinction between the primary and secondary reflections.

Despite the lack of explicit references to Marcel in *Fallible Man,* this chapter will trace Marcel's influence therein. I will begin with an overview of Ricoeur's relation to Marcel, followed by a summary of the key Marcellian ideas that inform Ricoeur's work in *Freedom and Nature* and then *Fallible Man*: for example, Marcel's critique of objectivity, his distinction between problem and mystery, and his distinction between the primary and secondary reflections. These themes will reveal Marcel's influence in Ricoeur's analyses of such mysteries as Transcendence, embodiment, and fallibility, as well as the affective relation of having. But we will also see that while Ricoeur is sympathetic to Marcel's critique of objectifying thinking, he is also determined to give objectivity and primary reflection their due, which is why *Fallible Man* is full of transcendental arguments more akin to Kant and Husserl than Marcel. This approach will become the *modus operandi* of Ricoeur's work: like Marcel, he wants a philosophy that is both rooted in concrete existence and that leads to a deeper participation in being. But instead of taking a shortcut to this destination, he insists on the detour through more rigorous, objective modes of reflection.

MARCEL'S PHILOSOPHY OF EXISTENCE

The year 1934 was momentous for Ricoeur, as he was in Paris working on his master's thesis and preparing for the *agrégation* at the Sorbonne. This year also marked his first encounter with phenomenology as well as the philosophy of existence, as practiced by Karl Jaspers and Gabriel Marcel. These two movements would go on to shape much of Ricoeur's early work. But Ricoeur's encounter with Marcel went beyond the printed page, as the two philosophers met and became lifelong friends, with the elder Marcel becoming a mentor to the younger Ricoeur. Marcel wrote letters to Ricoeur when the latter was a prisoner of war in a German camp during the 1940s (Reagan 1996: 9), and their dialogue lasted through the decades that followed. Near the end of his life, Ricoeur confessed that of all French philosophers, "Marcel is by far the person with whom I maintained the deepest relationship" (Ricoeur 1998: 23).

Ricoeur originally met Marcel through a mutual friend, and he began to attend the philosophical "*salons*" Marcel hosted at his home on Friday afternoons and evenings. These gatherings were devoted to philosophical exploration and dialogue, and the list of attendees would become something of a Who's Who of French philosophy; in addition to Ricoeur, attendees included Jean-Paul Sartre,[1] Emmanuel Levinas (Malka 2006: 148), and Jean Wahl, among others. The discussions proceeded in a Socratic fashion, focusing on familiar philosophical topics like truth, reality, and the a priori, as well as "experiences that were at once ordinary and puzzling, such as promises or the feeling of injustice" (Ricoeur 1995: 6). The rules of engagement in these conversations were that participants could not appeal to familiar philosophical reference points such as the names of important philosophers, texts, and jargon. In academic circles it is customary to refer to a position as Cartesian, or Scholastic, or Kantian, for example; this is a perfectly reasonable custom, but it can become a kind of shorthand that skims the surface of ideas rather than plunging in and thinking through philosophical questions in an original manner. This shorthand also makes it possible to fall into habitual modes of evaluation and argument, and to endorse or dismiss a position with facile references to schools or thinkers, thereby mimicking the philosophical act without undertaking the more difficult task of thinking. Marcel's Socratic dialogues were meant as an exercise in the discipline of thinking, which is one of the reasons why they became a recurring event with regular participants. Ricoeur describes the exhilaration of these conversations, recalling that "at Marcel's one had the impression that thinking was alive, that it was doing the arguing" (Ricoeur 1998: 23).

During this period Ricoeur read all of Marcel's published works, and was particularly influenced by the *Metaphysical Journal, Being and Having,* and the essays "Existence and Objectivity" and "On the Ontological Mystery." Ricoeur's most sustained examination of Marcel's work appeared in 1947, when he published *Gabriel Marcel et Karl Jaspers: Philosophie du mystère et philosophie du paradoxe.* The book is a work of secondary rather than primary scholarship, devoted entirely to a comparative study of Marcel and Jaspers and their respective approaches to "the philosophy of existence." It is worth noting that Ricoeur uses this term rather than "existential*ism.*" When that label came into vogue during the 1940s, Marcel—like Sartre—found himself obligated to comment on it: "Hardly a day goes by without my being asked what is existentialism."[2] But whereas Sartre decided to embrace the term and give it his own definition, Marcel preferred to designate his style of thinking as "Neo-Socratism," as this was "the least misleading" term (Marcel 1973: 251). Marcel rejected Sartre's definition of existentialism, which holds that existence precedes essence, but he did continue to undertake his philosophical investigations in an existential key—that is to say, by taking his starting point in concrete existence rather than abstract ideas, and focusing on such existential themes as freedom, hope, being in situation, communication, the relation to the You, Transcendence, and faith.[3] Ricoeur examines each of these themes in his book on Marcel and Jaspers, discerning a common "intention and rhythm" between the two thinkers (Ricoeur 1947: 33). At the same time, he also draws out some of their significant differences in order to critique and improve the other's thinking. Most relevant to our concerns in this chapter, Ricoeur finds in Jaspers a "vigor and a rigor" that can help to read Marcel in a "more systematic manner" (Ricoeur 1947: 206, 243).

REFLECTION, OBJECTIVITY, AND EXISTENCE

When Ricoeur met Marcel, he was writing his master's thesis on the problem of God in Jules Lachelier and Jules Lagneau, two philosophers who belonged to the French tradition of reflexive philosophy. This tradition was a continuation of the work of thinkers like Descartes, Kant, and Fichte, and it was practiced in Ricoeur's time by thinkers like Léon Brunschvicq and Jean Nabert. Its aim was for the thinking *I* to undertake an act of self-reflection and identify itself as the radical origin of acts of knowing, willing, and judging. In reflection, the self gathers itself up from its dispersal among mundane activities and comes to know its true nature.[4] The self thereby recovers, or returns to, that which it most truly is: the self-positing origin of all its conscious acts.

Ricoeur aligns himself with the reflexive tradition throughout his entire career, but his model of reflection was seriously chastened as a result of his encounter with Marcel. Whereas reflexive philosophy argues that the act of thinking is prior to being, Marcel insists that being is prior to act. The act of thinking is only possible because we are always already situated in being. For the philosopher of existence, ontological participation is the soil from which any act of thinking whatsoever can arise.

Like the reflexive philosopher, Marcel recognizes that there is a way in which thinking collects itself, gathers itself up into unity out of its dispersal—an act he describes in terms of "recollection." For Marcel, however, this act is not set in distinction to being. Recollection is not an abstraction from being or a reduction to a transcendental ego; rather, "*in this retreat I bring with me what I am and what my life perhaps is not.*" Likewise, recollection is not a kind of speculative gaze that consists in "looking at something"; rather, it is "a retrieval, a renewal." It is not an intellectual intuition but an "assurance." Recollection renews the self by plunging deeper into its source of being. Thus while the act of recollection consists in taking a position, this is not a self-positing act in which the self secures itself. Rather, "this gathering together, this concentration is also a relaxation, a letting go. It involves *abandoning to . . ., relaxing in the presence of*" (Marcel 1998: 181–83). Instead of a proud self-positing, recollection is best characterized as a "humble withdrawal" (Marcel 1998: 188) that renews our participation in being.

On Marcel's account, philosophers have overlooked the primacy of this ontological participation because they misconstrue the act of knowing. This is particularly true of modern philosophy, which describes knowledge as a relation between a subject and an object. This subject/object dualism tends to bring with it a conception of sensation in which the senses deliver information about the world, and the subject forms an idea about the object. According to Marcel, this account construes the subject and object as telegraph stations, with the subject receiving a transmission from the object tower (Marcel 1952: 327). One problem with this dualism is that it is immediately susceptible to skepticism. How do we know that our ideas correspond to the world? How do we know that our senses are transmitting accurately? According to Marcel:

If sensation is to appear in some way intelligible, the mind must establish itself at the outset in a universe which is not a world of ideas. If it be possible to prove, as I think it is, that sensation is not susceptible of being conceived as a message, as a communication between different stations, it must involve the immediate participation of what we normally call the subject in a surrounding world from which no veritable frontier separates it.[5]

Marcel's appeal to this "immediate participation" is similar to Heidegger's idea of being-in-the-world: we are first and foremost engaged as participants in the world. Reflection, ideas, concepts, and the distinction between subject and object are all secondary, derived from this more primordial engagement.

Marcel makes a similar point about this subject/object dualism in *Being and Having*, observing our tendency to "forget how untenable, metaphysically speaking, is the position of a thought which believes that it can place itself over against things in order to grasp them. It can certainly develop a system of taking its bearings by things, a system of increasing and even infinite complexity: but its aim is to let the essence of things go" (Marcel 1965: 168).

Mystery and Problem

Another problem with objectivity is that it distorts our encounter with the mystery of being. Marcel suggests the term *mystery* as the best way to think about realities like love and hope, faith and fidelity, the encounter with evil, and the union of mind and body. Mysteries like these should be distinguished from *problems*, which is how philosophers usually frame their questions: the mind/body problem, the problem of other minds, the problem of evil. A problem is something we can relate to objectively, standing over and against it. Even the word "problem" suggests a puzzle waiting to be solved. The problem with "problems" is that this kind of objectifying thinking closes us off from the deepest levels of reality—what Ricoeur calls the ontological mystery.

As Ricoeur observes, Marcel's use of the term "mystery" comes from the Christian tradition (Marcel 1973: 238), from the Latin *mysterium* and the Greek *mysterion*. We should not think of mystery in the sense of a mystery novel, where we are simply waiting for the right clues to solve the puzzle. For Marcel, mystery is not properly understood in negative terms, as the mere lack or absence of an answer. It is not merely the unknown (Marcel 1952: 160–61). Instead, mystery is "a positive value" (Marcel 1973: 234). It is a presence, a surplus, an ontological abundance in which I encounter a reality that cannot be reduced to the register of objectivity or the merely problematic.

Talk of mystery makes the objectivist uncomfortable, to the extent that "the objective order" aims to exclude mystery altogether.[6] Whatever doesn't show itself to the objective gaze must be unreal, an illusion. Marcel's point is that under the bright lights of its interrogation, realities like these tend to be ontologically shy.[7] They do not make themselves readily available to the hard-nosed, no-nonsense critic who is determined to avoid error above all else. But if philosophy is going to be faithful to reality rather than its own epistemological and metaphysical preferences, it must confront such mysteries. And not only confront, but in some way inhabit them and take them as they are given. As Marcel writes, "There are certain higher relations which are only defined and elucidated by communion in mystery" (Marcel 1952: 160). When I treat these realities as problems to be solved, as things to explain functionally, I step out of the mystery. When I assume the posture of an objective observer, I am no longer dealing with the same reality. In order to reflect on mysteries appropriately, I must be a participant, encountering them in their concreteness.

PRIMARY AND SECONDARY REFLECTION

How is it possible to reflect without betraying this ontological participation? This is a difficult question, since it is reflection, after all, that reduces—or "degrades"—mysteries to the level of the problematic (Marcel 1998: 179). Is there a way for reflection to approach these mysteries without desecrating them? In Marcel's view, the true role of reflection "consists not in cutting to pieces and dismembering," but rather "in re-establishing in all its continuity that living tissue which impudent analysis tore asunder" (Marcel 1952: 334). Marcel thus complements his distinction between problem and mystery by distinguishing between two modes of reflection: *Primary* reflection is "purely critical or analytic," and proceeds by "dissolving the concrete into its elements." It aims at objectivity and leads to objectification. Consequently, this kind of reflection must be "itself reflected upon" (Marcel 1998: 179). Marcel calls this meta-reflection *secondary* reflection, since it aims to resituate reflection, regaining more immediate contact with reality by taking concrete existence as its starting point. Secondary reflection is reconstructive: where primary reflection breaks down and dissolves the concrete, secondary reflections aim to reconstruct "that concrete state of affairs which had previously been glimpsed in a fragmented or pulverized condition." Marcel insists that this reconstruction occurs "at the level of thought," "in an intelligent and intelligible way," and is not merely an "appeal to purely subjective intuitions" (Marcel 1973: 229, 235). For Marcel, secondary reflection is a way for thinking to attend more fully to ontological mystery. It is a way for philosophy to reflect on those aspects of reality that are so fundamental to our concrete experience, but are so often dismissed by objective, reductive modes of thinking as mere illusions.

ONTOLOGICAL MYSTERY IN RICOEUR

Marcel's reflections on the mystery of being were very influential on Ricoeur and play an important role in his early work on the *Philosophy of the Will*. We find the theme of mystery in several areas, most notably (1) the mystery of Transcendence, (2) the mystery of one's own body, and (3) the mystery of fallibility.

Presence and Transcendence

For Marcel, being is best understood not in terms of objects or things, but as a presence, a nourishing source that resides at the roots of the human being. In his words, "existence is not only given, but giving" (Marcel 1973: 221). This vision became highly influential for Ricoeur, who found similar descriptions in Spinoza, Nabert, and Schelling. For Ricoeur, the subject is not the self-founding and self-grounding source of itself; its own act of self-positing is not a *creatio ex nihilo*, but instead an affirmation or attestation of itself that is more deeply rooted in the soil of being.

This vision figured prominently in Ricoeur's plans for the final volume in his trilogy on the *Philosophy of the Will*—the unfinished and unpublished *Poetics of the Will*. Whereas *Fallible Man* deals with the human as capable of falling, and *The Symbolism of Evil* deals with the human as already fallen, the *Poetics of the Will* was meant to deal with the way Transcendence heals the broken will. Transcendence is a creative power that is the true source of subjectivity, prior to the acts of the subject. Ricoeur uses a Marcellian term, describing Transcendence as "a presence which constantly precedes my own power of self-affirmation" (Ricoeur 1966: 32–33).

Transcendence is, however, a difficult topic for philosophical reflection to address. This is why Ricoeur kept the topic in brackets in *Freedom and Nature* (Ricoeur 1966: 29). Marcel makes a similar observation in his *Metaphysical Journal*, writing that "we cannot really think grace," because thinking wants to treat it as a mode of causal explanation. As a result, the thinking subject concludes that "grace must be rejected out of hand." Is there any way for grace to be thought? According to Marcel, only insofar as "the *I think* is capable of transcending itself, and of becoming faith" (Marcel 1952: 57). Faith "posits transcendence" as a kind of a grace, "a radically independent power" to which we are related. There is some precedent among philosophers to speak of something like this as an impersonal power—for instance, Spinoza, as well as numerous Romantics, Idealists, and Transcendentalists. But Marcel is no more satisfied with identifying grace or transcendence as an impersonal power than he is with reducing it to an objective causal explanation. Instead, he describes it as a meeting of two freedoms, and thus two persons.[8] The best term to describe this relation, Marcel proposes, is *love* (Marcel 1952: 58).

Love is similarly difficult—indeed, impossible—to think in a purely objective manner. "The more I love a being and the more I participate in his life the less adequate this way of thinking is shewn to be. The beloved is beyond all these questions"—that is, the vital statistics that make up an objective knowledge (Marcel 1952: 158). Instead of investigating love as a reality of its own, reflection reduces it to abstractions like "the will to live, the will to power, the libido, etc." (Marcel 1998: 179). From that perspective, talk of love is ontologically suspect and must therefore be reduced to and explained in some other categories that are easier to verify. Marcel's point is that reflection needs to take the mysteries of these interpersonal relations on their own terms, rather than trying to reduce them to some other principle.

The Mystery of My Body

Another mystery that Ricoeur takes up is the theme of embodiment, or what Marcel sometimes call "incarnate being." For Marcel, the body is "the landmark of all existing things," and "incarnation is the central landmark of philosophical reflection" (Ricoeur 1947: 100). His point is that our relation to our own body is unlike our relation to other physical things in the world. It can be viewed as an objective thing, but that is not my more primordial relation to my body. My body is not an instrument to which I am externally related, something I merely *have*: "I do not *make use of* my body, I *am* my body" (Marcel 1952: 332–33). My body is thus my starting point, the most fundamental root in my concrete, existential situation.

Ricoeur's takes up "the mystery of my body" in *Freedom and Nature*, where he uses Marcel's descriptions to challenge the Cartesian primacy of the *I think*. "The Cogito's experience, taken as a whole, includes 'I desire,' 'I can,' 'I intend,'" and these are not disembodied activities. Instead, they all implicate "my existence as a body" (Ricoeur 1966: 9). Thus even my thinking, my engagement with the world, and even with ideas, is a bodily affair. Incarnate being is essential to the philosophy of the will: "The bond which in fact joins willing to its body requires a type of attention other than an intellectual attention to structures. It requires that I participate actively in *my incarnation as a mystery*. I need to pass from objectivity to existence" (Ricoeur 1966: 14).

That last line is a clear allusion to Marcel, and it is characteristic of Marcel's prominent role in *Freedom and Nature*. As Ricoeur puts it: "Meditation on Gabriel Marcel's work lies at the basis of the analyses in this book" (Ricoeur 1966: 15). Given Marcel's prominent role in *Freedom and Nature*, it is puzzling that Ricoeur never directly mentions Marcel anywhere in *Fallible*

Man. Nevertheless, Marcel's influence remains, since the mystery of the body is still operative there; Ricoeur simply does not need to say as much about it, since he is building on the earlier analyses from *Freedom and Nature*.

In *Fallible Man*, Ricoeur is able to focus more specifically on the body as a transcendental condition of knowledge. My body is "a mediation of appearance." It is my opening "onto the world." My body is "an originating mediator 'between' myself and the world . . . either allowing perceived things to appear or making me dependent on things I lack" (Ricoeur 1986: 19). There are thus dual aspects to how the body shows itself: from an external, third-person perspective it can appear as a thing among things, but from a first-person perspective, I encounter the world through my body: "It opens me to others insofar as it expresses, that is to say, displays the interior upon the exterior and becomes a sign for others, decipherable and offered to the reciprocity of consciousness. In a word, my body opens me to the world by everything it is able to do" (Ricoeur 1986: 19). In descriptions like these, Ricoeur is building on the phenomenology of the embodied "I can" in *Freedom and Nature*.

What Ricoeur adds to the earlier analyses is his emphasis on the essential finitude of embodied knowing. My body is what gives me a view from somewhere; it is my "center of orientation, the zero origin, the 'here from where' I see all that I can see." My body gives me a perspective on the object. This perspective is finite, because I always perceive objects from a partial perspective.[9] This perspective is always partial because of my embodiment. At the same time, I am able to take in different profiles by moving my body: "by changing my position I *can* make the object's aspect change." As I move around an object, or it moves around me, I see a series of profiles, a "flow of silhouettes," but intentional consciousness perceives a unity (Ricoeur 1986: 21). In this perception there are "unnoticed aspects of bodily mediation: my perceiving body is not only my openness onto the world, it is also the 'here from where' the thing is seen" (Ricoeur 1986: 21–22). Marcel's reflections on the mystery of the body continue to inform Ricoeur's reflections on how we know objects in the world. He is not describing a detached, disengaged subject observing an object but rather an embodied agent whose knowing is rooted in participation in the world.

The Mystery of Fallibility

We can also detect Marcel's influence in Ricoeur's overall approach to the mystery of fallibility, that is, the human capacity for evil. For Marcel, the encounter with evil is one of the preeminent mysteries with which philosophy must contend. But philosophers are not accustomed to treating evil in terms of mystery; instead, we habitually refer to "the problem of evil," by which we typically mean a logical trilemma: if God is both omnipotent and perfectly good, then why is there evil? Framed in this way, the problem is looking for a conceptual solution, and the "solution" starts to look like one has simply moved around ideas to balance a conceptual ledger (Ricoeur 1965: 171–72).

There is a time and place to address the logical problem of evil, and to show that the trilemma does not defeat theism. For those in the thick of real suffering, however, it is likely to be cold comfort. It's an abstraction,[10] and as Marcel observes, when we treat evil as a problem to be solved, explained, or treated, "we are perhaps no longer speaking of evil but of something else, from which it would be very simple to liberate ourselves."[11] The best response, according to Marcel, is not abstract but personal, when we enter into relations of communion with those who suffer.[12]

Suffering is not, however, the only aspect of the mystery of evil. There is evil suffered, and there is evil *committed*—"the evil that men do."[13] This is the theme of *Fallible Man*: for example "the constitutional weakness that makes evil possible" (Ricoeur 1986: xliii). What is it about human beings that makes us fallible—that is, capable of falling?

Like Marcel, Ricoeur sees this question as central to the mystery of the human being. The possibility of evil is "inscribed in the innermost structure of human reality" (Ricoeur 1986: 1). It is not a problem sociology, psychology, or biology can solve. As Ricoeur puts it, "psychology will never show me the birth of the impure."[14] It can only be addressed at the level of ontological mystery. According to Ricoeur, this possibility arises out of the human being's ontological disproportion, the "non-coincidence" of the self with itself (Ricoeur 1986: 1).

This description is very similar to the premise of Walker Percy's 1971 novel *Love in the Ruins*. Percy (who, like Ricoeur, was deeply influenced by Marcel)[15] gives us a protagonist and narrator named Tom More, a physician asking the same question as Ricoeur: "How to account for man's wickedness?" Like Ricoeur he thinks it has something to do with our ontological disproportion, but unlike Ricoeur, more has high hopes that the cause—and cure—of our propensity for evil might be found with the right technology. More has invented a device to give readings of our fallenness: an aptly named device called "More's Qualitative Quantitative Ontological Lapsometer" (Percy 1971: 30). He has grand dreams for what this techno-therapeutic device might accomplish:

> If you measure the pineal activity of a monkey—or any other subhuman animal—with my lapsometer, you will invariably record identical readings at Layers I and II. Its self, that is to say, coincides with itself. Only in man do you find a discrepancy: Layer I the outer social self, ticking over, say, at a sprightly 5–4 mmv, while Layer II just lies there, barely alive at 0.7 mmv, or even zero!—a nought, a gap,

an aching wound. Only in man does the self miss itself, *fall* from itself (hence *laps*ometer!). Suppose—! Suppose I could hit on the right dosage and weld the broken self whole! What if man could reenter paradise, so to speak, and live there both as man and spirit, whole and intact man-spirit, as solid flesh as a speckled trout, a dappled thing, yet aware of itself as a self! (Percy 1971: 36)

Percy's novel satirizes the idea that we could devise any objective, technical means of diagnosing and treating evil. Like Marcel and Ricoeur, he rejects the idea that we can find an explanation in science or a cure in technology. The possibility of evil lies in the more fundamental disproportion of the human being with itself, and this radical evil needs a more radical cure.

According to Percy's novel, two common ways in which the self falls out of line with itself are *angelism* and *bestialism*. The former is a distorted identification with one's spiritual existence, the latter with one's animal existence. This is a clear allusion to Pascal, for whom the human being is neither angel nor beast (Pascal 1941: 118). We are intermediate beings, between angel and beast, the infinite and nothing.[16] This is where Ricoeur makes an original contribution: he agrees with Pascal that the human is an intermediary being, but argues that the human being "is not intermediate because he is between angel and animal; he is intermediate within himself, within his *selves*. He is intermediate because he is a mixture, and a mixture because he brings about mediations" (Ricoeur 1986: 3). This mixture, or intermediate existence, is the locus of the mystery of human evil. The human being is the intermediary between the poles of the finite and the infinite, and human fallibility arises out of this mediation. Ricoeur is not attempting an explanation of the origin of evil, but rather a description of its locus—the place where fallibility emerges (Ricoeur 1986: xlvi).

Ricoeur also argues that this intermediacy is the central locus of mystery in the human being. Oddly, Ricoeur never uses the term *mystery* in *Fallible Man*,[17] but in his 1960 essay "L'homme et son mystère," published the same year as *Fallible Man*, Ricoeur does explicitly treat this analysis of disproportion, intermediacy, and mixture in terms of mystery (Ricoeur 1960: 119). He writes: "If there is a mystery of the human being, it seems to me it is because the human, disproportionate in himself, exists as an intermediary being, as a mixture, forever obscure for himself" (Ricoeur 1960: 125). The human mystery lies in this intermediary, mixed condition.

REHABILITATING PRIMARY REFLECTION AND OBJECTIVITY

The theme of mystery clearly plays a prominent role throughout Ricoeur's *Philosophy of the Will*. But as helpful as this framework of mystery may be, he does not want philosophy to end in contemplative silence. In this regard he agrees with Marcel, whose notion of secondary reflection is meant to provide a way for philosophical reflection to remain faithful to ontological mystery. Ricoeur embraces Marcel's model of secondary reflection, since he too wants reflection to lead to recovery, to a restored immediacy, a renewed participation in the fullness of being. In Ricoeur's terms: a "second naïveté." In Ricoeur's mature philosophy, the counterpart of this secondary reflection is a hermeneutics that offers a recuperative, restorative interpretation (Ricoeur 1995: 20). But Ricoeur is afraid that Marcel wants to rush ahead and get there too quickly. In his view, the moment of recovery, restoration, and renewal can only take place on the far side of rigorous reflection, critique, and objectivity.

Ricoeur recognizes this point early in his career. It shows up in his critical comments in his book on Marcel and Jaspers. Where Marcel's thinking tends to emphasize the personal against the impersonal, the concrete against the abstract, and existence against objectivity, Ricoeur argues that these oppositions are oversimplified. Marcel needs to offer a more "positive evaluation of objectivity in general, a more nuanced description of its diverse levels and mainly the search for a less degraded form of objectification than that of positivist empiricism" (Ricoeur 1947: 108). Marcel fails to recognize (1) that not all forms of objectivity are equally objectifying and (2) that philosophical reflection requires some form of objectivity.[18] The trick is to pursue objectivity in the right way.

This is one reason why Ricoeur found phenomenology attractive: it can provide a way to pursue objectivity without falling into the metaphysical assumptions of naturalism or reductionism. As Ricoeur argues in *Freedom and Nature*, "objectivity is not naturalism." Phenomenology is an objective mode of inquiry that seeks to intuit the essential structures of appearance (Ricoeur 1966: 15–16). This is also why Ricoeur's subsequent work takes detours through genuinely reductive methodologies like psychoanalysis and the hermeneutics of suspicion, structuralism, and the natural sciences. He is well aware that these disciplines can be reductive and objectifying, but he thinks that good-faith philosophical reflection must contend with these challenges, and maybe even learn something from them. The danger with Marcel's approach is that if we move too quickly to the post-critical moment of recovery, we short-change our own philosophical work.

According to Ricoeur, Marcel conceived of secondary reflection "as a sort of revenge" on "primary reflection" (Ricoeur 1995: 20). Ricoeur wants to give objectivity its due, by intensifying the rigor of the reflective process beyond what Marcel would allow. If primary reflection can degrade, it is nevertheless a necessary moment in philosophical activity. There is still much to be learned from these long detours through these critical, objective modes of inquiry, and so Ricoeur takes them, in the wager that greater understanding will come at the end of the journey.

From the *Pathétique* to the Transcendental Reflection on the Object

We find an early version of Ricoeur's model of detour and return[19] in *Fallible Man*. Although fallibility is part of the mystery of the human being, it is nevertheless in principle accessible to pure reflection (Ricoeur 1986: 1). In Chapter 1 Ricoeur opens his reflections with what he calls a *"Pathétique of 'Misery.'"* The phrase is an allusion to a section early *in Pascal's Pensées: The Misery of Man without God*, but Ricoeur's discussion is less of an *apologia* for Christian faith than Pascal's. Instead, Ricoeur draws on Pascal—as well as Plato, Descartes, and Kierkegaard—to provide a "pre-comprehension," or hermeneutical preunderstanding, of the theme of disproportion. Ricoeur draws on these pre-reflective sources to gain preliminary orientation in the pathos of human misery. The goal is a participatory understanding of the existential experience of this disproportion.

Although these texts are a rich source of poetic insight into the human condition, for Ricoeur's purposes they are still too close to direct introspection. Ricoeur is looking for the added rigor of pure, transcendental reflection in order "to break down the nebula of 'misery' into distinct forms" (Ricoeur 1986: 15, 18). That is what Ricoeur attempts in Chapter 2, The Transcendental Synthesis, where he shows himself to be a disciple of not only Marcel, but also Kant and Husserl. Whereas the *pathétique* of misery in Chapter 1 gives the existential content to reflection, the transcendental synthesis of Chapter 2 takes an objective turn. That is to say, it takes its starting point with the thing, the object of cognition. As Ricoeur writes, "Reflection is not introspection; for reflection takes the roundabout way via the object; it is reflection *upon* the object" (Ricoeur 1986: 18).

Ricoeur undertakes a "transcendental reflection" on the object—*transcendental* in the sense that it examines the power of knowing in order to identify the conditions that make knowledge of objects possible (Ricoeur 1986: 17). This is also where Ricoeur deepens his account of disproportion. All human knowing is subject to an internal disproportion, since it is a synthesis of finite and infinite aspects. Our knowing is finite because it is always perspectival and thus incomplete (Ricoeur 1986: 20–21, 23). This is part of our being embodied knowers, situated and thus seeing the object from a limited viewpoint. But knowing also includes an infinite aspect, since it transcends my perspective in signification, or speech. While I am immersed in my finite point of view in the world, language also allows me to intend "the thing in its meaning that is beyond all point of view" (Ricoeur 1986: 31). The thing, or the object, is a synthetic unity realized in the meeting between the finitude of my point of view and the infinitude of speech; it is a synthesis of appearance (or presence) and meaning (Ricoeur 1986: 37–39). What makes this synthesis possible, however, is a third element or power, the intermediate term itself: the pure imagination (Ricoeur 1986: 17–18, 37). Ricoeur derives this point from Kant, but in his essay "*L'homme et son mystère*" he also uses Marcellian language, arguing that the imagination is where the human mystery resides (Ricoeur 1960: 126).

Ricoeur's transcendental reflection marks a significant departure from Marcel, who sees the object as an abstraction from concrete existence. For Marcel, existence and objectivity are two rival orientations and ways of doing philosophy, and he finds a philosophy that takes its bearings from things, objects—that which stands over and against the subject—to be metaphysically "untenable" (Marcel 1965: 168). But Ricoeur challenges Marcel's opposition of existence and objectivity, arguing that they need not be mutually exclusive. In *Freedom and Nature* he writes that "the meaning of 'existence' excludes the meaning of 'objectivity' only when the latter is already degraded" (Ricoeur 1966: 15). Objectivity does not have to adopt the dualistic view in which an object is thrown over and against a detached, disengaged, disembodied thinking subject. Pursued rightly, it can deepen our understanding of being.

HAVING: FALLEN OR FALLIBLE?

Ricoeur's critical engagement with Marcel can also be seen in one other place in *Fallible Man*, namely in Ricoeur's discussion of *having*, which is a prominent Marcellian theme. Philosophers spend a lot of time reflecting on being, but what about having? This phenomenon has received much less philosophical attention (Marcel 1965: 157), and yet it is a central feature of human existence. What does it mean to *have* something? We talk about having things, like a book or a pen. We also use the word to describe personal relations, like having a spouse and children, as well as enemies and friends. I can have feelings as well as ideas. I have memories, commitments, goals, and a story. To paraphrase Aristotle, "having" is said in many senses.

Marcel pays considerable attention to this theme, and his reflections are characteristically exploratory. One of his most basic definitions is that having means "being able to dispose of, having a power over." It is a kind of "assimilation" of something to my being. Having is also "always the way in which I give suffering a hold upon me" (Marcel 1965: 82, 83, 86). If having entails a kind of power over things, this relation can also make us passive (Marcel 1965: 147). In this regard having has "a tendency to destroy and lose itself in the very thing it began by possessing, but which now absorbs the master who thought he controlled it" (Marcel 1965: 164). In having, I end up being had.

Marcel's reflections on having are not exclusively negative, and he does recognize the necessity of having in human life. But in his reflections, having ends up looking less than laudable. For instance, at one point he suggests that having is coextensive with the problematic. It belongs to the realm of objectivity (Marcel 1965: 172). Having stands opposed to being, so that having is to being as problem is to mystery.

By contrast, Ricoeur offers a more positive take on having in *Fallible Man*. The topic comes up in Chapter 4, where Ricoeur examines the way our ontological proportion manifests as the level of feeling. Ricoeur examines the fallibility of three affects in particular: the desires for having, power, and worth. We often experience these affects in their fallen form, as "passions," but Ricoeur tries to imagine them at a more primordial level, as modes of desire that are fundamentally human and would exist even in a prelapsarian condition (Ricoeur 1986: 111–12).

It is easy to identify the desire to have in its fallen form, as the passion for possession. The more difficult task is to determine whether there is a "possibly innocent quest for having." Is every desire to have a symptom of our fallenness, or could having be part of a more fundamental ontology of the human? Ricoeur suggests that *Habsucht*, or greed, is "a perversion" of a more primordial quest for having (Ricoeur 1986: 116). "This quest is a quest of humanity in that the 'I' constitutes itself therein by founding itself on a 'mine'" (Ricoeur 1986: 113). Whereas Rousseau identifies the fall with possession, when humans start to say "mine," Ricoeur locates having at a more fundamental level: having is ontologically prior to fallenness. The capacity to be an I, a subject, a human self is in fact bound up with our capacity to have. "I cannot imagine the I without the mine, or man without having" (Ricoeur 1986: 115). The *mineness* of having provides a certain "anchorage" for the I.

Some thinkers, like Rousseau, might imagine a scenario—a romantic state of nature, or an eschatological condition like the kingdom of God or a socialist utopia—in which there is no *mine* and *yours*. But Ricoeur argues that "If man's goodness is to be possible, even as a past or future utopia, this goodness would require the innocence of a certain having." Even if one seeks to move beyond private property, this would still require a relation of having "on the level of a 'We.' Through the mediation of the 'we' and the 'our,' the I would again join itself to a 'mine'" (Ricoeur 1986: 115).

Ricoeur does not go into much detail about this positive vision of having, but he does conclude that an "innocent" mode of having is imaginable and thinkable. Similar to Marcel, he describes having in terms of the object's availability for me. When I have something, it is an "available good." But Ricoeur also subtly distances himself from Marcel when he writes: "It should be possible to draw a dividing line that cuts not between *being and having*, but between unjust having and a just possession that would distinguish among men without mutually excluding them" (Ricoeur 1986: 115). Ricoeur's description is preparing the way for a more affirmative analysis of having and the feelings it entails: "Insofar as the thing is 'available' it creates the whole cycle of feelings relative to acquisition, appropriation, possession, and preservation." These terms often have negative connotations, but Ricoeur intends them as fundamentally neutral—potentially fallen, but innocent in themselves.

Ricoeur shows that the affect of possession needs to be distinguished from the passion of possessiveness. We should also recognize that possessiveness is not the only way to go wrong in relation to one's things: the opposite of possessiveness is not indifference to one's things. It is not negligence—a careless disregard for one's property. There is a proper kind of care and responsibility for what is ours, for instance, the way someone "keeps" their house, tends to their yard, maintains their vehicle, curates a personal collection, or cares for their tools. As Ricoeur puts it, the desire to preserve what one has is part of the "cycle of feelings" related to having. The proper practice of preservation is distinguishable from distorted forms of preservation in which I become obsessed, jealously guarding my possessions like fetish-objects. This is a kind of virtuous care that is clearly recognized in its absence, when someone neglects their things. When a car falls into disrepair or a house falls into ruin, we recognize this as a kind of irresponsibility. How a person disposes of their possessions tells us something about their disposition, their habits, and the kind of person they are.

Could we go so far as to suggest that virtuous having is analogous to Marcel's idea of creative fidelity—as a kind of faithfulness to that with which one has been entrusted? Consider Marcel's description: "Creative fidelity consists in actively maintaining oneself in a state of permeability, and we see that there occurs here a sort of mysterious interchanging between this free act and the gift given in response to it" (Marcel 1998: 190). Marcel conceives of this permeability as a responsiveness to other persons, to the exigencies of the situation. But is there also a positive permeability to the things we *have*? Theologians sometimes describe this in terms of stewardship. It is a way of faithfully administering that with which one has been entrusted—not for the sake of my own egoistic enjoyment, but for the benefit of other people.

Perhaps a faithful having could be a mode of creative fidelity—not simply to preserving the having as an end in itself but so the having transcends itself for the sake of others. This fidelity would be a virtuous mode of caring for that which is mine. Perhaps, though, we must also recognize that this would be a fragile, deeply fallible fidelity, the point on which having is particularly susceptible to falling. But such is the way with all the capacities of the self: subject to disproportion, and thus capable of falling.

CONCLUSION

Early in *Fallible Man*, Ricoeur writes that the "whole movement of this book consists in an attempt to enlarge reflection step by step" (Ricoeur 1986: 6). The first step, as we have seen, was to dive into the *pathétique* of misery and immerse reflection in the preunderstanding of human disproportion. The second step was to use transcendental argumentation to gain a degree of rigor that will raise the reflection to the "genuinely philosophical." This is where Ricoeur goes beyond Marcel, and follows in the footsteps of Kant, Hegel, and Husserl. The ideal limit of this reflective ascent would be a "total comprehension" in which pure reflection "would be equivalent to the *pathétique* of misery." That said, this total comprehension is always out of reach, "because in man's pre-comprehension of himself there is a wealth of meaning that reflection is unable to equal" (Ricoeur 1986: 6). Like the disproportion of the fallible human being, the two never perfectly coincide.

Reflection never becomes fully adequate to reality. This is a very Kantian point, but one that Ricoeur also shares with Marcel. Even phenomenology, which cleaves closely to the concrete, remains a kind of conceptual thinking and as such involves "a definite loss of being."[20] The result is a "loss of presence," a "conceptual de-incarnation" in which the I is cut off from the presence of reality (Ricoeur 1966: 16). Reflection—whether primary or secondary—is not the same as being.

Nevertheless, if reflection is going to lead to a deeper understanding of being, then Ricoeur believes it must be thoroughly rigorous. As we have seen, this is why Ricoeur sees more of a need for primary, objectifying modes of reflection—not because these methods alone give us the best account of reality, but because they add a critical, rigorous perspective that philosophy needs. Ricoeur makes this point years later in his essay "Gabriel Marcel and Phenomenology," which he contributed to a volume of essays in honor of Marcel. Ricoeur argues that

> even if reflection must finally be discovered within being, it is first necessary to constitute it as reflection. It is perhaps in the nature of the original affirmation that it should engender a second Copernican Revolution, a second naïveté presupposing an initial critical revolution, an initial loss of naïveté. This hard destiny is perhaps what distinguishes philosophy from poetry and faith. (Ricoeur 1984: 492)[21]

Poetry and faith may in fact be the deepest source of existential nourishment. But if philosophy seeks to understand them, Ricoeur argues, it must not mistake itself for either poetry or faith. This tension—between rigorous critique and existential conviction—resides at the heart of Ricoeur's thinking.

And it is in this tension that we see the ongoing influence of his debate with his friend and master, Gabriel Marcel.

NOTES

1. Marcel recounts a time when Sartre presented a paper at Marcel's home (Marcel 1956: p. 53).

2. "Usually it is a society lady who asks for this information, but to-morrow it may be my charwoman or the ticket-collector on the Underground" (Marcel 1956: 91).

3. Marcel 1973: 221, 237. See also Ricoeur 1995: 7. Elsewhere Marcel writes: "If there is, as I think there is, a philosophy of existence, I don't believe it can become an ism without betraying itself" (Marcel 2003: 193). Marcel also writes: "for me, 'essence' constitutes the locus of a renewed meditation, and I would be wholly against subordinating it in any way to the notion of 'existence'" (Marcel 1973: xxxii).

4. For a fuller discussion of reflexive philosophy and its influence on Ricoeur, see Gregor 2019: 12–14.

5. Marcel 1952: 331–32. Ricoeur credits Marcel with having a major influence on French philosophy, as being "the one who made the connection between the philosophy of sensation and that of existence." In his interview Ricoeur tells him: "Sensation was no longer just the business of psychophysiology. According to you, sensation testified to our participation in existence, the participation of my own self in the world of existing things. When you criticized the conception of sensation as a message passing between one thing and another, between a transmitter and a receiver, you laid the foundation of what Merleau-Ponty and others later called phenomenology of perception" (Marcel 1973: 222).

6. "By its very essence the objective order excludes all mystery" (Marcel 1952: 161).

7. My thanks to Bob Doede for this turn of phrase.

8. In a pair of entries from December 1918 in the *Metaphysical Journal*, Marcel discusses the way in which God goes beyond being a *he* or an *it*—someone or something spoken of in the third person: "when we speak *of* God we should realise that it is not of *God* that we are speaking" (Marcel 1952: 159)—to being addressed in the second person, as *You* or *Thou*. Marcel finds this second-person language in prayer: "To pray is actively to refuse to think God as order, it is to think him as really God, as pure *Thou*" (Marcel 1952: 160).

9. "Now the 'I' of the 'I see' is *here* only insofar as the body as a whole has a position from which it effectuates all its perceiving acts" (Ricoeur 1966: 23).

10. Philosophers are tempted by other abstract approaches to evil, such as metaphysical dualisms that treat evil as the dark counterpart of the good; in Hegelian and Marxist views of evil as the work of the negative, to be overcome by historical synthesis, and in our own technological age it is tempting to see evil as malfunction, to be treated with the right technique (Marcel 1973: 141, 145).

11. Marcel 1973: 133. In the interest of approaching the mystery of evil in its concreteness, Marcel offers something like a phenomenological description of the

encounter with evil. Evil in this description "appears as wholly unsusceptible of being characterized and classified like an object, which we control to the extent that we describe it." Evil shows itself as outside our control, and "surprises us with its treachery," such that we are at a loss for how to interpret it, to locate it objectively, or to identify its origins: "I am disoriented. I am plunged into darkness" (Marcel 1973: 135, 137).

12. According to Marcel, this encounter with evil calls for "concrete communication" between persons, who enter into relations of communion or participation (Marcel 1973: 140–41). This kind of communion is the basis for hope. There is hope only for a *we*: "all hope is at bottom choral" (Marcel 1973: 143). The solitary individual is far more susceptible to despair; "it is not by turning in on myself that I will manage to overcome [the temptation to despair]; for solipsism cannot be a liberation. My only recourse is to open myself to a wide communion, perhaps an infinite one, at the heart of which this evil which has come on me in some way changes its nature. For in becoming *our* evil it ceases to be a blow struck at a self-centered love. It becomes the evil over which *you, you have triumphed*" (Marcel 1973: 145). "Who is this 'you'?" Marcel asks. It might be the person who has come alongside me. It might also be the comfort that comes with participation in the communion of saints, as well as the example of Christ, in the cross and resurrection. This possibility of knowledge is a matter of faith and hope, nourished by grace (Marcel 1973: 145–46).

13. William Shakespeare. *Julius Caesar*, III.ii.76.

14. Ricoeur laments the way these disciplines distort our self-understanding, so that we come to resemble their descriptions. He writes that "most often we treat ourselves as objects. Working and social life require this objectification; our very freedom depends on these social regularities which give us a routine existence. And so we create ourselves and in ourselves the conditions of validity of the concepts of modern psychology. These concepts are adapted to the man who adapts himself" (Ricoeur 1986: 101).

15. Jay Tolston discusses Marcel's influence on Percy in Tolson 1992: 238–39. I have been unable to uncover any evidence that Percy read *Fallible Man*, and there is no copy of the book in his personal library. Late in his life Percy did read Ricoeur's essay "What is a Text? Explanation and Understanding," collected in Lambropoulos and Miller, 1987. Percy's underlining and marginalia suggest he studied the essay closely, but this reading came too late to influence any of his novels. My thanks to the Special Collections department in the Wilson Library at the University of North Carolina for consulting their archive of Percy's personal library.

16. As Pascal writes in an entry called "Man's disproportion": "For in fact what is man in nature? A Nothing in comparison with the Infinite, an All in comparison with the Nothing, a mean between nothing and everything. Since he is infinitely removed from comprehending the extremes, the end of things and their beginning are hopelessly hidden from him in an impenetrable secret; he is equally incapable of seeing the Nothing from which he was made, and the Infinite in which he is swallowed up" (Pascal 1941: 21–22). Ricoeur cites this passage from Pascal in his own discussion of human disproportion (Ricoeur 1986: 12).

17. Though he does write of the "riddle" of Fault, or the enslaved will (Ricoeur 1986: xlv, 142).

18. Ricoeur does not cite Jaspers as the ultimate guide to objective thinking, but only as a way of highlighting this need in Marcel's work. For example, Ricoeur compares and contrasts the two thinkers on the topic of communication and the relation to the second person, the *You*—a point where Ricoeur discerns "considerable resemblance" between Marcel and Jaspers (Ricoeur 1947: 157). For Marcel, the solitary thinking I is not the sum total of existence, since the I is always interrelated with the *You*. I am an I only in relation with the You. Marcel opposes this interpersonal relation to the kind of anonymous, depersonalized relations that govern so much of modern society, but Ricoeur argues that Marcel "lacks a positive reflection" on the meaning of the abstract frameworks that belong to every human institution. Philosophy has a double task of affirming the place of impersonal, abstract institutions and orders, while at the same time "recognizing their ultimate poverty." These institutions and orders are no substitute for the fullness of interpersonal relations, and yet they do play an important role in mediating our social relations. On Ricoeur's reading, Jaspers offers a more satisfactory account of this "double exigence" than does Marcel (Ricoeur 1947: 177).

19. A phrase I am borrowing from Boyd Blundell, who argues that Ricoeur takes primary reflection as a way to deepen secondary reflection (Blundell 2010: pp.60–62). For a more elaborate discussion of Ricoeur's relation to Marcel, see also Blundell 2003:89–102.

20. "I appropriate what I understand, I lay a claim to it, I encompass it by a definite power of thought which sooner or later comes to regard itself as positing, forming, and constitutive with respect to objectivity" (Ricoeur 1966: 16).

21. Ricoeur makes a similar point in *Freedom and Nature*. Concepts may never be fully adequate to being, but they can serve as *"indications"* of a living experience in which we are submerged," rather than as "signs of mastery which our intelligence exercises over our human condition." And philosophy must use concepts, since "it is the task of philosophy to clarify existence itself by use of concepts. And this is the function of a descriptive phenomenology: it is the watershed separating romantic effusion and shallow intellectualism" (Ricoeur 1966: 17).

REFERENCES

Blundell, Boyd. 2003. Creative Fidelity: Gabriel Marcel's Influence on Paul Ricoeur. In *Between Suspicion and Sympathy: Paul Ricoeur's Unstable Equilibrium*. Ed. Andrzej Wierciński. Toronto: The Hermeneutic Press, pp. 89–102.

———. 2010. *Paul Ricoeur between Theology and Philosophy: Detour and Return*. Indiana University Press.

Dosse, François. 2008. *Paul Ricoeur: Les sens d'une vie (1913–2005)*. Édition revue et augmentée. Paris: La Découverte/Poche.

Gregor, Brian. 2019. *Ricoeur's Hermeneutics of Religion: Rebirth of the Capable Self*. Lanham, MD: Lexington Books.

Kearney, Richard. 2004. *Debates in Continental Philosophy: Conversations with Contemporary Thinkers*. New York: Fordham University Press.

Lambropoulos, Vassilis and David Neal Miller. 1987. *Twentieth Century Literary Theory: An Introductory Anthology*. Albany, NY: State University of New York Press.

Malka, Salman. 2006. *Emmanuel Levinas: His Life and Legacy*. Pittsburgh, PA: Duquesne University Press.

Marcel, Gabriel. 1952. *Metaphysical Journal*. Trans. Bernard Wall. Chicago, IL: Gateway/Henry Regnery Company.

———. 1956. *The Philosophy of Existentialism*. Trans. Manya Harari. Seacaucus, NJ: Citadel Press.

———. 1965. *Being and Having: An Existentialist Diary*. New York: Harper & Row.

———. 1973. *Tragic Wisdom and Beyond*. Trans. Stephen Jolin and Peter McCormick. Evanston, IL: Northwestern University Press.

———. 1998. *Gabriel Marcel's Perspectives on The Broken World*. Trans. Katharine Rose Hanley. Milwaukee, WI: Marquette University Press.

———. 2003. *Awakenings (Gabriel Marcel's Autobiography)*. Trans. Patrick L. Bourgeois. Milwaukee, WI: Marquette University Press.

Pascal, Blaise. 1941. *Pensées*. Trans. W.F. Trotter. New York: Random House.

Percy, Walker. 1971. *Love in the Ruins*. New York: Picador.

Reagan, Charles. 1996. *Paul Ricoeur: His Life and Work*. Chicago: University of Chicago Press.

Ricoeur, Paul. 1948. *Gabriel Marcel et Karl Jaspers: Philosophie du mystère et philosophie du paradoxe*. Paris. Éditions du Temps présent.

———. 1960. L'homme et son mystère. *Le Mystère*, XII semaine des intellectuels catholiques, 1959. Ed. Pierre-Horay, pp.119–30.

———. 1966. *Freedom and Nature: The Voluntary and the Involuntary*. Trans. Erazím V. Kohak. Evanston, IL: Northwestern University Press.

———. 1970. *Freud and Philosophy: An Essay on Interpretation*. Trans. Denis Savage. Yale University Press.

———. 1974. *The Conflict of Interpretations: Essays in Hermeneutics*. Edited by Don Ihde. Evanston, IL: Northwestern University Press.

———. 1984. Gabriel Marcel and Phenomenology. *The Philosophy of Paul Ricoeur: (Library of Living Philosophers Vol. 17)*. Eds. Paul Arthur Shilpp and Lewis Edwin Hahn. Chicago, IL: Open Court Publishing, pp. 471–494.

———. 1986. *Fallible Man*. Trans. Charles A. Kelbley. New York: Fordham University Press.

———. 1995. Intellectual Autobiography. *The Philosophy of Paul Ricoeur: Library of Living Philosophers*. Eds. Lewis Edwin Hahn. Chicago and LaSalle, IL: Open Court Publishers, pp. 3–53.

———. 1998. *Critique and Conviction: Conversations with François Azouvi and Marc de Launay*. Trans. Kathleen Blamey. New York: Columbia University Press.

Tolson, Jay. 1992. *Pilgrim in the Ruins: A Life of Walker Percy*. New York: Simon & Schuster.

Chapter 4

The Limitation of the Ethical Vision of the World
The Influence of Jean Nabert
Scott Davidson

The influence of the French reflexive philosopher, Jean Nabert, might not be readily apparent to the casual reader of *Fallible Man*. Although Ricoeur dedicates the book to Nabert in the original French text, the dedication page is omitted from the English translation of the book. Moreover, neither reflexive philosophy in general nor Nabert's philosophy in particular is widely read or discussed in the English-speaking world, and so Nabert's influence on Ricoeur is not likely to be detected by readers, except where it is explicitly mentioned by Ricoeur. And even though Ricoeur does refer to Nabert's work in the "Preface" and "Conclusion" of *Fallible Man*, these two separate discussions do not appear to have any clear or systematic unity and Nabert's work is not engaged elsewhere in the body of Ricoeur's text. Even if these obstacles may make it difficult to perceive Nabert's influence on the surface of the text, the aim of this chapter is to show how Nabert's thought is essential to Ricoeur's argument in *Fallible Man*.

Nabert's influence becomes evident first in how Ricoeur defines the task of *Fallible Man* in relation to its predecessor, *Freedom and Nature*. The earlier work bracketed and set aside any evaluative questions that might concern the morality of the will; its focus was restricted to providing a value-neutral description of the will. But with *Fallible Man*, Ricoeur announces the removal of those brackets so that he can engage the realm of "the fault," a concept that is borrowed directly from Nabert's *Elements for an Ethic*.[1] In taking up the notion of the fault, Ricoeur is not only able to account for the human possibility to err [*posse peccare*] but also able to articulate the limitations of the so-called "ethical vision of the world" in which the experience of evil is always traced back to some form of wrongdoing.[2] Nabert's philosophy thematizes the excess of an evil that surmounts the ethical vision and posits an undeserved suffering of evil that escapes rational justification.

THE METHODOLOGICAL INFLUENCE OF FRENCH REFLEXIVE PHILOSOPHY

Jean Nabert's work is often located within the tradition of French reflexive philosophy, a tradition whose influence has scarcely been touched in the now voluminous secondary literature on Ricoeur.[3] One initial indication of this influence on Ricoeur, however, is offered by his remark that his own thought "stands in the line of a *reflexive* philosophy; it remains within the sphere of Husserlian *phenomenology*; it strives to be a hermeneutical variation of this phenomenology" (Ricoeur 1991: 12). Reflexive philosophy is a movement that draws its inspiration from Cartesian philosophy, beginning with Maine de Biran and extending through the work of nineteenth-century thinkers such as Félix Ravaisson, Jules Lachelier, and Jules Lagneau. When Ricoeur places himself in the lineage of this tradition, he often attributes this inspiration to the work of Nabert in particular.[4] And Nabert, in turn, situates his own work within the reflexive tradition in a 1952 entry he composed on "Reflexive Philosophy" for the *Encyclopédie Française* (Nabert 1994). Understanding Nabert's unique place within the French reflexive tradition, in my opinion, can help to shed light on Ricoeur's own practice of reflexive philosophy.

Nabert begins by noting that the reflexive tradition, instead of forming a shared orthodoxy, develops along two distinct trajectories: for some, it leads to a reflection on the conditions of the possibility of true knowledge and of the universality of reason (the Kantian path); for others, it is the intimacy of conscious life that prevails (the Biranian path). To be sure, it would be fair to say that Ricoeur is inspired by both of these directions in certain respects. All reflexive philosophers, to be sure, would agree with Kant's assertion that the self—the "I think"—accompanies every representation and action. What distinguishes the Biranian path, however, is that it challenges the formal and impersonal nature of the Kantian ego and instead seeks to "promote a self-consciousness that does not lack the dimension of intimacy that is missing from the transcendental consciousness of criticism" (Nabert 1994: 404). And this search for a personal self-relation is an important impetus that propels the progression of the argument in *Fallible Man*.

The role of reflection, from the Biranian perspective, is to recover a personal dimension of the self and restore an intimate relation with oneself. Nabert describes this recovery in the following manner:

in all of the domains where the spirit reveals itself as creative, reflection is called on to retrieve the acts which works conceal, because, living their own life, these works are almost detached from the operations that have produced them. It is a question of bringing to light the intimate relationship between an act and the significations in which it is objectified. (Nabert 1994: 406–07)

The activity of reflection, then, is necessitated by a self-forgetting that occurs with respect to the acts and meanings that are objectified in the world. Due to the possibility to detach an action from its agent or a meaning from its initial intention, we can easily lose sight of the personal connection with what exists in the objective realm. Reflexive philosophy, as Lagneau puts it, seeks "to rediscover thought even in the very least object" (see Nabert 1994: x). In this way, the act of reflection attempts to recover what Nabert calls the "intimate relationship" between the power to act and the products in which it is objectified; it rediscovers the self's personal presence in the world.

One way to think about the role of reflection is to situate it within a contrast between different perspectives from which events can be described: either objectively from a third-person point of view or subjectively from a first-person point of view. It is with this distinction, in fact, that Nabert's *Elements for an Ethic* opens: "There are two ways to treat historical events. One way aims at a determinist explanation, the other seeks to recapture the decisions, moral energy and ideals expressed by the events" (Nabert 1969: 3). That is to say that, on the one hand, any action can be described as an event, as something that takes place in the world: "Person x raised his hand." Under such a description, the action is neutralized and treated as an event that can be observed publicly and described in the same way by any external observer. Furthermore, this external observation of an action allows it to be explained in relation to a series of other observable events; it can be described as the effect of a prior causal chain of events. Hence, one could say that "Julius Caesar crossed the Rubicon, because y and y occurred, because z, and so on." In contrast with this third-person perspective, the task of reflection is to describe the same action from a first-person point of view. In so doing, reflection sets out to recover the set of motives and reasons which lead to an action: "I raised my hand, because I considered myself to be responsible for that action and because so and so." Nabert's practice of reflection offers what Ricoeur calls a via media between the Kantian and Biranian paths, because it recognizes the need for both perspectives (Nabert 1969: xxii).[5]

Returning to Ricoeur's claim that his own thought "stands in the lineage of a *reflexive* philosophy" I would suggest that Ricoeur's use of reflexive philosophy in *Fallible Man* likewise pursues a middle ground between the Kantian and the Biranian paths. The Kantian path is evident in chapter 2 "The Transcendental Synthesis," whose analysis is outlined in the Introduction to this volume. While the transcendental synthesis is necessary in order to bring intelligibility to the pathos of human misery, its contribution to reflection is limited. It provides only a formal conception of the person as an "I think" that would be valid for each and every person. The Kantian path of reflection needs to be complemented by a second mode of reflection—carried out along the Biranian path—that attains the uniqueness of the self. This form of reflection is operative in *Fallible Man*, when Ricoeur utilizes reflection in the subsequent chapters to recover the self in its concrete, personal reality. The combination of these two different types of reflection is present in Ricoeur's description of the work of reflection in terms of "the appropriation of our effort to exist and our desire to be by means of works which testify to this effort and this desire" (Ricoeur 1974: 329).This conception of reflection avoids the extremes of either a Kantian or a Biranian path. Unlike the Biranian path, it does seek to attain an immediate or direct intuition of the personal self; unlike the Kantian path, it does not approach the self as an abstract or formal reality. Instead reflection proceeds indirectly and passes through the external world.[6] And this detour of reflection through the external world is first disclosed as a possibility for Ricoeur through Nabert's distinctive interpretation of the reflexive tradition. Following Nabert's middle path, reflection proceeds through works and signs in the external world with the ultimate goal of bringing about a regeneration, a rebirth, of the self.

ELEMENTS FOR AN ETHIC AS A MODEL OF REFLEXIVE SELF-RECOVERY

In the "Preface" of *Fallible Man*, Ricoeur claims that Nabert's *Elements for an Ethic* is worthy of being regarded "as the canonical work of the reflective method" (Ricoeur 1986: xxv), and Ricoeur later wrote a preface for the English translation of the work. In the most general terms, Ricoeur's interpretation of *Elements for an Ethic* identifies a dialectical progression that leads through the three major divisions of the text. Starting from the negative feelings described in the first part of the work on "The Givens of Reflection," the second part of Nabert's work proceeds to what is called "The Originary Affirmation" in which the self discovers itself as a truth of reflection. But there is no repose to be found in this retrospective recovery of the self, because the originary affirmation immediately points outside of the self, specifically to its role in constituting the external world through action. On the level of action, this converts the inner motives of the self into external actions which serve as the visible signs of the self's intentions. This process of externalization of the self in a world of values and goals is described in the third part of the book, "Existence." In what follows, the steps of this dialectical progression will be traced in more specific detail, which ultimately will help to show how the Nabertian dialectic comes to be incorporated into the progression of Ricoeur's own argument in *Fallible Man*.

A. The Givens of Reflection: The Experience of Fault

Importantly, Nabert's reflection does not begin in a vacuum or with a merely voluntary act of introspection, instead it is motivated by what is already there in experience. As Ricoeur observes, this means that the task of reflection is not so much to establish a first starting point, as was the case for Descartes, and to coincide with it; instead, it is initiated by what precedes reflection. Nabert thus sets out "to reveal the structure of what precedes reflection" (Nabert 1969: xviii) through a process that resembles what Husserl would call a "questioning back" [*Rückfragen*]. This is why Nabert's book finds its starting point under the heading of "The Givens of Reflection." Its reflection proceeds from a set of negative experiences—fault, failure, and solitude—that have already occurred in the mode of feeling. These initial negative feelings serve as the initial givens or material that motivates reflection.

It is in this context that Nabert introduces his influential discussion of the "experience of fault," a concept which Ricoeur borrows in *Fallible Man*. Nabert's notion of the fault is not limited to our ordinary usage of the term. That is to say that it does not refer to a cognitive error in which we would make a false judgment, nor does it refer to the violation of a moral rule or obligation, nor to the internal pangs of conscience that might result from the violation of such norms. Instead, the experience of fault is more fundamental; it goes beyond the categories by which we understand moral experience (Nabert 1969: 8). To be precise, the fault refers to a more general opacity within oneself, "which insinuates itself into all the actions of the self and delays or obstructs the development of its own aspiration." Second, unlike an individual action, the fault is not something whose origin can be located at any given moment or event in time. Without a clear beginning or end point, the experience of fault accordingly reveals that the self participates in a broader world that "cannot be reduced to the operations of individual consciousness." Lastly, the experience of fault, together with the analogous experiences of failure and solitude, enables us to apprehend an insurmountable inadequacy of the self; in other words, it opens up an unbridgeable gap between what we are and what we desire to be (Nabert 1969: 57). Although the experience of fault is broader than ethics in these respects, the awareness of our lack of being is nonetheless what motivates an ethics, at least in the sense of a Spinozistic ethics of self-realization.

Under the influence of Spinoza, Nabert's conception of ethics does not conform with more familiar versions of normative ethics. Instead of prescribing a set of moral rules or formulae, Nabert understands ethics in terms of Spinoza's conception of the *conatus essendi*.[7] Ethics in this sense is rooted in a personal history and a struggle to be that leads the self "from servitude to beatitude" (Ricoeur 1974: 340). To the extent that its goal is to lead the individual to a higher degree of self-realization, such an ethics could be classified more accurately as an ethics of authenticity. Its goal is to grasp the ego in its effort to exist, in its desire to be, which is taken as an affirmation of being (Ricoeur 1974: 341). And the experience of the negative is the starting point for self-reflection, insofar as the negative presents an obstacle or roadblock in relation to the self's own desire to be. The experience of the negative produces the feeling of sadness—or what Ricoeur calls the pathos of misery in *Fallible Man*—a feeling which Spinoza defines as "a passion by which the soul passes to a lesser perfection" (Ricoeur 1974: 318). To suffer is thus to undergo a decrease or limitation in one's own being. And when Ricoeur talks about reflection, he likewise situates it in relation to a prior pathos, an experience of misery; from this starting point, reflection then involves a "reappropriation of our effort to exist" (Ricoeur 1974: 328). This is the reason why the dialectical progression that proceeds from the fault is not simply a journey that leads to a positing of the existence of the self; more profoundly, it is a journey of authenticity and self-realization that leads toward the generation of an ideal self.

B. Originary Affirmation

The realization of the self through self-reflection signifies both a struggle and an achievement for Nabert. The struggle to be, as we have seen, begins with the initial feelings of fault, failure, and solitude—feelings that stand in conflict with the desire for self-realization. Under the sway of these negative feelings, I might find myself to be lost, wayward, or led astray, somehow separated from myself. The act of reflection is itself an attempt to recover those aspects of oneself which have been diminished or lost. And this reflection itself is an expression of the more general desire to be or to realize oneself, and its relation to the accomplishment of this goal is what defines the process of reflection as a task, instead of a given. Through a reflection on the experience of the negative, the self seeks to arrive at what Nabert calls an "absolute and originary affirmation."

To arrive at this affirmation, the reflective method must first bring these experiences of our past into a "present congenial to reflection" (Nabert 1969: 41). This reflection on the present, as Nabert explains, is a movement "which goes from action in its spontaneity to reflection on action" (Nabert 1969: 41). Through this reflexive relation to oneself, the self arrives at an originary affirmation that resembles the Cartesian affirmation "I am, I exist." Elsewhere

Ricoeur further echoes the Cartesian doctrine of continual creation in stating that "this affirmation must be attained and reattained indefinitely, even though basically this affirmation is not subject to loss, is inalienable, primordial" (Ricoeur 1974: 341). What is surprising, nonetheless, is that when Nabert affirms the *cogito*—the "I am, I exist"—this does not lead him to advocate for an autonomous or self-enclosed subject. Concerning this self-affirmation, Nabert instead raises a question concerning its source: to paraphrase, does my originary affirmation establish the certitude of that which is doing the affirming (the act of self-positing) or does the source of this affirmation come from the side of what is affirmed (the posited self)? This question concerning the ground of the originary affirmation retains traces of the famous Cartesian circle which raised a similar question concerning the ground of knowledge. And Nabert's answer to this question is perhaps also inspired by Descartes, at least in the sense that he rejects either of these two alternatives. Instead of seeking to secure the originary affirmation either subjectively or objectively, he conceives the originary affirmation as a twofold relationship. What characterizes the "I am"—invoking the thetic judgment of Fichte—is its dual reference: I affirm myself at the same time as I enter into relation with a principle that stands outside myself.

This dual character of the originary affirmation leads Ricoeur to observe that it is "an affirmation of being in the lack of being" (Ricoeur 1974: 341), which is a way of saying that the originary affirmation at once posits the self and continues to bear the mark of a self-division. Insofar as a distance stands between the existence of the "I am" and the affirmation which grounds it, "the impossibility of self-adequation enters into the constitution of subjectivity" (Nabert 1969: 51). Accordingly, even within the originary affirmation, the self continues to be defined by an "inadequation of existence to itself" (Nabert 1969: 57).[8] And if this inadequation persists and if a Spinozistic ethics seeks to fulfill the desire to be, it means that reflexive philosophy cannot achieve its aim simply by accomplishing the act of reflection and by affirming the existence of the self. As Nabert says, "the movement of reflection does not direct itself toward primary reflection so that it may settle down in it" (Nabert 1969: 57). The originary affirmation, in order to realize the self, must extend out to the world in a movement that Nabert places under the heading of "existence."

C. Existence

There is, as we have noted, a temporal dimension to the progression of Nabert's book, and this temporality continues into the third main division. Whereas the givens of reflection put the self in relation to its past and the reflection on consciousness concentrated its focus on the affirmation of the self in the present, the third movement is primarily directed toward the self's aspirations for the future. This affirmation calls for concrete perpetuation and realization in human existence. The reflexive return to the concrete world constitutes the authentic orientation of the ethical life, for Nabert. The ethical life differs from the ordinary relation to the world precisely in the sense that it includes the reflective movement that has passed through the originary affirmation. In its reorientation toward the world, individual freedom seeks to affirm itself by expressing itself in the world, not simply in reflecting how the world actually is but by directing itself toward the world in an ideal manner, or as the world ought to be. Values, Nabert asserts, "are the modes in which a real consciousness in its commerce with the world verifies its own relationship to pure consciousness. But this verification can be made only indirectly by means of goals and tasks for which the will acts" (Nabert 1969: 100). Without going into the complete details of Nabert's discussion of values, goals, duties, and other related concepts that belong under the rubric of existence, suffice it to say that these affirmations of the world become the means by which the self affirms itself and accomplishes its aspirations for self-realization. The ethics that is outlined here, then, is one which seeks to produce a deepening of the self through its self-expression in the actions in the world (see also Ricoeur 1974: 342).

What is interesting to Ricoeur about this passage from an inner motive to an external action is that it gives rise to a fundamental paradox. There are two different types of activities involved here: reflection, which concentrates the self at its source, and action, which extends the self into the world. And these two activities do not necessarily coalesce. The originary affirmation, on the one hand, is the source and generative principle of all value, but the action which extends it to the world entails a certain "obfuscation of the generative principle of value," on the other hand. At best, actions can only serve as signs or indicators of the reflexive acts in which they originate. In the transition that leads from the reflexive determination of a value and into the actions which are its signs, there is a possible loss of their original generative principle. The self who stands behind an action is no longer evident within the action itself. As a result, the action can come to be viewed simply on its own terms from a third-person standpoint, without reference to the agent's motivations or even to the agent who made it happen at all. Yet, this effacement of the agent stands in direct contrast with what was said at the outset of this discussion of Nabert, where the purpose of the reflective method was defined precisely as an attempt to recover the lost motives that vanish from the external actions that are described in the third-person. With this final passage into existence in the concrete world of action, then, has Nabert's reflexive philosophy undone itself and erased its own first-person contribution? What are we to make of this paradoxical result?

Nabert was not unaware of this paradox, and Ricoeur's solution provides a key indication of Nabert's influence on *Fallible Man*: he suggests that the solution to this paradox requires a continual "alternation between two movements" (Ricoeur 1974: 220). In other words, there is a continual back and forth that takes place between the regressive movement that proceeds reflexively from the action back to the motive and the progressive movement that leads from the motive to the action. The phenomenon of action, or the action in its appearing, is the observable expression of an inner operation which we have defined as an originary affirmation, and this inner operation, in turn, can only establish itself by expressing itself outwardly. The necessary detour of the originary affirmation through the external world, according to Ricoeur, is "based on the very structure of the originary affirmation as both difference and relation between pure consciousness and real consciousness" (Ricoeur 1974: 222). So if there is a dialectical progression to be found in the unfolding of Nabert's *Elements for an Ethic*, Ricoeur's point is that this dialectical conflict can never be closed or resolved. It must remain a continual or "open" dialectic. Instead of providing the fulfillment and closure that the desire for self-realization seeks, the open dialectic frustrates the search for wholeness or to form a totality. The result is perfectly clear: if the task of reflexive philosophy is to carry out a self-recovery, this remains an infinite task.

This section has outlined Nabert's *Elements for an Ethic* in order to underscore its influence on Ricoeur's argument in *Fallible Man*. This influence is first and foremost methodological. In Nabert's practice of the reflexive method, Ricoeur discovers an activity of self-recovery that passes through the external world. In this respect, it could be said that Nabert's practice of the reflexive method is aligned with the development of Ricoeur's hermeneutics. And indeed, it is the quest for self-recovery, in the guise of the renewal of a personal self-relation, that propels the dynamic of *Fallible Man*, as it moves through the theoretical, practical, and affective levels of human experience. Each stage of this reflection leads to a greater degree of inwardness, unveiling an increasingly intimate self-relation. But, Nabert's influence is not only methodological but also substantive. To pursue this aspect of Nabert's influence, I now want to provide a close reading of the specific passages in *Fallible Man* which refer directly to Nabert. The first reference pertains to the "ethical vision of the world" discussed in the "Preface," while the second concerns Ricoeur's treatment of the dialectic of self-affirmation and negation that takes place in the "Conclusion."

THE ETHICAL VISION OF THE WORLD

Ricoeur's "Preface" to *Fallible Man* attests explicitly to Nabert's influence, but it does so in the context of a brief response to Kant's *Essay on Radical Evil*. Ricoeur describes the Kantian account of evil as the ultimate expression of "an ethical vision of the world." But what exactly does this "ethical vision" imply? To answer this question, Ricoeur's reference to the ethical vision should be situated, in turn, in relation to his identification of three other "visions of evil" in *The Symbolism of Evil:* the ritual vision, the tragic vision, the eschatological vision. While he does not mention the ethical vision of evil in the world there, this notion is introduced later in the essay "The Hermeneutics of Symbols: I" where Ricoeur observes that "reflection upon the symbolism of evil reaches its peak in what we shall henceforth call the ethical vision of evil" (Ricoeur 1974: 300). The ethical vision of evil signifies the culmination of the three visions of evil that are elaborated in *The Symbolism of Evil*, insofar as it offers the most fully developed philosophical interpretation of evil. Such an approach seeks, first of all, to demythologize the dualistic myths of evil that depict evil as a substance, and furthermore it interprets the eschatological vision—or the Adamic myth of the fall—as a mere allegory for the human will. As a result, the ethical vision of the world locates the problem of evil entirely within the purview of the free will, such that freedom and evil allow for a mutual explanation of one another. The "grandeur" of the ethical vision is that it takes us "as far as possible in this direction" (Ricoeur 1986: xlvi).

To elaborate the ethical vision, Ricoeur draws from Kant's account of evil in *Religion within the Boundaries of Mere Reason* which, Ricoeur says, represents its "first maturity." Taking a purely secular approach to the problem of evil, Kant's aim is to make sense of three apparently conflicting features of human being: (1) we are radically free; (2) we are by nature inclined toward the good; and (3) we are by nature inclined toward evil. To account for this simultaneous inclination toward good and evil, Kant develops a "philosophical anthropology" that is comprised of three levels: animality, humanity, and personality. Animality is Kant's term for the natural self-concern formed around our natural needs for food, sex, and social interaction. Humanity corresponds to what Rousseau describes as *amour-propre*, or, our social concern for esteem and the admiration of others. Personality refers to a conception of the self as a moral being who possesses unconditional dignity as an end in itself. While each of these aspects of the human being has a proper use that leads to development of the individual as a biological, social, and moral being, each of these three aspects of the human being also admits a propensity to evil.

Based on this account of the human being, Kant identifies three gradations of evil which correspond with increasing levels of corruption of the will. The first of these is *frailty*. A person with a frail will attempts to perform morally right actions because these actions are morally right but is ultimately too weak to follow through with them. Due to weakness of the will (Kant 1998: 24–25), the frail person yields to the temptations of self-love in spite of maintaining a commitment to morality. This leads natural appetites for food and sex, for instance, to turn into the vices of gluttony and lust. The next level of corruption of the will is *impurity*. A person with an impure will does not strive to perform morally right actions for the right reasons. Even if such a person were to act rightly, they act on the basis of some other incentive, such as social conformity or approval. The impure person is satisfied as long as no one else accuses them of wrong action, in other words, as long as their actions appear to be right in the eyes of others. Kant believes that this defect in the will is worse than frailty, even though the frail person does wrong and the impure person may do right. What makes impurity worse is that the impure person has followed another incentive than the moral law (Kant 1998: 25–26). The final stage of the corruption of the will is *depravity*. A person with a perverse will inverts the proper order of moral incentives. Such a person prioritizes another motive, such as self-love, above the moral law. The will which subverts the moral law and obeys a different type of law displays the worst form of evil possible for a human being; for Kant, this characterizes a truly evil person (Kant 1998: 25). The most extreme evil, according to Kant, is not attributed to the mere violation of moral duty; it involves the subversion of reason through fraud—through the mere semblance of morality—or to put it in existentialist terms, bad faith. Extreme evil occurs when the pure motive of respect is subverted by sensible motives and when these ulterior motives are accepted as if they were rational maxims. By locating the origin of evil within a maxim of the free will, the Kantian account articulates "the very essence of the ethical vision of evil" (Ricoeur 1986: xlvii).

But in his criticism of the Kantian account of evil, Ricoeur first objection is that Kant does not go far enough in articulating "the ethical vision of the world" and that the ethical vision of evil "is complete only when, in turn, we realize its benefit for the understanding of freedom itself" (Ricoeur 1986: xlvii). In addition to utilizing freedom to illuminate evil, as Kant does, Ricoeur asserts that it is also possible to pursue the reverse movement and to utilize the experience of evil in order to illuminate freedom. This is precisely the path that is attributed to Nabert, whose reflexive approach to evil is described by Ricoeur as "a model of reflection that is not content with illuminating the problem of evil by means of the doctrine of freedom, but constantly enlarges and deepens the doctrine of freedom under the sting of evil it has incorporated within itself" (xlvii). In reversing the course of the Kantian analysis, Nabert's reflexive philosophy is able to articulate the full maturation of the ethical vision of evil.[9]

We have already seen this reverse path at work in Nabert's *Elements for an Ethic*, insofar as Nabert's analysis starts from the givenness of the experience of fault and then illuminates freedom through a subsequent act of reflection. Accordingly, in Nabert's version of the ethical vision, the relation between freedom and evil is reversed, such that here "the avowal of evil is the condition of the consciousness of freedom" (Ricoeur 1986: xlix). In the "Preface" to *Fallible Man*, Ricoeur outlines three key implications that follow from Nabert's account of the reflexive avowal or recognition of the fault. First, this avowal of the fault is not limited to the present; it has a temporal extension according to which retrospection overlays a past occurrence with remorse and where the projection of the future emerges as repentance. Second, this penitent retrospection also reveals the self in its freedom, as a total and undivided cause in relation to its action. In other words, in confessing to a fault, I attest to myself as the cause or the agent of the wrong that has been done. Finally, in taking responsibility for its own wrongdoing, the self discovers a discrepancy between its own desire for wholeness or completion and the disappointment of this demand, which is to say that it gives rise to an experience of nonbeing or of a lack within oneself. The future-oriented aspect of the avowal of fault gives rise to a new project of freedom—a penitent freedom—that seeks to overcome this lack and fulfill the desire for self-realization.

But, after laying out the ethical vision in its full grandeur, Ricoeur raises the following question: "Can an ethical vision give an all-embracing explanation of evil?" (Ricoeur 1986: xlix). This leads to his second objection to the Kantian account of evil, which asserts that what is missing from the ethical vision is the "tragic" dimension of evil. This signifies an antecedent evil that precedes the awakening of my consciousness and is already given. Although Kant does not thematize this dimension of evil, it can already be glimpsed in his reflection on the ground of wrong maxims. The source of such maxims points beyond the specific details about an individual's motives, about the specific harms done, and the specific feelings that an individual might have about doing wrong. It points toward a natural propensity to subordinate the moral law that stands outside of the boundaries of human experience. This predisposition, as Ricoeur sees it, implies that "evil, which always begins by freedom, is always already there for freedom: it is act and habit, arising and antecedence" (Ricoeur 1974: 308). This "tragic" dimension of evil also comes to the surface in Nabert's 1955 *Essay on Evil*, where evil is treated in its facticity. Actual evil is presented as a hindering force—an intrusion—that comes from the outside. Unlike the negative feelings—fault, failure, solitude—that initiate his *Elements for an Ethic* but are ultimately recuperated by reflection, the experience of evil gives rise to a feeling of the unjustifiable, the irredeemable. Evil, as unjustified, cannot be recovered by the understanding or balanced out by reason. If evil is unjustifiable and if it remains inscrutable, it would seem that the self has already been taken hold of and possessed by evil as an outside force, prior to anything that has been experienced or willed. The preexistence of evil establishes a limit—an absolute other—that prevents evil from being assimilated into the ethical vision.

This is why Ricoeur proposes that an apt subtitle for *Fallible Man* would have been "The Grandeur and Limitation of an Ethical Vision of the World" (Ricoeur 1986: xlvi). In its full grandeur, the ethical vision is able to locate evil in human actions and human motives. The suffering of evil would always be traceable to an act of evil and to someone who is responsible for it. The "grandeur" of this vision is that it offers a rational world in which the cause of evil can ultimately be explained and justified; its source can be pinned down and ascribed to someone who is held accountable for wrongdoing. But in spite of the grandeur of such an attempt, Ricoeur insists, in both *Fallible Man* and *The Symbolism of Evil*, on the limitations of this "ethical vision of the world."[10] What escapes the ethical vision of the world is the other side of the experience of evil, not the doing of evil but the suffering of evil. The suffering of unjustifiable evil highlights the fact that the human being is "no less a victim than guilty," no less a sufferer than an agent of wrongdoing (Ricoeur 1986: xlix). This is why it is necessary to go beyond the ethical vision in order to articulate the experience of evil in its full breadth: only in such a way is it possible to account for a self who is capable of acting *and* suffering.

THE OPEN DIALECTIC OF *FALLIBLE MAN*

The "Conclusion" of *Fallible Man* outlines Ricoeur's attempt to take the human experience of limitation seriously. The initial reference point for Ricoeur is to define this dialectic in terms of Kant's categories of quality: affirmation, negation, limitation. In his *Critique of Pure Reason*, Kant applied these categories on a purely formal level to the limitation of all things in general. On the formal level, there is nothing more to limitation that the positing and negating of something. But this formal account yet does not provide an account of what is specific to human limitation. Ricoeur wants to express the categories of quality in terms of his philosophical anthropology, and it is in transposing the Kantian categories to human limitation that Nabert's influence becomes clear. In what follows, we will trace out the three stages of this dialectic—originary affirmation, existential difference, human mediation (Ricoeur 1986: 135).

Ricoeur begins with the notion of an originary affirmation, which is borrowed directly from the second section of the same name in Nabert's *Elements for an Ethic*. He observes that each level of the preceding analysis—the theoretical, practical, and affective levels—has passed through its own moment of originary affirmation. And furthermore, each of these levels leads to a progressively richer and more inward affirmation. On the theoretical level, the originary affirmation is identified in the word which asserts the existence of what is signified. But it is the self that is affirmed in the practical idea of totality or happiness on the practical level. While the practical ideal gives rise to the humanity of the person, it does not yet establish that I myself am this humanity. This is what is revealed on the level of feeling through eros, or the happy heart, which affirms the joy of one's own existence. Even if this originary affirmation, for Ricoeur, is necessary to thinking about the meaning of human limitation, it alone is not sufficient. It requires a passage through the experience of existential negation. As Ricoeur explains in his essay "Negativity and Primary Affirmation," to start with an act of reflection means to start with the acts in which we become aware of our finitude: "it means to start with the connection between an *experience* of finitude and a *movement* which transgresses this finitude" (Ricoeur 1965: 306). The experience of self-affirmation, in other words, is always accompanied by the experience of one's limitations.

The next stage of the dialectic, accordingly, is to pass through existential difference, or in other words, a series of negations. On this stage of the dialectic, my identity comes to be defined by the experience of negation. Each level of the analysis in *Fallible Man*, likewise, has passed through its own distinctive type of negation. Furthermore, each type of negation has become moved progressively from the exterior to the interior, from a "difference between myself and the other, then as a differing of myself from myself, and finally internalizing itself in the sorrow of the finite" (Ricoeur 1986: 138). On the theoretical level, the experience of negation is tied to perspective, which reveals the opposition between my own perspective and those of others. On the practical level, this difference becomes a difference of myself from myself. Ricoeur connects this feeling of self-difference to the feeling of contingency which arises from the nonnecessity of my existence. This contingency also gives rise to negative feelings, or in other words, what Ricoeur calls "the sorrow of the no." These sorrows are associated with suffering, not the suffering of physical pain, but the suffering of limitations: "lack, loss, dread, regret, deception, dispersion, and the irrevocability of duration" (Ricoeur 1986: 139). These negative affects attest to a diminishment of one's being, or suffering.

From this, it is clear that the third stage of the dialectic—limitation—will be a mixture of originary affirmation and existential negation. In this respect, Ricoeur is establishing an account of the human that diverges from Sartre, for whom the self is defined as a power of negation. To be sure, Ricoeur does not deny the role of negation, but he does not believe that it can be a stopping point. It is necessary to pass through the work of negation in order to recover a concrete mediation between these two opposites. This "mixture" of originary affirmation and existential negation is not simply something that human beings accomplish with respect to the external world; humans also carry out fragile mediations of themselves. This mediation is expressed in what is perhaps the most famous line in *Fallible Man*: "Man is the joy of the yes in the sadness of the finite" (Ricoeur 1986: 140). But such a mediation—which affirms human existence with both its joys and sorrows, its accomplishments as well as its setbacks—is always a fragile and precarious accomplishment. The self, located in a liminal space between the yes and the no, remains ever precarious.[11]

If this is the result of the dialectical development of *Fallible Man*, how does it reflect the influence of Nabert? We have seen that *Elements for an Ethic* follows a trajectory that begins with the negative experiences—such as the fault—that are given to reflection, passes to the originary affirmation, and then culminates in a concrete existence which is able to mediate between them. *Fallible Man* follows a similar development but alters its order by beginning with the originary affirmation, passing through the givens of reflection in existential difference, before culminating in a concrete mediation of human limitation. But this difference does not seem to alter the results in any significant manner: Nabert's concrete existence is tantamount to Ricoeur's notion of limitation and vice versa. For both Nabert and Ricoeur, what is essential is that the experience of limitation can be traced back to a fault that is not simply individual but ontological. To be sure, individuals are capable of erring and of wrongdoing. But if the experience of fault were merely personal, then it would be possible to give a full account of one's own wrongdoing and to repair it fully through acts of repentance, apology, or forgiveness. Without denying the importance of such efforts to make amends for personal faults, it is important to add that the fault is also ontological, so to speak. This means that self-division does not simply occur through one's own actions; it is already embedded within oneself prior to any thought or action performed by oneself. The suffering of the fault opens the door for thinking about the evil that one suffers. The suffering of evil can be brought up to the level of reflection, but it cannot be fully justified by reason or undone by works. This is why the pathos of suffering exposes the limits of an ethical vision of the world.

NOTES

1. It should be noted that the notion of fault likewise plays an important role in *The Symbolism of Evil*, where Ricoeur identifies three moments of fault: defilement, sin, guilt (Ricoeur 1967: 100). These three moments are the vehicle by which Ricoeur approaches the "symbolic richness" of the fault (Ricoeur 1967: 26).

2. More broadly, it could be argued that this influence overflows *Fallible Man* and runs throughout the three books comprising his "philosophy of the will." Close consideration suggests that there is a sort of interweaving of the topics taken up in Ricoeur's "philosophy of the will" with three books by Nabert: *Freedom and Nature* corresponds with the *Inner Experience of Freedom*, *Fallible Man* corresponds with *Elements for an Ethic*, and *Symbolism of Evil* aligns with the *Essay on Evil*.

3. Significantly, Ricoeur's master's thesis, has recently been published in France, was written on the reflexive philosophy of two nineteenth-century French thinkers: Jules Lachelier and Jules Lagneau. See Ricoeur 2017.

4. In his "Intellectual Autobiography," Ricoeur writes: "On the one hand, this tradition [of French reflexive philosophy] led back, through E. Boutroux and F. Ravaisson, to Maine de Biran; on the other hand, it tended toward Jean Nabert who, in 1924, had published *L'expérience intérieure de la liberté* . . . Jean Nabert was to have a decisive influence on me in the 1950s and 1960s" (Ricoeur 1995: 6). See also Ricœur 1991: 1–20.

5. For instance, Nabert writes in the Encyclopedia article that "It was necessary for a critical theory of knowledge to establish the priority in the 'I think' of its function of objectivity and truth so as to keep reflection, immediately attentive to the concrete forms of inner experience, from indulging in sterile irrationalism" (Nabert 1994).

6. Later Ricoeur describes reflection in the following terms: "having completely incorporated the corrections and the lessons of psychoanalysis and semiology, takes the long and roundabout route of an interpretation of private and public, psychic and cultural signs, where the desire to be and the effort to be which constitute us are expressed and made explicit" (Ricoeur 1974: 266).

7. Interestingly on this point, Ricoeur also describes Spinoza's ethics as fundamental and says that he would search for it along the lines of Nabert's reflexive philosophy. See Ricoeur 1974: 340.

8. Indeed, already in *The Inner Experience of Freedom* (1924), Nabert rejects the very possibility of the self to coincide with itself. Instead, the concentration on myself in the originary affirmation leads me toward the world.

9. This relation between Kant and Nabert calls for a much deeper analysis than can be provided here. Ricoeur's "Preface" to the English translation of *Elements for an Ethic* describes it as a contrast between the moral formalism of Kant and the more concrete ethics of Nabert. Whereas Kant's formalism allows for a separation of duty from the pathology of desire, Nabert carries out on action which "rediscovers a meaning of "ethics" which is closer to Spinoza than it is to Kant" (Ricoeur 1969: xxi), primarily because it is rooted in desire.

10. In order to highlight the pathos of suffering, *The Symbolism of Evil* will call attention to the symbolism of captivity whose significance is to establish a dimension of the experience of evil that is "contracted" prior to consciousness or freedom of the will and undergone by the victim who suffers from it.

11. Ricoeur's notion of the fragile self anticipates in profound and interesting ways with Judith Butler's notion of precarity. See Butler 2004.

REFERENCES

Butler, Judith. 2004. *Precarious Life: The Powers of Mourning and Violence*. London: Verso.

Kant, Immanuel. 1998. *Religion within the Boundaries of Mere Reason*. Trans. Allen Wood and George Di Giovanni. Cambridge: Cambridge University Press.

Nabert, Jean. 1994. *L'expérience intérieure de la liberté et autres essais de philosophie morale*. Paris: PUF.
Nabert, Jean. 1969. *Elements for an Ethic*. Trans. William J. Petrek. Evanston: Northwestern University Press.
Nabert, Jean. 1955. *L'Essai sur le mal*. Paris: P.U.F.
Nabert, Jean. 1924. *L'expérience intérieure de la liberté*. Paris: P.U.F.
Ricoeur, Paul. 2017. *Méthode réflexive appliqué au problème de Dieu chez Lachelier et Lagneau*. Paris: Cerf.
Ricoeur, Paul. 1995. "Intellectual Autobiography." In *The Philosophy of Paul Ricoeur. The Library of Living Philosophers, vol. XXII*. Ed. L.E. Hahn. Chicago: Open Court, pp. 3–53.
Ricoeur, Paul. 1991. *From Text to Action*. Evanston: Northwestern University Press.
Ricoeur, Paul. 1974. *The Conflict of Interpretations*. Ed. Don Ihde. Evanston: Northwestern University Press.
Ricoeur, Paul. 1970. *Freud and Philosophy*. Trans. Denis Savage. New Haven and London: Yale University Press.
Ricoeur, Paul. 1967. *The Symbolism of Evil*. Trans. Emerson Buchanan. Boston: Beacon Press.
Ricoeur, Paul. 1965. *History and Truth*. Trans. Charles A. Kelbley. Evanston: Northwestern University Press.

Part II

THEMATIC AVENUES

Chapter 5

The Imagination

From Ideation to Innocence

Luz Ascárate

Fallible Man provides a broadening of Ricoeur's anthropological perspective on the eidetics of the will that was developed in *Freedom and Nature*. It places the concept of fallibility within a broader dialectic than the eidetic description of the voluntary and the involuntary: a dialectic between the finitude and the infinitude of the human being. While the influence of Husserlian phenomenology is evident in Ricoeur's eidetics, it is commonly believed (Reeder 2010; Romano 2010; Stevens 1990) that he abandons this method in the second volume of his *Philosophy of the Will* in which his hermeneutics is born. This chapter will show, on the contrary, that phenomenology remains a decisive resource on the way to his hermeneutics, specifically in the philosophical anthropology developed in *Fallible Man*. Ricoeur's reinterpretation of the Kantian concept of the imagination and his concept of innocence are made possible by a detour through Husserlian phenomenology. To demonstrate this point, this chapter will return to Ricoeur's translation of *Ideen I*, in which he initially elaborates his own conception of the imagination, ideation, imaginative variation, and intentionality.

The importance of this insight is twofold. On the one hand, it strengthens the overall unity of Ricoeur's theory of the imagination, based on a phenomenological conception of the imagination underlying the transition from his eidetic to his anthropology. On the other hand, it situates Ricoeur's philosophy of the imagination within the context of the history of philosophy. The argumentation of this chapter will be developed as follows. First, Ricoeur's comments to his own translation of *Ideen I* will be examined in order to highlight how he aims to go further than Husserl in formulating a phenomenology of the imagination. Second, it will be shown that Ricoeur's unique approach to the imagination is put to use in the *Fallible Man* and that it provides new access to the realm of the possible which is concealed by modern ontology.

Third, the importance of phenomenology for the establishment of Ricoeur's notion of innocence and the formulation of an affirmative philosophical anthropology will be made explicit. In this sense, the access to the world of possibilities will demonstrate that the phenomenological notion of imaginative variations plays a central role in the overall argument of *Fallible Man*: despite the actual reality of actual human beings, it establishes innocence as a fundamental human possibility.

FROM IDEATION

In the section of *Ideen I* entitled "Eidetic Seeing and Phantasy. Eidetic Cognition Independent of All Cognition of Matters of Fact," Husserl establishes that "pure eidetic truths contain not the slightest assertion about matters of fact" (Husserl 1983: 11). Although the *eidos* "can be exemplified for intuition in experiential data" (Husserl 1983: 11), it can also be grasped by what is given in the imagination. That is to say that in order to know an essence, according to Husserl, one can start either from empirical or from purely fictional intuitions. The intuition of an essence thus does not require the positing of an individual existence. As a consequence, from the pure truths of the essences, "not even the most insignificant matter-of-fact truth can be deduced from pure eidetic truths *alone*" (Husserl 1983: 11). This leads Husserl to establish a sharp distinction between *facts* and *essences*. In his footnote commentary on this paragraph, Ricoeur takes a step further. Indeed, his comment deserves particular attention, insofar as it sheds light on the close relationship between the imagination, imaginative variation, and phenomenology:

> *The Illustrative Function of Imagination* must not be overlooked: fiction is the true revealer of essence. The function of serving as an example can thus be accomplished by something other than experience. Fiction allows for experimenting with unlimited variations which yield the eidetic constant. Husserl says further on: "Fiction is the vital element of Phenomenology as well as of all eidetic science" (§ 70). In fact, fiction breaks the circle of facticity which culminates in empirical law and which gives its domain over to the freedom of ideation. (Ricoeur 1996: 68)

Whereas fiction is one of the possibilities for grasping essences for Husserl, Ricoeur goes further in stating that fiction is "the true revealer" of essences. The radicality of Ricoeur's point of view is based on Husserl's reflections on imaginative variations in paragraph 70. Ricoeur holds that fiction "allows for experimenting with unlimited variations which yield the eidetic constant" (Ricoeur 1996: 68). In fact, by establishing a parallel between the geometer and the phenomenologist, Husserl underscores the importance of the freedom of the imagination in order to access infinite eidetic configurations. It is in this context that he affirms that fiction is a vital element of phenomenology. Nevertheless, in the first part of this paragraph, Husserl makes explicit the superiority of perception over all other types of *presentations*, including the imagination, both for the observation of existence and for the phenomenological apprehension of essences. This is the reason why Husserl introduces some nuances that Ricoeur does not take into account:

> Thus if one is fond of paradoxical phrases, one can actually say, and if one means the ambiguous phrase in the right sense, one can say in strict truth, that *"feigning" [Fiktion] makes up the vital element of phenomenology as of every other eidetic science,* that feigning is the source from which the cognition of "eternal truths" is fed. (Husserl 1983: 160)

It is in terms of the question of whether perception or the imagination is superior that phenomenology is "paradoxical" and has an "ambiguous" sense. Ricoeur, however, in his commentary on paragraph 70, radicalizes the role of imagination in eidetic apprehension: "Imagination [. . .] is the principal weapon of these tactics through examples" (Ricoeur 1996: 119). What is clear in this paragraph is Husserl's intention to respond in a provocative way to naturalism. It should be remembered that *Ideen I* was written, at this period of Husserl's thinking, with the aim of criticizing naturalism. In a footnote, Husserl himself claims that "feigning is the source from which the cognition of 'eternal truths' is fed" (Husserl 1983: 160), and that this claim "should be especially suitable for a naturalistic ridiculing of the eidetic mode of cognition" (Husserl 1983: 160). Ricoeur is well aware of this. At the end of his commentary, he points out that fiction breaks the circle of facticity and opens the door to the "freedom of ideation."

In section of *Ideen I* entitled "The Spontaneity of Ideation. Essence and Fictum," Husserl clearly establishes a parallelism between the work of ideation and that of fiction in order to make the role of intentionality explicit. Both ideation and fiction are psychic products. Here Husserl mentions the example of the "the flute-playing centaur," who "is nothing psychical; it exists neither in the soul nor in consciousness, nor does it exist somewhere else" (Husserl 1983: 43). The imagined centaur belongs to conscious experience itself, but it is necessary to distinguish between this experience and the object of the experience which is not a product of the mind. In the same way, ideation is an act of the mind but not of the essence. The confusion between ideation and essence often results from a psychologistic-naturalistic interpretation of consciousness. But the ideation or intuition of essences is an original giving act like sense perception. It is here that, according to Husserl, eidetic intuition is distinguishable from fiction which, at least in *Ideen I*, would not be an original act of giving meaning. But here again Ricoeur emphasizes the importance of the analogy between ideation and fiction for his own understanding of the meaning of intentionality by asking: "why doesn't Husserl posit the principle of intentionality directly rather than through the analogy of fiction? Because the 'nothingness' of a centaur is clear proof that it transcends what is experienced" (Ricoeur 1996: 82). But it is surprising that Ricoeur does not comment on the fact that for Husserl fiction is not an original act of giving meaning,[1] whereas the kind of suspension implied in fiction will be the source of ideation and of phenomenology itself for Ricoeur.

In fact, in his comments to the French translation of *Ideen I*, Ricoeur establishes the relationship between the phenomenological *epoche*, the neutrality modification, and the imagination. In "The Neutrality Modification and Fantasy," Husserl makes an effort to distinguish the neutrality modification from fantasy. The former is of universal significance: it can be applied to all conscious experiences. The latter, by contrast, is just a modification of memory (Husserl 1983: 260). In paragraph 32, Husserl defines the phenomenological *epoche* as the act of putting out of play the general thesis of natural attitude (Husserl 1983: 60). Like the modification of neutrality, it can be applied universally to all conscious experiences: "we parenthesize everything which that positing encompasses with respect to being, *thus the whole natural world* which is continually 'there for us', 'on hand', and which will always remain there according to consciousness as an 'actuality'" (Husserl 1983: 61). For Husserl, the *epoche* is thus, in addition, an "operation" of consciousness that can be carried out "with complete freedom" (Husserl 1983: 61). For his part, Ricoeur's commentary on paragraph 111 points out that "the close connections between imagination and neutralization account for why the imagination has been able to play such a great role in the 'destruction' of the world which rids us of the habit of naïve belief in existence itself" (Ricoeur 1996: 147). In this sense, the neutrality modification, according to Ricoeur, is at work in the epoche and thus "has made phenomenology possible" (Ricoeur 1996: 147). In this way, the epoche and neutralization have a radical meaning for Ricoeur and both are the expression of an operation of consciousness. But what type of operation is implemented?

By recalling the importance of the imagination in breaking from the realm of facticity, we can say that this operation can be defined negatively in its relation to "empirical laws": it is an act of suspension. The realm of facticity and empirical laws belongs to the natural attitude, and the phenomenological epoche is an operation or act that liberates us from this attitude. Thus, the neutralization that takes place through the phenomenological method constitutes an overcoming of the empirical order. The neutralization function, in this way, opens the door to the realm of possibility. Liberation from the actual world thus stands at the base of the Ricoeurian account of phenomenology. The exploration of the realm of possibility is at the heart of Ricoeur's recovery and reinterpretation of the Kantian concept of the transcendental imagination.

THE TRANSCENDENTAL IMAGINATION

Ricoeur's analysis of fallibility is developed on three levels in *Fallible Man*: (1) a theoretical level, (2) a practical level, and (3) an affective level.[2] On each level, there is a corresponding intermediate concept through which the analysis unfolds: (1) imagination, (2) respect, and (3) affective fragility. According to Ricoeur, fallibility is accessible to pure reflection on the theoretical level as "a way of understanding and being understood that can reach a certain threshold of intelligibility where the possibility of evil appears inscribed in the innermost structure of human reality" (Ricoeur 1986: 1). In confronting this threshold of intelligibility, the imagination occupies a fundamental place in this transcendental consideration of human being. Ricoeur characterizes this type of reflection as a reflection that "begins with the object or, to be more precise, with the *thing*" (Ricoeur 1986: 18).

But, what is the starting point of a transcendental reflection of this kind? Ricoeur answers that it begins with a reflection on the experience of a thing. Here we can already observe that "the break introduced by reflection between sensibility and understanding is the point of departure of a transcendental study on man as intermediate and on the intermediate function of the imagination" (Ricoeur 1986: 18–19). Transcendental reflection thus discovers the disproportion "between the verb that gives expression to being and truth at the risk of falling into error, and, on the other hand, the passive look that is riveted to appearance and perspective" (Ricoeur 1986: 37). From this discovery of disproportion between language and sense experience, there arises the problematic of the third term—the intermediate term—which Ricoeur calls the *imagination*. This term is not given in itself, but in "the thing."

Ricoeur defines the thing as "the unity that is already realized in a correlate of speech and point of view" (Ricoeur 1986: 37). Inspired by a Kantian language, for Ricoeur, the unity of the thing is a synthesis "projected outside" (Ricoeur 1986: 18). This synthesis, as a unity of expression and appearance, produces the "thing" in its "objectivity." It does not exist in consciousness, nor in scientific objectivity, instead the synthesis is "first intentional" (Ricoeur 1986: 38), which means that "consciousness makes itself an intermediary primarily by projecting itself into the thing's mode of being" (Ricoeur 1986: 38). In this sense, as Helenius points out, Ricoeur is clearly inspired by Kant insofar as he places the pure imagination in between empirical intuition and the concepts of the understanding (Helenius 2015: 43). Indeed, in his *Critique of Pure Reason*, Kant makes this mediating character of the imagination explicit:

> The imagination [*Einbildungskraft*] is to this extent a faculty for determining the sensibility a priori, and its synthesis of intuitions, in accordance with the categories, must be the transcendental synthesis of the imagination, which is an effect of the understanding on sensibility and its first application (and at the same time the ground of all others) to objects of the intuitions that is possible for us. (Kant 1998: 257).[3]

But unlike Kant, for Ricoeur objectivity—as a synthesis of perspective and speech—is related to the object itself instead of the categorical framework of consciousness: "here consciousness is nothing else than that which stipulates that a thing is a thing only if it is in accordance with this synthetic constitution, if it can appear and be expressed, if it can affect me in my finitude and lend itself to the discourse of any rational being" (Ricoeur 1986: 38). That is why I agree with Helenius that "for Ricoeur, the synthesis concerns that which appears, and to which a meaning is given, that is, an object in its objectivity, as opposed to Kant who emphasizes the formal condition of the one and self-same consciousness" (Helenius 2015: 43). Whereas Kant seems to place the foundation of the synthesis carried out by the imagination on the *principles* of understanding, for Ricoeur the objectivity of the object is a synthesis of meaning:

> Consequently, in order to stress that the objectivity of the object is constituted on the object itself, I prefer to say that the synthesis is primarily one of meaning and appearance rather than a synthesis of the intelligible and the sensible. The point where I differ from Kant is clear: the real a priori synthesis is not the one that is set forth in the "principles," i.e., in the judgments that would be prior to all the empirical propositions of the physical domain. (Ricoeur 1986: 38)

Ricoeur's reformulation of the Kantian role of the imagination implies a new sense of objectivity related to the phenomenological discovery of intentionality.

This discovery can be understood, as Robert Hanna does, on the basis of Kantian theory's own role in giving rise to this tradition. According to him, in the foundational book of phenomenology—*Psychology vom empirischen Standpunkte* (1974)—Brentano refers to the Kantian critique of rational psychology. According to Kant, *rational psychology* is the a priori science of consciousness. In response, Brentano defines descriptive psychology as the "*a posteriori* science of *mental phenomena*" (Hanna 2008: 158). Unlike Kant, Brentano follows an Aristotelian-scholastic tradition and understands mental phenomena in terms of the concept of intentionality as "a necessary and sufficient condition of mental phenomena" (Hanna 2008: 158). According to Brentano himself:

> Every mental phenomenon is characterized by what the Scholastics of the Middle Ages called intentional (or mental) inexistence of an object, and what we might call, though not wholly unambiguously, reference to a content, direction toward an object (which is not to be understood here as meaning a thing), or immanent objectivity. (Brentano 1995: 68)

To understand Brentano's statement, it is important to remember the Scholastics' critique of Descartes's *Metaphysical Meditations* in which we can identify the passage from the representational theory of knowledge of modernity to a theory of knowledge based in the theory of intentionality.

According to Descartes, ideas have a dual reality: (1) "actual or formal reality" from whose point of view all ideas have the same ontological degree as *res cogitans* and (2) "objective reality" which differentiates them from the point of view of their content. Giving an actual or formal reality to ideas—like substances have—was *sui generis* in his time. In fact, the radical departure from scholasticism is that, according to Descartes, this *objective reality* was produced by an efficient cause.[4] It was no longer *flatus vocis*: "something cannot come from nothing" (Descartes 1996: 28). In this regard, the first objections to Descartes's *Meditations* clearly attest to the astonishment of the scholastics of the time, for whom ideas do not have actual reality since they add nothing to the world of things. The definition of an idea is precisely the *absence* of reality. This, as the first objections to the *Meditations* show, seems to lead Descartes into a contradiction:

> So why should I look for a cause of something which is not actual, and which is simply an empty label, a non-entity? "Nevertheless, says our ingenious author, 'in order for a given idea to contain such and such objective reality it must surely derive from some cause." On the contrary, this requires no cause; for objective reality is a pure label, not anything actual. A cause imparts some real and actual influence; but what does not actually exist cannot rake on anything, and so does not receive or require any actual causal influence. Hence, though I have ideas, there is no cause for these ideas, let alone some cause which is greater than I am, or which is infinite. (Descartes 1996: 85)

In the epistemology implicit in *Fallible Man*, it likewise seems that the ideas have no substance because they belong to the realm of the possible and not the actual. In Ricoeur's own words, they are "nowhere." So contrary to Descartes, for the Scholastics ideas are not products of something, instead they are distinct from reality. The reference of consciousness to ideas is the intentionality taken up by Brentano. Ideas are intended and not part of an actual reality that requires an efficient cause. On the contrary, Descartes erased the difference between the possible and the actual ideas absorbing the entire field of the possible into that of the actual.

The first thinker who advocated for the distinction between the actual and the possible was Suarez, who influenced Descartes. According to Gilson, Suarez first took up the distinction between the objective and the formal concept in regard to being; then he distinguished—in a new way for this epoch—between *ens* as present participle and *ens* as a noun. In this latter meaning, *ens* designated the real essence (*essentia realis*), leaving actual existence out of account (*praecisive tantum abstrahendo*) (Gilson 1952: 98). As participle, *ens* designated for Suarez the *being* with real essence and actual existence (Gilson 1952: 98). To Gilson, in this reformulation of *ens*,

> existing being represents a restricted area of being in general which [. . .] includes both possible and actual being. This is a statement which necessarily implies that both possible and actual being are the same being and, furthermore, that actual being is a particular case of being at large. Exactly: actual being is being in general. (Gilson 1952: 98)

The consequence is the conception of *essence* as true actual being (*verum actuale ens*) (Gilson 1952: 101); therefore the disappearance of the distinction between essence and existence, and finally the dissolution of the possible. That is, according to Gilson, the origin of ontology as we know it today. In Kantian epistemology, the representational relation between consciousness and world is based on a Cartesian presupposition. This modern ontology has lost the meaning of the imagination as an opening to the possible. In this sense, I think that it is the concept of intentionality—also lost in modernity and restored by phenomenology—that allows Ricoeur to recover the possible.

More precisely, we can say that Brentano's rediscovery of intentionality—which allows the foundation of phenomenology—is already an answer to representationalism. However, it is thanks to the amendment of Brentano's psychology made by Husserl that Ricoeur can recover the field of the *possible*. According to Zahavi, with the *Logical Investigations*, Husserl inaugurates the meaning of the phenomenological method as a method of the study of consciousness which modifies, while being inspired of it, Brentano's concept of intentionality:

> The aim was to explore the intentional structures involved in our perception, thinking, judging, etc. This might seem like a simple continuation of the project commenced by Brentano in his *Psychologie vom epirischen Standpunkt* of 1874. But although Brentano should be praised for his rediscovery of the concept of intentionality, his analysis of intentionality remained—as Husserl points out—naturalistic and psychological, whereas Husserl's own analysis was neither. (Zahavi 2008: 666)

In order to move away from psychologism, Husserl had to make a distinction between two approaches of consciousness: one psychological and the other transcendental (Zahavi 2008: 667). The first raises the psychological question of knowing how a preexisting reality is grasped by the subject (Zahavi 2008: 667). But the transcendental approach, specific to phenomenology, is concerned "with the question of what it means for something to be real and objective in the first place and in particular with the transcendental questions concerning the very condition of possibility for manifestation" (Zahavi 2008: 667). The shift from psychologism to the transcendental attitude takes us back to the point at which Ricoeur diverged from Kant with regard to the synthesis performed by the transcendental imagination. This synthesis is no longer based on the categories of the understanding, but on the nature of the object itself (the conditions of possibility of its manifestation).

The importance of the theme of intentionality for this modification of the Kantian conception of the imagination is now clear. It is in this sense that the Ricoeurian critique of Kant's philosophy of the imagination should be understood:

> The real *a priori* synthesis does not appear even in the first principles; it consists in the thing's objectival character (rather than objective, if objective means scientific), namely that property of being thrown before me, at once given to my point of view and capable of being communicated, in a language comprehensible by any rational being. The objectivity of the object consists in a certain expressibility adhering to the appearance of anything whatsoever. (Ricoeur 1986: 38–39)

The fact that Ricoeur emphasizes the language or communicative aspect of the constitution of the subject makes explicit the change of emphasis from eidetics to symbolics, if we understand these two moments of his philosophy as two different facets of the same path toward deeper senses and meanings. The property of being "thrown before me" is clearly intentional and takes place in the world of the possible. Indeed, in the third part of this book, when Ricoeur opens a parenthesis at the same time as he introduces a summary of his interpretation of Kant's transcendental imagination, he asserts:

> We may remember that, for a merely transcendental analysis, the third term, the term of synthesis, the one Kant calls transcendental imagination, is nothing but the possibility of the synthesis in the object. It is in no way an experience capable of being dramatized; the consciousness to whose province it belongs is by no means self-consciousness, but the formal unity of the object, a project of the world. (Ricoeur 1986: 106–07)

Ricoeur ends up by restoring *the possible*—in the theory of knowledge— that was concealed by modern representationalism. The imagination provides phenomenological access to the possible. This world of possibilities, which is explored through imaginative variations, will enable a phenomenological formulation of the imagination of innocence.

... TO INNOCENCE

The next level of this anthropology of fallibility is the practical level where the intermediate or *third* term between character and happiness is respect,[5] and it is followed by the affective level where "affective fragility" constitutes the intermediate term between pleasure and happiness. It should be noted that Ricoeur was heavily preoccupied with the philosophy of feeling at this time. He presents much of the same analysis in a text, written at the same time, that was published on the occasion of the centenary of the birth of Husserl (Ricoeur 2004). In addition, he devotes a chapter of the Appendix to the *Histoire de la philosophie allemande* (Bréhier 1967) to Scheler's phenomenology of feeling. But the key question here is: how should we understand the relationship between affective fragility and imagination? I propose that this relationship should be understood in a sense that is at first analogical and then "overlapping." On the one hand, it is in feeling that affective fragility shows its character as both intermediation and conflict (Ricoeur 1986: 106). This double nature of feeling makes the analogy with the imagination difficult. Although it is also a *third term and a mediator*, it operates in a distinct way from the imagination. On the other hand, as far as the overlapping is concerned, it should be noted that each of the three levels, analyzed by Ricoeur, interconnects with the others, including their intermediate terms. It is in this way that we ought to understand the interconnection between imagination—characterized as transcendental in the first chapter of the book—and feeling at this stage of the Ricoeurian analysis.

In Ricoeur's description of feelings, a reference to Kantian anthropology appears. In this anthropology, according to Ricoeur, the passions are understood initially as figures deprived of human affectivity. On the contrary, in an affirmative philosophical anthropology such as Ricoeur wants to propose in this book other types of requirements are needed: "it must attempt to restore the primordial state that is at the root of the fallen. Just as Aristotle described the perfection of pleasure beyond all 'intemperance'" (Ricoeur 1986: 111). Is a change of order of perspective necessary? Ricoeur answers "yes." First must there be indeed an understanding of the original and then of the fallen "in and through the primordial?" (Ricoeur 1986: 112). And its understanding, according to him, requires a certain type of imagination: the imagination of innocence. On my opinion, this imagination is not itself an emotional feeling or nostalgia. Its function is more theoretical, consistent with what Ricoeur has shown it in the first part of his book. The imagination provides the *access to the possible* that enabled us to make explicit the phenomenological conception of the imagination that he has elaborated in its translation of *Ideen I*. In Ricoeur's own words:

> But this imagination is not a fanciful dream; it is an "imaginative variation," to use a Husserlian term, which manifests the essence by breaking the prestige of the fact. In imagining another state of affairs or another kingdom, I perceive the possible, and in the possible, the essential. The understanding of a passion as bad requires the understanding of the primordial by the imagination of another empirical modality, by exemplification in an innocent kingdom. (Ricoeur 1986: 111)

Although Ricoeur attaches great importance to the creative dimension of the imagination, he "considers the negative theories of imagination very seriously, with their denunciation of its capacity for concealing reality and for evading it" (Lafuente 1999: 246). In Ricoeur's announcement of the theme of the second volume of the *Philosophy of the Will* that he established in the first volume of this book, he affirmed a close relationship between the imagination in the negative sense—sense developed in the first volume—and the fault whose parentheses have been removed to make possible the analysis of the anthropology of fallibility:

> according to our account imagination is *in addition* a privileged point of entry of what in subsequent works we shall call the fault. This corruption is in part binding oneself by nothing; the vanity "spreading to all things" is this captivity of which we are at the same time jailers and prisoners. But it is projected outside of us, as the nothing which lures, seduces, and captivates, as a magic potion which we drink in together with the world. The charm of imagination, the magic power of absence, thus seems to us to go back to a guilty consciousness, a consciousness which has already given in to temptation. (Ricoeur 1966: 98)

Nevertheless, the *charm* of the imagination of guilt and fault is subverted by imaginative variations that allow us to distinguish the originary innocence from the description of evil through which it is perceived. The imagination, although theoretical, is thus curative and therapeutic. Ricoeur cannot be more clear on this point: "Can we, then, isolate this representation of the primordial from the description of evil through which the primordial was perceived? Yes, but only in an imaginary mode" (Ricoeur 1986: 144). When the imagination is thus turned toward the primordial, it is possible to speak about the "imagination of innocence," which frees us from the slavery that brings awareness to itself. Ricoeur here understands innocence as "fallibility without fault" (Ricoeur 1986: 144).

In that respect, the imagination of innocence makes possible an affirmative anthropology, and this affirmative anthropology is made possible by a phenomenological account of the imagination. Consider Ricoeur's description of the imagination of innocence at the end of the *Fallible Man* in support of this point:

> There is in this imagination nothing scandalous for philosophy. Imagination is an indispensable mode of the investigation of the possible. It might be said, in the style of the Husserlian eidetics, that innocence is the imaginative variation that makes the essence of the primordial constitution stand out, in making it appear on another existential modality. At that moment, fallibility is shown as pure possibility without the fallen condition through which it ordinarily appears. (Ricoeur 1986: 145)

In fact, Ricoeur is able to describe the imagination of innocence in this way precisely because of his phenomenological heritage. The imagination elevates innocence to its philosophical-existential formulation: it opens to the possible, creating new possibilities and constituting existence, more precisely, the proper, the origin, or the *essence* of existence. In this sense, Ricoeur affirms: "My innocence is my primordial constitution projected in a fanciful history" (Ricoeur 1986: 145). But one must not understand this "fanciful history" in the sense of an *unreality* but rather as part of a *history of possibilities*. The purpose of the imagination of innocence is to realize the pure possibilities of our existence—in short, "the imagination of innocence is nothing but the representation of a human life that would realize all its fundamental possibilities without any discrepancy between its primordial destination and its historical manifestation" (Ricoeur 1986: 144).

The manifestation of this "fanciful history" presupposes the Ricoeurian treatment of myth developed in *The Symbolism of Evil* (1967).[6] How do we imagine our primordial constitution as the sum of possibilities of our existence ("fanciful history")? Only from the symbols which denouncing the decay make it possible to grasp the primordial. In other words, it is the symbols that mobilize the imagination and make its *innocent* manifestation possible. In this sense, the affirmative anthropology of fallibility will require a symbolism in which the imagination will be able to deploy its path toward possible meanings of existence.

To summarize, starting from Ricoeur's formulation of a phenomenology of imagination in the comments of his own translation of *Ideen I*, this chapter has shown the relationship between ideation, imaginative variation, suspension and the access to a world of possibilities in the Ricoeurian sense. Then, regarding the imagination's fundamental role for the "transcendental" determination of the human, the chapter has shown that Ricoeur reformulates the Kantian account of the imagination and that this reformulation is made possible thanks to the notion of intentionality discovered by Brentano and reformulated by Husserl. In this sense, Ricoeur recovers the status of the possible. On the affective level, this conception of the imagination allows him to recover what he calls the primordial through the imagination of innocence. The conceptual ground for a *hermeneutics of the symbol*—as the possibility of grasping the primordial through the fallen—is thus prepared.

NOTES

1. This is going to change in *The Lectures on Imagination* (1975). In the article "The Phenomenological Contributions of Ricoeur's Philosophy of Imagination," George Taylor shows that it is for this reason that Husserl's imaginative variations are placed within the Ricoeurian framework of the reproductive imagination. However, Taylor believes that the Husserlian sense of intentionality is the greatest contribution to Ricoeur's phenomenology of the imagination. Ricoeur gives importance to the "nothingness" of the centaur in the analogy established by Husserl through which the essences do not exist "anywhere" like fictions. George Taylor precisely identifies, in this "nowhere" of the intentional aim, the point of conjunction between the *Lectures on Imagination* and the *Lectures on Ideology and Utopia:* "By contrast, Ricoeur strikingly elevates the application of phenomenological intentionality to imagination by requiring consideration of consciousness as the *consciousness of* something where the 'something' is no longer real, not even the absent that is elsewhere, but the 'absolutely nowhere.' Ricoeur requires us to think through what it means to have *consciousness of* the 'absolutely nowhere.' This to me is a remarkable contribution to the theory of intentionality. Consideration of what this *consciousness of* may entail is the task of a theory of productive imagination and one that Ricoeur undertakes in his theory of fiction. Here his lectures on imagination rejoin with his lectures on ideology and utopia, because, we recall, the utopia is also the 'nowhere.' Ricoeur poses whether a theory of fiction can connect the unreal with the real by reshaping it intentionally. When the image has no original referent, then fictions may provide an original of their own. Fictions may produce their own world, which may in turn enlarge our world" (Taylor 2015: 20). This perspective has been discussed in Ascárate (2018). For a different approach to the phenomenological heritage of this hermeneutic period of Ricoeurian thought, see MacAvoy (2016).
2. Lafuente names the three levels "knowledge, action and feelings" (Lafuente 1999: 246).
3. "So ist die Einbildungskraft sofern ein Vermögen, die Sinnlichkeit a priori zu bestimmen, und ihre Synthesis der Anschauungen, den Kategorien gemäß, muß die transzendentale Synthesis der Einbildungskraft sein, welches eine Wirkung des Verstandes auf die Sinnlichkeit und die erste Anwendung desselben (zugleich der Grund aller übrigen) auf Gegenstände der uns möglichen Anschauung ist" (Kant 1967, III. B152).
4. "Now it is manifest by the natural light that there must be at least as much <reality> in the efficient and total cause as in the effect of that cause. For where, I ask, could the effect get its reality from, if not from the cause? And how could the cause

give it to the effect unless it possessed it? It follows from this both that something cannot arise from nothing and also that what is more perfect—that is, contains in itself more reality—cannot arise from what is less perfect. And this is transparently true not only in the case of effects which possess what the philosophers call actual or formal reality, but also in the case of ideas, where one is considering only <what they call> objective reality" (Descartes 1996: 28).

5. According to Amalric, respect is a kind of "practical imagination" (Amalric 2013: 180). This interpretation relies on the following statement made by Ricoeur: "The 'practical' mediation that extends the mediation of the transcendental imagination, projected into the object, is the constitution of the person by means of "respect'" (Ricoeur 1986: 50). Amalric understands the word *"extends"—prolonge* in the original French text (Ricoeur 2009: 90)—as a characterization of the imagination called "respect" in its practical sense. I believe that the relationship between imagination and respect has to be understood as an analogy and that Ricoeur used the word "prolonge/extends" differently in this analogy, for two reasons. First, Ricoeur clearly distinguishes a transcendental reflection (imagination) from a practical one (respect). Transcendental reflection "starts from the thing; it is a reflection on the conditions of possibility of the objectivity of the thing" (Ricoeur 1986: 47). It is within the framework of this reflection that transcendental imagination corresponds to the synthesis in the object. Second, practical thinking is a reflection on *the person*. It is the *person* who occupies, in this practical space, the place of *objectivity* in the theoretical space: "What we must first establish is that the person is primarily a project which I represent to myself, which I set before me and entertain, and that this project of the person is, like the thing but in an entirely irreducible way, a "synthesis" which is effected" (Ricoeur 1986: 69–70). It is on the basis of this distinction that Ricoeur thus speaks of an extension of "mediation." In practical space, it is indeed a "mediation" which is extended in respect and not the imagination. On the other hand, in the section of the book dedicated to respect, Ricoeur only speaks of the imagination to make explicit the "analogical" relationship between imagination and respect: "Just as the transcendental imagination was the third term homogeneous with both understanding and sensibility, so also respect is a paradoxical 'intermediary' that belongs both to sensibility, that is, to the faculty of desiring, and to reason, that is, to the power of obligation that comes from practical reason. Imagination was the condition of the synthesis in the object; respect is the condition of the synthesis in the person" (Ricoeur 1986: 73).

6. "It matters little that I can depict innocence only by way of myth, as a state realized "elsewhere" and "formerly" in localities and in times that have no place in the rational man's geography and history. The essence of the myth of innocence is in giving a symbol of the primordial which shows through in the fallen and which exposes it as fallen" (Ricoeur 1986: 144–145).

REFERENCES

Amalric, J.-L. 2013. *Paul Ricoeur, l'imagination vive. Une genèse de la philosophie Ricoeurienne de l'imagination*. Paris: Hermann.

Ascarate, Luz. 2018. L'utopie: du réel au possible. *Etudes Ricoeuriennes / Ricoeur Studies* IX.1: 55–69.
Bréhier, Emile. 1967. *Histoire de la philosophie allemande*. Paris: Vrin.
Brentano, Franz. 1995. *Psychology from an Empirical Standpoint*. Trans. Antos C. Rancurello, D.B. Terrell, and Linda L. McAlister. New York: Routledge.
Descartes, Rene. 1996. *Meditations on First Philosophy. With Selections from the Objections and Replies*. Trans. and ed. John Cottingham. Cambridge: Cambridge University Press.
Gilson, Etienne. 1952. *Being and Some Philosophers*. Toronto: Pontifical Institute of Mediaeval Studies.
Helenius, Timo. 2015. Between Receptivity and Productivity. Paul Ricoeur on Cultural Imagination. *Social Imaginaries* 1.2: 32–52.
Husserl, Edmund. 1983. *Ideas Pertaining to a Pure Phenomenology and to a Phenomenological Philosophy. First Book: General Introduction to a Pure Phenomenology*. Trans. Fred. Kersten. The Hague: Martinus Nijhoff.
Kant, Immanuel. 1967. *Kritik der reinen Vernunft*. Hamburg: Verlag.
———. 1998. *Critique of Pure Reason*. Trans. and ed. Paul Guyer and Allen W. Wood. Cambridge: Cambridge University Press.
Lafuente, M. A. C. 1999. Imagination and Practical Creativity in Paul Ricoeur. In *Analecta Husserliana. The Yearbook of Phenomenological Research, Vol. LX: Life—The Outburst of Life in the Human Sphere, Book II. Scientific Philosophy / Phenomenology of Life and the Sciences of Life*. Ed. A.-T. Tymieniecka. Dordrecht: Kluwer, 243–261.
MacAvoy, Leslie. 2016. Distanciation and *Epoché*: The Influence of Husserl on Ricoeur's Hermeneutics. In *Hermeneutics and Phenomenology in Paul Ricoeur: Contributions to Hermeneutics*. Eds. Scott Davidson and Marc-Antoine Vallée. Springer.
Reeder, Harry. 2010. Husserl's Hermeneutic Phenomenology. 41st Annual Meeting of the Husserl Circle, June 21–23: 15–36.
Ricoeur, Paul. 1966. *Freedom and Nature: The Voluntary and the Involuntary*. Trans. Erazim V. Kohák. Evanston: Northwestern University Press.
———. 1967. *The Symbolism of Evil*. Trans. Emerson Buchanan. Boston: Beacon Press.
———. 1975. *Lectures on the Imagination*. Unpublished tapescript of George Taylor.
———. 1986. *Fallible Man*. Trans. Charles A. Kelbley. New York: Fordham University Press.
———. 2004. *À l'école de la phénoménologie*. Paris: Vrin.
———. 2009. *Philosophie de la volonté, t. 2. Finitude et Culpabilité*. Préface de Jean Greisch. Paris: Points.
Romano, Claude. 2010. *Au cœur de la raison: la phénoménologie*. Paris: Gallimard.
Stevens, Bernard. 1990. L'évolution de la pensée de Ricoeur au fil de son explication avec Husserl. *Études phénoménologiques* 11: 3–29.
Taylor, George. 2015. The Phenomenological Contributions of Ricoeur's Philosophy of Imagination. *Social Imaginaries* 1.2: 13–31.
Zahavi, Dan. 2008. Phenomenology. In *The Routledge Companion to Twentieth Century Philosophy*. New York: Routledge: 661–692.

Chapter 6

"Making Sense of (Moral) Things"
Fallible Man *in Relation to Enactivism*
Geoffrey Dierckxsens

In a previous paper I examined the general overlap between Paul Ricoeur's philosophy and enactivism (Dierckxsens 2018a). I argued that Ricoeur's philosophy of the will in *Freedom and Nature* is remarkably close to enactive cognition theory, insofar as he understands cognition in terms of an embodied interaction with the natural and cultural environment, which is, generally speaking, also how enactivists understand cognition (see Varela et al. 1991). Moreover, Ricoeur's critical attitude toward representationalism, so I argued, is similar to enactivism's view that cognition results from subjective interaction, rather than being modeled on a theory of representations, that is, a theory which specifies the world in ways which can be, with respect to how the world actually is, true or accurate, versus false or inaccurate.

This chapter will focus more closely on the second volume of Ricoeur's philosophy of the will, *Fallible Man* (1986), in particular on the notion of imagination which is developed in that work. The reason for choosing this particular concept is not only that it is a central notion in that work, but also that it demonstrates, so I will assert, the significance of *Fallible Man* for recent discussions in enactivism. The concept of imagination that Ricoeur develops in *Fallible Man* is close to an enactivist understanding of the imagination, according to which the imagination is the (re-)enactment of (past) experiences that are familiar and that make sense of the world through embodied interaction with it (see Gallagher 2017). For Ricoeur, imagination allows us to mediate between our embodied condition and the external world, that is to say, it allows a mediation between the experiences we have—such as desires, needs ("sensibility") but also reason ("understanding")—and the things we encounter in the world (Ricoeur 1986: 45).

What is more, consideration of Ricoeur's concept of the imagination as a mediation of feelings with the world, yet understood also in the sense of the social imaginary (see also Ricoeur 1992; 2007), enables the further extension of an enactivist understanding of cognitive interactions to moral contexts, an aspect of cognition which enactivists have largely overlooked so far. If the imagination is connected to basic cognitive capacities that mediate between experiences and the world (e.g., perception, but also love or hate), then this mediation also likely entails a socially and morally extended cognitive process, because the others with whom we interact through imagination are not only the objects and partners of our needs and desires, but also the others whom we care for, and with whom we can share moral values, norms, institutions, and symbols. This idea, which I take from Ricoeur, not only fits onto the theoretical framework of an enactivist understanding of "simulation,"[1] it also has empirical validity, insofar as cognitive science shows a link between perceptual activity of the senses (e.g., taste perception), which is connected to imagination, and ethico-political opinions (e.g., moral disgust) (Eskine et al. 2011).

This chapter is thus divided into two main parts. The first part examines the similarities between Ricoeur's concept of imagination in *Fallible Man* and an enactivist approach to the imagination, based on the notion of enactive simulation, or, the idea that we use imagination for re-enacting past experiences, which allows making sense of present experiences and situations (see Gallagher 2017; Hutto and Myin 2017). The point I intend to make is that Ricoeur's account of the imagination should be understood ontologically, as a way of expressing being, of making sense of life's experiences, which also functions as a motivating factor for acting and for making sense of present situations. In this sense, Ricoeur is close to enactivism. Yet, the second part of this chapter will argue that where Ricoeur differs from enactivism is that for him the imagination also has moral significance.[2] We use the imagination to re-enact experiences and place them in a larger perspective, both on an individual level and on the level of social groups, in order to make moral decisions, to create social and political ideas and to understand the values of communities (e.g., we learn how to sympathize or feel with others through the different experiences and relations we have with others) (see Ricoeur 1992). My conclusion will be that this notion of imagination, even though it goes beyond enactivism, can nevertheless contribute to enactivism by showing how cognitive interactions with moral contexts can be understood from an enactivist perspective.

IMAGINATION, SYNTHESIS, AND SIMULATION

Imagination: A "Scattered" Concept

Before going into closer detail concerning Ricoeur's concept of imagination in *Fallible Man*, it is important to clarify that Ricoeur does not have one single concept of imagination. In fact, as has been pointed out by several scholars, the imagination is a central notion in Ricoeur's thought as a whole, yet it has several different meanings (e.g., Taylor 2006; Amalric 2013). Ricoeur does not offer a theory of the imagination, as is clear from the fact that he did not devote a separate volume on the topic, as he has done, for example, for the concept of the metaphor (Ricoeur 1975).[3] According to Jean-Luc Amalric (2012), it is both in a practical and in a poetic sense that Ricoeur understands the imagination, which means that he defines it both in the sense of a capability that is central to acquiring knowledge of the world (Ricoeur 1986, 1966) *and* in the sense of the creative process of narrating, of placing life experiences into the setting of a story, fictional, or historical (Ricoeur 1984, 1986, 1990).

Moreover, it is possible to distinguish further between several different "layers" of meaning in Ricoeur's account of imagination. Along with imagination as a cognitive process, he also understands it in the sense of "imagination in discourse," that is, as the capacity of "semantic innovation" which gives meaning to objects metaphorically (Ricoeur 2007: 171). Thus, we use language to "label" objects ("this is water"), and we create new meanings by shifting concepts metaphorically, by "labeling" an object with a concept that it was not originally designed for ("the water is gentle"). Next, there is the imagination in its relation to fiction, which designates the capacity to "*redescribe* reality," to create a fictive reality in a story, whether or not by referring directly to the "real" world (Ricoeur 2007: 175).

Ricoeur also defines imagination as part of action; as such, it is the capacity to create a plan or "project" by which one aims to guide one's actions (imagination in this sense is close to imagination as a cognitive process of organizing experiences). Further, Ricoeur connects imagination to intersubjectivity (Ricoeur 2007: 179). Imagination in this sense is the ability to imagine oneself as another, in the place of the other, which possibly finds an expression in the historical narrative that recounts the stories of others in the past (e.g., historical film). Imagination can also enable the creation of a narrative identity, a reworking of our life experiences into a life story, which we can share with others (Ricoeur 1992). Finally, Ricoeur understands imagination as the "social imaginary," a social group's set of values, norms, institutions, and symbols that have ethico-political meaning and that are possibly translated into an ideology or, conversely, a utopia (Ricoeur 2007: 181).

In recent years, a number of studies of Ricoeur's conception of the imagination have already been published, and it is not my intention here to discuss all of these different meanings of the imagination at length (e.g., Amalric 2013; Kearney 2016). What I will focus on instead is an examination of the relevance of Ricoeur's conception of the imagination, in particular, his conception of the imagination in *Fallible Man*, for recent theories of enactivism. This paper is thus part of my larger project to bring Ricoeur's thought into current enactivist debates, through which I aim to show both the timeliness of certain of Ricoeur's ideas and to investigate the moral meanings of enactive cognitive relations (see Dierckxsens 2018b).

Transcendental Synthesis, Embodied Synthesis

At first sight Ricoeur's notion of imagination in *Fallible Man* would seem to have little in common with enactivism. There Ricoeur discusses Kant's concept of "transcendental imagination," which seems to suggest a defense of representationalism, understood in the sense of a defense of a model of cognition, according to which the manipulation of mental content is how we obtain knowledge in the world (Ricoeur 1986: 18). Kant's idea of imagination, in Ricoeur's interpretation, is based on a priori principles, which represent the functioning of pure reason. It is part of a model of the mind, which represents how the process of gaining knowledge actually works. The imagination is then the cognitive capacity that allows for a synthesis or schematization between the mind and the external world, that is to say, cognitive activity through which principles of reason allow making sense of experiences (Ricoeur 1986: 38).

In fact, in the *Critique of Pure Reason*, Kant defines cognitive synthesis through imagination as follows:

> By synthesis in the most general sense, however, I understand the action of putting different representations together with each other and comprehending their manifoldness in one cognition. Such a synthesis is pure if the manifold is given not empirically but a priori (as is that in space and time). (Kant 1998: 210)

Understood in this sense, Kant's notion of imagination thus designates a cognitive capacity that is purely mental. It is an a priori capacity that we do not obtain through empirical knowledge. Rather, it is a cognitive capacity, a part of the mind, that allows us to connect representations with each other. Surely, certain representation can be the result of empirical knowledge. Nonetheless, for Kant imagination does not mediate between body and world. It is a "part of the soul" (Kant 1998: 211).

In contrast, Ricoeur states that this "epistemology" of the transcendental synthesis is exactly the "point where [he] differ[s] from Kant" (Ricoeur 1986: 38). He adds that the synthesis of imagination he has in mind occurs "neither in consciousness nor in the principles of science," but rather as a "mode of being" (Ricoeur 1986: 39). Certainly, like Ricoeur, imagination for Kant also has a mediating function, "without which we would have no cognition at all, but of which we are seldom even conscious" (Kant 1998: 211). Simply put, for both Kant and Ricoeur, imagination allows us to make sense of things by connecting experiences. However, imagination understood in this sense is not representational. It is an ontological notion that designates the activity of making sense of the world, giving meaning to its objects. It should not be understood on the basis of a representational theory of mental content, that is, of representations that specify the world in ways it would actually be. Instead, in Ricoeur's ontology the emphasis is foremost on subjective (inter) action and discourse with the surrounding world, rather than on epistemology (see his critique of Descartes in the introduction of *Oneself as Another* (Ricoeur 1992)).

It is perhaps also for this reason that he states later in *From Text to Action* that the imagination, in its most basic sense, takes place in speaking, when we connect different semantic meanings (sentences, metaphors, speech acts). Imagination is thus *not* the creation of an "image to be first and foremost a "scene" unfolding in some mental "theater" before the gaze of a "spectator"'" (Ricoeur 2007: 171). This would be a classical theory of representation. Yet, imagination for Ricoeur is neither to "tailor our abstract ideas, our concepts [. . .] some sort of mental alchemy" (ibid.). This would be closer to a computational or functional model of imagination and representationalism.

Indeed, if we take a closer look at the function of the imagination in *Fallible Man*, then it is clear that Ricoeur uses it to stress the embodied condition of knowledge and the entanglement between body and mind. The process of gaining knowledge from the world is not explained in *Fallible Man* in terms of a mind–body dualism. Rather, the human being, as understood in this book, is "a mixture" between reason and desire (Ricoeur 1986: 3). Characteristic of this mixture is that humans mediate between their different cognitive capacities (synthesis) and that this mediation implies a mediation with the external world. Humanity's "ontological characteristic of being-intermediate consists precisely in that his act of existing is the very act of bringing about mediations *between all the modalities and all the levels of reality within him and outside him*" (ibid., my emphasis). In other words, the mediation of which the imagination is the central cognitive capacity should be understood, in *Fallible Man*, as a direct embodied and intelligible interaction between the senses and the external world.

Hence, when Ricoeur announces, in the introduction of *Fallible Man*, the central thesis of the book that the "specific weakness and [. . .] essential fallibility [of human beings] are ultimately sought [. . .] between the pole of [. . .] finitude and the pole of [. . .] infinitude," he does not mean that reason is infinite and therefore higher, and that the body is infinite and thus lower (Ricoeur 1986: xliv). Reason is itself mediated by the senses and in that sense is already a mixture between finitude and infinitude. Ricoeur is critical of Descartes and defends that "we must also abandon the idea of linking the finite to one faculty or function and the infinite to another" (Ricoeur 1986: 2).

Ricoeur's philosophical anthropology aims in *Fallible Man* to explain human fault as a mixture of the incapacity of body *and* of reason.

As I said, the function of the imagination is to mediate between these faculties, but also with the external world. Essentially, imagination is a key concept for Ricoeur here, because "understanding without intuition is empty" (Ricoeur 1986: 10). Without an intuitive synthesis between different experiences, consciousness would be a stream of experiences without any meaning. We find this idea, as explained above, also in Kant's theory of the transcendental synthesis. Yet, Ricoeur's idea of imagination in *Fallible Man* is not purely Kantian. In fact, he also refers to the imagination in Plato and Pascal. The reason for this is that Ricoeur wants to stress the imperfection of knowledge itself. We do not have absolute knowledge because reason is mediated by the senses (Plato), but also because reason itself cannot grasp the infinite in an absolute sense (Pascal) (Ricoeur 1986: 9, 14). There is always something ungraspable and mysterious in the process of gaining knowledge. Moreover, as will become clear later, this mysterious aspect also allows pointing out some of the moral aspects of embodied and enactive cognition, in that cognition can "fail." It is not a clean process. We make mistakes and this can imply harm, or even violence, which has consequences that are morally significant. Further, morality finds its roots in myths, in which primordial ethical meaning relates to the body through symbols (stain, impurity, shame, etc.) as described in *The Symbolism of Evil*.

By introducing his notion of imagination in *Fallible Man*, Ricoeur therefore offers more of a critique of representationalism than a representational theory of the imagination, and this critique is reflected in his later writings as well. Yet, he also maintains that imagination performs a transcendental synthesis, at least in *Fallible Man*. Nonetheless, he understands this in an unusual sense. He defines it as "a synthesis of speech and perspective" (Ricoeur 1986: 40). This means that imagination is a cognitive capacity that allows us to imagine an "absent" object or experience; it is an experience that differs from the object and/or experience we are looking at from our actual point of view. Because we have imagination, we are "not merely a situated onlooker, but a being who intends and expresses as an intentional transgression of the situation" (Ricoeur 1986: 27). Imagination is thus the capacity to transcend a certain perspective, to look at things differently or to create a different point of view (in relation to discourse). For example, if we feel cold while walking through the snow, we can imagine a different situation such as being in front of a warm fireplace, which would then result from an association of the sense of feeling warm with the semantic meanings we know from experience (e.g., warm, fireplace, inside, cold, and outside).

Transcendentalism and representationalism are thus two different things for Ricoeur. His idea of a transcendental synthesis is unusual, in that it describes an embodied relation that is not exclusively rational, but unfolds in the direct interaction between body and world. It is a cognitive capacity that mediates between the senses and the outside world, that in the first place "anticipates pleasure and pain, the joy and sadness of being joined to or separated from the desired object" (Ricoeur 1986: 54). In short, transcendental synthesis for Ricoeur is more of an embodied synthesis than a rational synthesis.

Understood in this sense, the imagination mediates our desires and needs. It is the creativity to imagine a joy or pleasure that is absent but that one would like or desire to experience. If we are thirsty, we can imagine drinking a glass of water. This does not necessarily imply, in Ricoeur's theory, that we have representations of the actual object "glass," "water" or "H_2O," because this would require a description or model of the functions that allow for such a representation, for instance, that enable translating the molecules of H_2O into the experience of the object water. And, as I am arguing, Ricoeur does not design such a model. Rather, imagining drinking a glass of water implies, if we follow Ricoeur's argument, knowing what it is like to drink water or, in other words, *re-enacting* past experiences of drinking water, of needing it and enjoying it, through language and the association of semantic meanings.

This concept of the imagination is in fact quite similar to the idea of imagination that Ricoeur developed ten years earlier in *Freedom and Nature*. This is not surprising, since the original French editions of *Fallible Man* and *Freedom and Nature* are part of the same project to develop a philosophy of the will: *Philosophie de la volonté*. In fact, Ricœur writes in *Freedom and Nature*: "Thus we are led to seek the crossroads of need and willing in imagination—imagination of the missing thing and of action aimed towards the thing" (Ricoeur 1966: 95). Therefore, in both *Freedom and Nature* and in *Fallible Man*, Ricoeur understands the imagination in terms of the cognitive capacity that enables one to imagine certain experiences that come with the satisfaction of needs and desires (what Ricoeur calls "willing" as well). Imagination in this sense is closely connected to embodiment and interaction with the different meanings that the world has to offer and which are expressed in discourse. The world affects the body and the imagination mediates in our understanding of the world and in the motivation to act in it accordingly.

In sum, Ricoeur defines imagination not in terms of having mental representations (representing the world in the mind), but instead as the imagination of experiences (as in the imagination of the satisfaction of needs). The difference between these two possible understandings of imagination (representational vs. nonrepresentational) is subtle. Yet it entails that Ricoeur's theory of imagination is closer to enactivism than to classical representational theory. Indeed, for Ricoeur, consciousness results from "incarnate existence" or from the body being affected by the world outside of it (Ricoeur 1986: 19). Similarly, Varela, Thompson, and Rosch, the founders of enactivism, define their program as a theory of cognition based on "lived human experience and the possibilities for transformation inherent in human experience," instead of being based on "the representation of a world that is independent of our perceptual and cognitive capacities" (Varela et al. 1991: xx).

Simulating Minds

I have argued in the previous section that Ricoeur develops a notion of imagination in *Fallible Man* that is nonrepresentational, at least if we understand representationalism as a theory or model of the mind that describes the manipulation of rational functions that represent the world. Yet, this does not mean that imagination cannot have, in Ricoeur's opinion, any mental content, such as beliefs, opinions, thoughts, and so forth. In order to understand this point, it is helpful to compare Ricoeur's theory of imagination with what enactivists call "simulation." The conception of imagination that Ricoeur proposes in his philosophy of the will resembles how certain enactivists understand "simulation" or "simulation vision" (e.g., Hutto and Myin 2017: loc. 3670). Versions of enactive simulation vision are designed to explain more complex forms of cognitive processes, including processes of imagination, in nonrepresentational terms, that is, as the simulation of past or known experiences.[4]

By doing so, these theories respond to the so-called "scaling-up" problem, pointed out by critics of enactivism (e.g., Shapiro 2014). As these critics point out, enactivism can explain basic types of cognitive capacities in nonrepresentational terms, such as our basic interaction with objects (which seems to be intuitive, without having any truth or content in mind). However, the explanatory force of enactivism seems much weaker when explaining more complex cognitive capacities, such as memory or imagination, because these capacities likely imply some kind of mental content (e.g., memory often implies a belief about what actually happened). Nonetheless, enactive simulation theories respond that, although complex forms of imagination and memory can imply mental content, even these types of imagination can be explained as nonrepresentational cognitive processes, if we conceive of them as "simulations" of perception (Gallagher 2017). Understood as such, the imagination works as the (re-)enactment of a perception that is absent and/or that one has experienced in the past, yet imagination in this sense also builds on lower-level sensorimotor activity. Moreover, there is no conflict between the idea that imagination is an intuitive re-enactment of episodic memories (past experiences) and the idea that imagination, in a more complex form, allows building autobiographical narratives that include mental content (Hutto and Myin 2017). Autobiographical narratives imply mental content (e.g., a belief of the kind of person one is), but this content can build on intuitive imaginings of past experiences without (clear) mental content. This model of imagination as simulation is also in line with the fact that young children are only capable of remembering scattered and fragmented experiences from their pasts, but when growing up they are gradually more capable of forming an autobiographical narrative and of remembering a specific episode from the past (while understanding one was actually there) (Hutto and Myin 2017: loc. 3670). This understanding of imagination is similar to Ricoeur's definition of imagination as the simulation of experiences of (the perception of) the satisfaction of needs and desires, at least if one understands perception not only as visual perception but as any kind of perceiving by the senses on which mental content can build.

To be sure, Ricoeur emphasizes in *From Text to Action* that imagination should not be confused with perception; it is not "a weak perception" or "a shadow of perception" (Ricoeur 2007: 175). However, in asserting this he is questioning the traditional theory of representationalism, which understood perception in terms of an "inner mental theater" (Ricoeur 2007: 171). This is surely not the way enactivists would understand perception and cognitive theories today are different from those of the time when Ricoeur wrote these lines. In fact, Ricoeur's point seems to be that perception and imagination are more of a linguistic and embodied process than classical representationalists would have it. Therefore, he defines imagination in terms of "apperception," the association of new meaning to knowledge one already has (Ricoeur 2007: 173). And to return to our text at hand, *Fallible Man*, Ricoeur asserts: "All perception is perspectival" (Ricoeur 1986: 26). The synthesis that the imagination makes possible is the mediation between the flux of fragmented perception that is consciousness, on the one hand, and the external world, on the other. Through this mediation we make sense of our perceptions. This also suggests that imagination is still close to perception for Ricoeur, even if it would be wrong to underestimate the force of imagination by categorizing it as mere fantasy or a lesser type of perception. This way of putting it thus stands very close to an enactive simulation theory of the imagination, according to which imagination is the (re-)enactment of perceptual associations (which are embodied rather than representational), yet on which more complex experiences including linguistic mental content can build. In fact, several enactivists hold that language is an essential component of embodied cognitive interactions as well (Di Paolo, Cuffari, and De Jaegher 2018).

We should therefore distinguish between two senses of the notion "representational." The first sense is in relation to a representational theory of the mind, according to which cognitive processes essentially or always imply representations, that is, the manipulation of mental content. Second, and in a weaker sense, representational can mean "having mental representations," such as beliefs or opinions. Enactivism questions the first sense of representational, but not the second. According to enactivism, cognition is best understood not on a representational model of the mind, but as the result of embodied interaction with the world. This does not exclude that we can and do have mental representations in several embodied cognitive interactions with the world. More complex types of imagination can then include mental content (representations) that is scaffolded on to these basic cognitive processes (see Hutto and Myin 2017) (e.g., I imagine that the houses in Prague are yellow and by doing so also believe it, because I've never been to Prague). There is also empirical evidence for these enactive simulation theories, to the extent that neuroscientific research has discovered that similar parts of the brain are active in perception and imagination (e.g., Clarke 2016). Ricoeur's early conception of imagination neatly aligns with this enactivist understanding of the imagination: for Ricoeur imagination is the re-enactment of basic cognitive processes, of perception of the senses, which find their roots in our embodied interaction with the world and which we come to understand through language and discourse (as in need and desire).

Fallible Man is therefore still relevant today for thinking about cognition, because the concept of imagination that Ricoeur develops is pertinent to contemporary discussions in cognitive science and in philosophy of mind in several key respects:

1. The concept of imagination in *Fallible Man* did not lose empirical credibility over time. This is not only because Ricoeur himself, as he states in the beginning of *Freedom and Nature*, developed an idea of imagination in dialogue with "empirical and scientific knowledge" (Ricoeur 1966: 19). Moreover, although empirical science of course evolves, Ricoeur's concept of imagination is not necessarily falsified by more recent developments of empirical science. On the contrary, as I mentioned, recent neuroscientific research shows that there is likely a cognitive link between imagination and perception, which does support Ricoeur's theory that imagination is the simulation of lived experiences, that is, of the senses. Even though Ricoeur holds that imagination is not the same as a weak perception, this idea proves to be quite ahead of its time, at least if one agrees with enactivism that embodied cognition is basically non-representational, but that complex forms of imagination with mental representation can nevertheless result from embodied cognitive processes. Ricoeur's notion of imagination in *Fallible Man* thus aligns more with contemporary cognitive theory than with the cognitive theories available at the time.
2. Ricoeur's conception of imagination in *Fallible Man* complies with the theoretical demands of enactivism in the sense that it questions classical representational theories which hold that cognition results from the manipulation of mental content that somehow represents the external

world. What Ricoeur understands as transcendental—and one might certainly question the use of this terminology—is closer to a theory of human embodiment and action. In other words, it is more anthropological than epistemological, more of a phenomenology of lived experience than a model of the inner human mind, more of an enactive theory than a representational one.

3. *Fallible Man* offers a concept of a "basic" type of imagination, understood as the simulation of perception, on which more complex forms of imagination can be scaffolded. Indeed, *Fallible Man* seems to make the transition between a transcendental or cognitive conception of the imagination (as we find in *Freedom and Nature*), and his later theory of the imagination in the poetic sense, as the capacity to create a narrative discourse, through which one can express beliefs, opinions, moral views, or other content. As Ricoeur argues in his later writings, imagination powers both fiction and historical narratives, and therefore enables not only creating narratives, but also a recollection of the past, its evaluation and examination of the moral lessons we can learn for the future (Ricoeur 1992: 164). Already in *Fallible Man*, Ricoeur seems to announce this later conception of imagination, by arguing that imagination is the mediator between the senses and meaning, and thus also makes us fallible. It functions as a medium to satisfy our needs and desires, which can lead to "egoism, as well as vice," the preference for one's own self-affection (Ricoeur 1986: 55). Yet, imagination also opens up to communication and reason, and considering Ricoeur's later writings on the social imaginary, it is the key to ethico-political values, norms, institutions and symbols. This idea is already anticipated in *Fallible Man*, where Ricoeur understands language as the way to make sense of fragmented perceptions: to signify is to intend, the transgression of the point of view is nothing else than speech as the possibility of expressing, and of expressing the point of view itself (Ricoeur 1986: 26).

Imagination in the poetic sense further allows for the development of a narrative identity, that is, of perceiving one's life experiences as a larger narrative that contains beliefs and evaluations that play a role in taking moral decisions (Ricoeur 1992: 127, 168). It is this idea of the moral significance of the narrative that leads Ricoeur to observe that "there is no ethically neutral narrative. Literature is a vast laboratory in which we experiment with estimations, evaluations, and judgments of approval and condemnation through which narrativity serves as a propaedeutic to ethics" (Ricoeur 1992: 115).

Whether or not literature has an essential moral function is a point of discussion and the task of literary theory and philosophy of literature (see Verheyen 2018). It is not my intention to take up this discussion here. Yet, it is clear that Ricoeur offers several different meanings of the notion of imagination, both in its basic sense and complexities, that are in line with recent cognitive theory. Moreover, his theories of narrative identity and moral implications of imagination already build on a cognitive theory of embodied imagination. And the connection that Ricoeur makes between morality and imagination, so I will argue in the next part, makes it possible to define some of the moral aspects of enactive cognitive relations.

MORAL ENACTIVE COGNITION

Interacting with Moral Contexts

In the previous part, my intention was simply to show that Ricoeur's notion of imagination comes close to how recent enactivist theories understand imagination, that is, as an embodied interaction with the external world that allows making sense of things through the simulation of perception (finding solutions to satisfy needs, desires, and understanding lived experiences). Yet, can we also learn something from *Fallible Man* that can actually bring something novel or unexamined into recent enactivist discussions? Indeed, one might argue that even though Ricoeur had certain ideas that are similar to ideas recently developed in cognitive theory, this does not really bring anything new to the field. These new ideas can be developed without reading Ricoeur. In this section my aim is to contest this view by arguing that Ricoeur's understanding of imagination as a capability to construe moral ideas, take moral decisions and actions in relation to the social imaginary extends enactive interactions to moral contexts (such as values, norms, institutions, and symbols). What I will aim to do is translate this understanding of imagination into enactivist concepts that help to explain this interaction. The argument will proceed as follows: if imagination enables for the simulation of experiences that are influenced and affected by others and social affordances, then this likely enables an understanding of the moral meanings of our surroundings as well, because they are part of these social contexts.

It is helpful to start by sketching briefly the context of the problem within the debates of enactivism. How do enactivists understand social relations? One of enactivism's central ideas is that cognitive relations are extended relations. This means that the mind should not be understood, as I have mentioned already, as a central machine that processes data input from the external world, but instead in terms of an extension of the body in the world, as a network of meaningful interactions between body and environment (e.g., Varela 1991). This is perhaps best understood on a biological level through the idea of autopoiesis (see Di Paolo 2005). Organisms are self-maintaining and the key to this is their engaging in a series of interactions with the environment (e.g., cell renewal). Yet, also on a social level we can see that interactions with the environment deeply influence and alter how we perceive the world (see Di Paolo and De Jaegher 2007; Gallagher 2017).

More exactly, social affordances influence self-awareness; our surroundings provide us with "clues" of how we can and/or should act and we are in that way influenced in how we perform socially (e.g., Gallagher 2017) This also has an impact on how we perceive ourselves in our environment. For example, the presence of others influences body awareness and body performance, as well as the body schema, which is a system of sensory-motor capacities that shapes perception, without the necessity of awareness (Gallagher 2017). I can feel uncomfortable, to give a more specific example, when others come too close. Another example: when on a hike I possibly feel less fatigue when seeing how easily the others reach the top of the hill.

Yet, despite the strong emphasis, enactivists put on the importance of social interactions for the understanding of cognition, they still rarely discuss the influence of the moral significance of the affection of others and moral interaction. What is overlooked in enactivist debates on social cognition is an examination of the interaction between, on the one hand, the presence of others and moral or ethico-political contexts (values, norms, institutions, and symbols), and on the other hand cognition, self-awareness and body awareness. I thus understand moral contexts here in the sense of the social imaginary.[5] Moreover, this interaction seems to go in two directions. Others and moral-political contexts influence how we feel, think, and are aware of things (e.g., moral shame). And conversely, how we feel, think, are aware of things influences how we see others and can ultimately lead to moral-political ideas, decisions, and actions (e.g., moral disgust).

To be fair, there are some enactivist theories that have addressed the relation between ethics and enactive cognition to some extent. In fact, in its original form, enactivism was modeled not only on phenomenology and cognitive sciences, but also on Eastern religion (Varela et al. 1991). Varela (1999) focuses on the ethical insights of Confucianism, Taoism, and Buddhism in order to investigate the ethical aspects of enactive cognition, which he describes in terms of a valuable knowledge of the good. This knowledge is obtained, according to Varela, by establishing harmony or an "immediacy in perception and action," which in turn means a harmonious coping with the situation, a *"know-how"* that results from the interaction between body and world (Varela 1999: 4). However, Varela steers enactivism in this context in the direction of a normative moral theory that promotes a harmonious outlook on the world, a type of Eastern mindfulness. Although his view is interesting in its own right, my intention in this paper is to examine moral enactive cognition in a different way. My aim is more descriptive than normative in that I focus on the question of how interactions with moral contexts (values, norms, institution, and symbols) work in enactive cognitive relations. What aspects of our relation with the world are parts of these interactions? The remainder of this chapter will pursue this question.

Moral Imagination as Simulation: Enacting Moral Meaning into Perceptual Relations

If we now return to Ricoeur's idea of imagination, we can find some clues that can help to define enactive interaction with moral contexts. Imagination, according to Ricoeur, is not only a significant tool for understanding our senses, but this understanding also has an immediate moral consequence. As I have argued above, imagination, as defined in *Fallible Man*, is a mediator for our needs and desires on one hand, and the environment on the other hand. For example, when in need of water, we find a creative solution to find water (we can go to the tap in the kitchen; we know that there will be water from previous experiences which we can re-enact, consciously, unconsciously or semi-consciously). Yet, this kind of direct interaction is interconnected with moral meanings, in that it is influenced by ethico-political values and norms (not necessarily always, but potentially). For example, we might be intuitively worried when seeing someone leaving the water tap open too long for no obvious reason, because we believe spillage is ethically and ecologically wrong. Another example: because the color red symbolizes socialism, a politician might intuitively (but also consciously) choose to wear a red tie in the morning, since he values the political values and ideas of socialism. These examples show that cognitive interactions with our environment have moral consequences and take on moral meaning because they are extended into moral contexts (e.g., values about the protection of the needs of others), and therefore require taking moral decisions and actions. Is it possible to translate this idea, that imagination mediates between cognition and morality, into enactivist terms? In order to see how this could be possible, I will discuss several enactivist concepts that support this idea and allow describing enactive interaction with moral contexts. These concepts are: *enactive simulation, affection,* and *social interaction*.

First, as I already argued in the previous part, the concept of *enactive simulation* supports Ricoeur's notion of imagination in *Fallible Man*. Enactive simulation explains imagination as a complex cognitive process that allows for the re-enaction of experiences in order to make sense of experiences and our surroundings. This theoretical model can explain cognitive tasks in a morally neutral way, such as memory being the re-enactment of past experiences (e.g., Gallagher 2017: 466). However, it can also pave the way for a better understanding of enactive interactions with moral contexts. Not only do enactivists use a similar conception of the imagination in order to explain cognitive tasks, such as tool-making, which implies a careful imagining and comparing of certain patterns as well as memory tasks (Hutto and Myin 2017: loc. 3245–3250). The tasks also seem to have moral consequences. For example, tools have an instrumental value but also influence the imaginative design of ethico-political symbols (e.g., flags, decorations, and drawings). The way we use tools also expresses cultural values (e.g., mining tools express our moral attitude toward the earth we inhabit in that it symbolizes natural exploitation).

Moreover, there is empirical support for the idea that in basic cognitive relations we consciously and/or unconsciously take on ethico-political meanings from our surroundings. For example, recent studies in cognitive psychology demonstrate that there exists a cognitive link between basic perception and basic motor bodily reactions, on the one hand, and moral judgment on the other hand. Chapman et al. (2009) published a study about the relation between facial motoric activity, in particular, the movement of the levator labii muscles in the face, and gustatory responses, including moral disgust (Chapman et al. 2009). How they understand moral disgust is not specified. Yet, for our purposes, it is possible to assume that moral disgust is based on the moral opinions or, more simply, beliefs one has, which would be based on different ethical and political values, norms, institutions, and symbols available (e.g., education of cultural moral values). This demonstrates, at least, that basic motor activity and more complex moral cognitive processes are connected.

To give another example, Eskine, Kacinik and Prinz (2011) found a similar link between taste perception and moral evaluation. They examined whether consuming different beverages (sweet, bitter, and neutral) would have any effect on moral evaluations of different situations. The study's participants were asked to label different moral transgressions (e.g., "second cousins engaging in consensual incest, a man eating his already-dead dog, and a student stealing library books") (Eskine, Kacinik, and Prinz 2011: 296). During the moral evaluation the test subjects were also provided with small amounts of Berry Punch, Swedish Bitters, and water. The results of the test showed that disgust caused by bad taste (caused by the bitter taste of the Swedish Bitters) evoked feelings of moral disgust that were stronger than the feelings of other test subjects who were asked to evaluate the same situation, while consuming the sweet beverage or water. Moreover, the test also showed that this effect was also influenced by the political opinions of the candidates. Test persons with conservative political views were more inclined to make a more severe moral evaluation than persons with a more liberal political opinion.

These empirical studies show that sense perception is influenced by diverse ethico-political meanings that are part of our social contexts and, conversely, that our social interactions influence our ethico-political opinions, beliefs, values, and norms. And if we recall the idea that perception can imply imagination (e.g., comparing of patterns), then we can translate Ricoeur's idea of moral imagination into an enactivist framework. If the senses work imaginatively by connecting and enacting experience, and if the senses are embedded and extended into their natural and social surroundings, then it is easy to see, for example, how they would be able to associate political opinion x or y with bad or good taste (bitterness, sweetness, visual harmony, etc.). This process might take place without us even knowing it. The persons in the taste test described above might not have been aware that their political conservatism/liberalism interacted with their taste experiences when performing moral evaluations (this would align with the concept of the body schema, according to which the control of the body through schematism works unconsciously). Yet, according to the enactivist response to simulation theory, more complex associations of meanings and experiences are scaffolded on lower end experiences (Hutto and Myin 2017). There is no giant leap between basic motor skills and culturally embedded meanings, if complex mental content results from the simulation of experiences through memory and ultimately through narratives. The capacity to build a narrative identity "around one's body" results then from an enactment of one's own experiences, beliefs, values, etc. This aligns well with Ricoeur's idea of practical synthesis in *Fallible Man*, which defines our mediation between body and mind through affectivity.

Affection as Ethical Concern and Moral Understanding through Stories

A second concept of enactivism that can lead the way toward an enactive conception of interaction with moral contexts is *affection*. Enactivists understand affection as "the relational process of signification between an autonomous, self-organizing subject and the world, on which she has a certain perspective based in her self-organization, which entails certain needs and concerns" (De Jaegher 2015: 123).

This autonomous process is not an isolated form of self-maintenance. On the contrary, while the relation itself has "interaction-autonomy" (Colombetti and Torrance 2009) as a network of processes and interactions between a subject and the surrounding world, it implies that others can influence an individual's intentions and assist in his/her needs and concerns. For example, in friendship our needs and concerns often change depending on the needs and concerns of our friends. To give another example, children typically initially lack a concern for the potential dangers of their surroundings (e.g., they try to touch pointy and hot objects), they partly learn this concern, not (only) by trial and error but (mostly) from affective interactions with their parents (through language (don't touch that!), body language (a concerned look), or touch (coordinating the child's actions).

Yet, one aspect that still remains undeveloped in enaction theory is the potential moral significance of such affective relationships. In fact, enactivists do question the significance of the ascription of personal responsibility (Colombetti and Torrance 2009). If our social relations are interaction autonomous, so they argue, then it is questionable whether and to what extent we can be held individually responsible for our actions. From an enactivist perspective, actions result from the interaction networks between subjects, rather than from an individual's personal choice. I will not go into further detail of this discussion here, because this would lead to a different debate, namely the free-will problem. However, another way of understanding responsibility in this context would be to describe it in terms of an ethical or moral concern of persons for each other *through affection* (e.g., care, love, and sympathy).

Ricoeur's notion of *feeling*, which is developed in *Fallible Man*, can offer some insight here. For Ricoeur, feelings toward others do not primarily imply mental content, such as beliefs or thoughts, but is rather a concern for the other produced in direct affective relation with this other: "Feeling [. . .] does not believe in the being of what it aims at, [yet] it manifests the way in which I am affected, my love and my hate, although it manifests it only through the lovable and the hateful, meant on the thing, on the person, and on the world" (Ricoeur 1986: 85). These lines suggest that affection has an ethical connotation as well, insofar it enables concern or disconcern for others, as manifested in love and hate.

If we reconnect this to the notion of imagination as simulation, we can put this idea into enactive theory. In fact, there are two possible ways of understanding this process of sympathy in terms of cognitive theory. One way would be to define feelings toward others as the simulation or manipulation of mental content by projecting one's own mental content into the mind of others, for instance, by comparing one's own beliefs, desires, and needs, with those of others. This understanding would be in line with a neo-pragmatic, mirror neuron theory, or simulation theory (see Gallagher 2017). Yet, this way of putting it does not fit Ricoeur's understanding of feeling. Rather than an intellectualistic kind of "pairing," it is a direct exchange of feelings in body language, or an "intention" that is at the same time "inwardness" (Ricoeur 1986: 84). Another way of putting this, more in line with enactivism, is that through embodied interactions with other persons, through communication and empathic imagination of their feelings, we come to learn their concerns and needs, which reorient our own concerns and needs. Moral imagination would then promote empathic understanding of others by re-enacting past experiences which are similar to or reflect the other's situation (e.g., I can feel with my friend who has a broken leg, because I also had a broken leg once or because I have seen others with broken legs in pain before).

Imagination relates in this context to narrative imagination. That is to say that the exchange of, and the interaction between, life stories aids in the care between persons. Ricoeur mentions the notion of "ethical imagination" in this regard, in a reference to Peter Kemp in *Oneself as Another* (Ricoeur 1992: 165). Moreover, he also introduces the idea that narratives offer a "laboratory" or "propaedeutic" to ethics (Ricoeur 1992: 115). What would this mean for enaction? The notion of the narrative has been widely discussed by enactivists (e.g., Caracciolo 2012, 2013, 2014). They argue that literary fiction can assist in imagining or enacting certain experiences, such as imagining what it feels like to experience certain kinds of pain.

Yet, these kinds of literary experiments are largely morally neutral. Ricoeur can help here. Not only can fiction have moral content through which we learn ethical values (e.g., the moral of a story). Fiction can be an ethical laboratory. Also, our own ethical and political values find their roots in our personal life stories. We do not just possess these values overnight, they get shaped by living through life's experiences, which of course interact with available social contexts (e.g., educational background, social and political engagement, opinions of friends). If we bring Ricoeur's idea that certain types of imagination and narratives are morally significant into an enactivist framework, we can thus conclude as follows: intersubjective self-organization of the subject implies the learning of moral meanings, because throughout the subject's life, he/she encounters others, as well as different ethico-political values, norms, institutions, and symbols. By interacting with these others and these ethico-political contexts the subject gets to form its own ethico-political ideas, interwoven into its life story, and can ultimately act accordingly as an individual. The possibility to act in this way is promoted by the capacity to (re-)enact (past) experiences that are morally valuable through imagination.

Enaction: Social and Moral Interaction

However, moral understanding (of values, norms, institutions, and symbols) does obviously not only take place on an individual level. Not only do persons have moral values and make moral decisions, but so too can social groups (this is, of course, already implied in the notion of the social imaginary). In fact, a personal value or norm taken on its own would not yet be a moral value or norm, since morality implies a community of shared principles. Ricoeur's idea of the social imaginary can put us on the way to define moral enactive interaction between individuals and groups. According to Ricoeur, the social imaginary is the capacity of a social group to design certain values, norms, institutions and symbols that have ethico-political meaning (Ricoeur 2007). This capacity has two extreme poles. On the one hand, it possibly results in ideology, through which a state controls the ethico-moral opinion, and in which there is no room for different values, norms, institutions, or symbols than those determines by the ideology (Ricoeur 2007: 184). On the other hand, the social imaginary can lead to utopia, understood not as a literary genre, but in the sociological sense, as the social group's imagination of radically new ethico-political values, norms, institutions, and symbols. "Utopia is the mode in which we radically rethink the nature of family, consumption, government, religion, and so on" (Ricoeur 2007: 184). In this respect, utopia leads the social imaginary into political dissent of the ideology.

To translate this into enactive theory, we can start by focusing on how enactivists understand social interaction, which they also define as "participatory sense-making" (De Jaegher 2015: 114). According to this principle, social interaction processes run deep into the core of our self-constitution and self-affection, to the point that social interaction changes how we perceive, think, and act (see the idea of social affordances). Empirical research illustrates this on several different levels, for example, by demonstrating that social interactions can influence humor in infants and also alter the development of their self-conscious emotions (De Jaegher 2015; Reddy 2008). Another example is that interactions with close others can influence how we experience pain (De Jaegher 2015; Krahé et al. 2013).

Yet, if this profound influence on self-awareness works on a social level, this surely implies moral influence as well. It is easy to see to what extent the realm of the social imaginary can penetrate our self-awareness and self-affection. Within affective relations with others we are the "self is inwardly affected" (Ricoeur 1986: 84). And this can go to the point of egoism and hostile feelings such as "aggressiveness, reprisals, resentment, and revenge" which result from not feeling recognized by or feeling superior to others (Ricoeur 1986: 125). For example, body images are shaped by larger institutional, ethico-political narratives by mediation of feelings toward others, sometimes in a violent fashion (racist discourse and misogyny in institutionalized societies). The experience of touch, for example, also has moral significance on the institutional level, insofar it relates to ethico-political narratives including mores about touching. We find various groups of "untouchables," stigmatized by societies and institutions (e.g., the *dalits* in India, *paekjong* in Korea, or *burakumin* in Japan (see Sarukai 2009)). Simultaneously, there exist communities in which untouchables are highly ranked, mainly kings or priests, due to their authority. Social, moral, and political actions occur within the context of such knowledge relations.

In sum, I have argued in this chapter that certain ideas of Ricoeur about morality, as connected to the imagination, are significant for recent enactivist debates, because they can be translated into enactive theory and define some of the moral aspects of enactive cognitive relations. As we have seen,

Ricoeur's idea of imagination allows us to define the moral aspects of enactive cognitive relations on three different levels.

First, I started from an enactive model of simulation to explain more complex cognitive tasks, such as memory and imagination. This model explains these cognitive tasks in terms of simulation of perception, such that memory is re-enactment of past experiences and imagination an enactment of absent experiences. This definition is close to how Ricoeur understands imagination in his early works, namely as an anticipation of an absent experience within embodied interaction with the world. What is more, the model can also explain why basic perception of the senses is not always morally neutral, as empirical research shows (e.g., interference of political opinion in taste associations). If we process knowledge through the simulation of experiences, which to a certain extent occurs unconsciously and spontaneously through the body schema and social affordances, then it is likely that what we already experienced and know, including morally significant knowledge, influences our senses. To put it more simply, if social interactions profoundly affect our self-awareness, then it is no surprise that ethico-political values, norms, institutions, and symbols influence how our senses work. This way of understanding sense perception is a translation of Ricoeur's idea that imagination is both cognitive and moral into enactivist theory.

Second, on the basis of this model of enactive simulation (or moral enactive simulation) it is possible to build a model of affection that explains moral intersubjectivity. Not only do ethico-political values, norms, institutions, and symbols interfere with the perception of our senses, but we are also capable of performing moral actions as a result of being deeply affected by others and in ways that profoundly affect others as well (e.g., love and care). In enactive theory this would be a sound statement, according to the idea of participatory sense-making: we make sense of the world, not alone but by engaging in social relations of affection. Ricoeur's notion of narrative imagination can further help understand here how these affective relations are intertwined with the realm of the social imaginary. By creating narratives and telling the stories of our lives we communicate with each other, try to understand each other's moral beliefs, opinions, and actions that are based on the social imaginary.

Last, the social imaginary not only plays a role on the intersubjective level between two persons, but also between social groups. Ricoeur's approach to the social imaginary is insightful here because it can be translated into enactivist theory as well. Ricoeur's idea that social groups communicate ethico-political ideas through narratives (e.g., the history of a subculture) leads the way to an enactivist conception of the social imaginary. This enactive social imaginary would then be an ethico-political realm that is not so much a whole of abstract theories, but rather a dynamic network of values, norms, institutions, and symbols of knowledge exchanged between social groups, which are mediated by feelings. This exchange obviously can take oppressive and violent forms (e.g., ideology) and can lead to the creation of new ethical and political ideas (e.g., utopia). Enactive cognitive interactions between social groups thus lead to shared ethico-political stories and also to abstract moral ideas (institutions, symbols, etc.). It is likely from an enactivist perspective that moral cognitive relations not only have an interaction autonomy (as an intersubjective relationship), but also are embedded and extended into the larger network of the social imaginary.

NOTES

1. I will refer to this concept hereafter as "enactive simulation."
2. As will become clear, imagination is not univocal for Ricoeur, but has several different meanings throughout his writings.
3. Ricoeur did, however, deliver a series of lectures on imagination at The University of Chicago in the 1970s.
4. They do not deny, however, that some forms of imagination include representations, mental content such as beliefs or opinions. Yet, they do deny that explaining imagination in its basic sense implies a representational model of the mind.
5. Understanding moral contexts in a social sense, as the social imaginary or the set of ethico-political values, norms, institutions, and symbols of social groups, has the advantage of defining morality in terms of social relations, rather than in terms of abstract principles. This social way of understanding morality aligns well with enactivism, which understands cognition in terms of social relations.

REFERENCES

Amalric, J.-L. 2012. L'Imagination poético-pratique dans l'identité narrative. *Études Ricœuriennes/ Ricœur Studies 3* (2), 110–27.
Amalric, J.-L. 2013. *L'imagination vive: une genèse de la philosophie ricœurienne de l'imagination*. Paris: Éditions Hermann.
Caracciolo, M. 2012. Narrative, Meaning, Interpretation: An Enactivist Approach. *Phenomenology and the Cognitive Sciences 11* (3), 367–84.
Caracciolo, M. 2013. Blind Reading: Toward an Enactivist Theory of the Reader's Imagination. In Bernaerts, L., De Geest, D., Herman, L., & Vervaeck, B. (Eds.), *Stories and Minds: Cognitive Approaches to Literary Narrative* (pp. 81–106). Lincoln, NE: University of Nebraska Press.
Caracciolo, M. 2014. *The Experientiality of Narrative: An Enactivist Approach*. Berlin and Boston, MA: De Gruyter.
Chapman, H.A., Kim, D.A., Susskind, J.M., & Anderson, A.K. 2009. In Bad Taste: Evidence for the Oral Origins of Moral Disgust. *Science 323*, 1222–1226.

Clark, A. 2016. *Surfing Uncertainty: Prediction, Action and the Embodied Mind.* Oxford: Oxford University Press.

Colombetti, G., & Torrance, S. 2009. Emotion and Ethics: An Inter-(en) Active Approach. *Phenomenology and the Cognitive Sciences 8* (4), 505–526.

De Jaegher, H. 2015. How We Affect Each Other: Michel Henry's "pathos-with" and the Enactive Approach to Intersubjectivity. *Journal of Consciousness Studies 21* (1–2), 112–132.

De Jaegher, H., & Di Paolo, E. 2007. Participatory Sense-making: An Enactive Approach to Social Cognition. *Phenomenology and the Cognitive Sciences 6* (4), 485–507.

Dierckxsens, G. 2018a. Ricœur's Take on Embodied Cognition and Imagination: Enactivism in Light of Freedom and Nature. In Davidson, S. (Ed.), *A Companion to Ricœur's Freedom and Nature* (pp. 191–205). London/New York, Lexington Books.

Dierckxsens, G. 2018b. Imagination, Narrativity and Embodied Cognition: Exploring the Possibilities of Paul Ricœur's Hermeneutical Phenomenology for Enactivism. *Philosophy South 19* (1), 41–49.

Di Paolo, E., Cuffari, E.C., & De Jaegher, H. 2008. *Linguistic Bodies: The Continuity between Life and Language.* Cambridge, MA: The MIT Press.

Eskine, J.J., Kacinik, N.A., & Prinz, J.J. 2011. A Bad Taste in the Mouth: Gustatory Disgust Influences Moral Judgment. *Psychological Science 22* (3), 295–299.

Gallagher, S. 2017. *Enactivist Interventions: Rethinking the Mind.* Oxford: Oxford University Press.

Hutto, D.D., & Myin, E. 2013. *Radicalizing Enactivism. Basic Minds without Content.* Cambridge, MA: MIT Press.

Hutto, D.D., & Myin, E. 2017. *Evolving Enactivism. Basic Minds Meet Content.* Kindle edition. Cambridge, MA: The MIT Press.

Kearney, R. 2016. Thinking the Flesh with Paul Ricœur. In Davidson, S. & Vallee, M.-A. (Eds.), *Hermeneutics and Phenomenology in Paul Ricœur* (pp. 31–40). New York, Springer. https://doi.org/10.1007/978-3-319-33426-4_3.

Krahé, C., Springer, A., Weinman, J.A., & Fotopoulou, A. 2013. The Social Modulation of Pain: Others as Predictive Signals of Salience — A Systematic Review. *Frontiers in Human Neuroscience 7*, 1–21. doi 10.3389/fnhum.2013.00386/.

Levitan, C.A., et al. 2014. Cross-Cultural Color-Odor Associations. *PLoS ONE 9* (7), https://doi.org/10.1371/journal.pone.0101651.

Reddy, V. 2008. *How Infants Know Minds.* Cambridge, MA: Harvard University Press.

Ricœur, P. 1966. *Freedom and Nature: The Voluntary and the Involuntary.* Kohák, E. (Trans.). Evanston, IL: Northwestern University Press.

Ricoeur, P. 1978. The Metaphorical Process as Cognition, Imagination and Feeling. *Critical Inquiry 5* (1), 142–159. https://doi.org/10.1086/447977.

Ricoeur, P. 1984, 1986, 1990. *Time and Narrative, 3 vols.* McLaughlin, K. & Pellauer, D. Chicago, IL: University of Chicago Press.

Ricoeur, P. 1986. *Fallible Man.* Kelbley, Charles A. (Trans.). New York, NY: Fordham University Press, 146 p.

Ricoeur, P. 1992. *Oneself as Another*. Blamey, K. (Trans.). Chicago, IL: Chicago University Press.

Ricoeur, P. 2007. *From Text to Action: Essays in Hermeneutics II*. Blamey, K. & Thompson, J.B. Evanston, IL: Northwestern University Press.

Sarukai, S. 2009. Phenomenology of Untouchability. *Economic and Political Weekly 44*, 9–48. https://www.epw.in/journal/2009/37/special-articles/phenomenology-untouchability.html.

Shapiro, L. 2014. Book Review: Radicalizing Enactivism: Basic Minds without Content. *Mind 123* (489), 213–20.

Taylor, G.H. 2006. Ricœur's Philosophy of Imagination. *Journal of French Philosophy 1/2*: 93–104. https://doi.org/10.5195/JFFP.2006.186.

Varela, F.J. 1991. Organism: A Meshwork of Selfless Selves. In Tauber A.I. (Eds.), *Organism and the Origins of Self*. Boston Studies in the Philosophy of Science, vol. 129. Springer, Dordrecht.

Varela, F.J. 1999. *Ethical Know-How: Action, Wisdom, and Cognition*. Stanford, CA: Stanford University Press.

Varela, F.J., Thompson, E., & Rosch, E. 1991. *The Embodied Mind: Cognitive Science and Human Experience*. Cambridge, MA: The MIT Press.

Verheyen, L. 2018. The Cognitive Value of Modernist Literature. Ricoeur's Conception of Productive Imagination Reconsidered. *Metodo 6* (1), 161, 175.

Chapter 7

The Self Is Embodied and Discursive

Tracing the Phenomenological Background of Ricoeur's Narrative Identity

Annemie Halsema

Paul Ricoeur's work is one of the main sources for the notion of "narrative identity," that is getting more and more attention nowadays. His book *Oneself as Another* (1992) and other articles published in the early 1990s (Ricoeur 1991a, 1991b) are important philosophical sources for this notion and are mentioned in debates on this topic.[1] Narrative identity is not uncontested, however. One of the most important critiques is that it doesn't constitute a sufficient account of the self. Narrative identity is seen as only one aspect of the self: the reflexive side, articulated in language and giving expression to an experiential self. It is claimed that this hermeneutical notion of selfhood needs a complement in phenomenal self-experience, in experiential subjectivity (Zahavi 2007: 182–84; 2014: 57–59).

It is well known that Ricoeur's intellectual trajectory starts phenomenologically, only to gradually develop into a hermeneutics. *Fallible Man* belongs to his early phenomenological work and aims to provide a philosophical anthropology, an account of what it is to be human. My question in this chapter is whether Ricoeur's early theorizing about the self provides the phenomenological notion of the self that Zahavi is after. What are the implications of his early account of the relation between the body, language, and self in *Fallible Man* for his later notion of narrative identity?

In this chapter I will read Ricoeur's account of the self backward. Starting from the notion of narrative identity developed in *Oneself as Another*, I will trace its phenomenological background to *Fallible Man*, published 30 years earlier (1960). I do not suppose that there have been no changes in Ricoeur's thinking, or that it hasn't been enriched over the years. Yet, there is an underlying continuity in Ricoeur's thinking, which he himself has outlined in various accounts of his intellectual trajectory (Ricoeur 1978, 1995), that legitimizes my form of reading backward. The chapter will first situate the notion of narrative identity in the contemporary debate and develop its main characteristics. Second, I will describe the main problems with this notion as well as Dan Zahavi's suggestion of a phenomenal pre-reflective subjectivity as presupposition for narrative identity. Third, I will turn to *Fallible Man*. I intend to show that Ricoeur provides a notion of the self that is not merely linguistic, but is the reflection upon itself of a subject born within language, culture, and history.[2] Taking into account the relationship between body, language, and self in *Fallible Man*, Ricoeur's "narrative identity" includes a self that is not merely a secondary construction, but that finds itself as an embodied and discursive being in the world. On this basis, phenomenal and narrative identity can no longer be distinguished.

NARRATIVE IDENTITY: THE SELF AS CONSTRUCTION

In current discussions of "the self" that take place in the philosophy of the cognitive sciences and the philosophy of mind, narrative identity is considered as one of its many manifestations. Sean Gallagher (2013) argues for a "pattern theory of the self," of which narrative identity is a part.[3] Likewise, Miriam Kyselo claims that the self in contemporary theories of the cognitive sciences is understood as pluralistic: "*minimal embodied, minimal experiential, affective, intersubjective, psychological/cognitive, narrative, extended,* and *situated*" (Kyselo 2014: 1, italics in original). In the context of such discussions, Ricoeur is often mentioned as one of the sources for the notion of narrative identity, along with the American philosopher Marya Schechtman.[4] Both Ricoeur and Schechtman hold the view that narrative identity is ontological, which includes the view that the self is constructed by telling its own life story. The self comes to exist through its being narrated. This position is described as "strong narrativism" (Hutto 2016). Schechtman, in her dissertation *The Constitution of Selves* (1996), argues for a "narrative self-constitution view" that is close to Ricoeur's view on narrative identity in many respects (Atkins 2004).[5] In this section, I will outline the main differences between Ricoeur's (1992) and Schechtman's (1996) accounts of narrative identity as well as develop its central characteristics on the basis of their similarities. I will not confine myself to Ricoeur's perspective on narrative identity, as one might perhaps expect in a volume about *Fallible Man*, because in the aforementioned debates his account of narrative identity is mentioned alongside Schechtman's more detailed notion of narrative identity. Reading their work together thus provides us with a richer and more precisely developed notion of narrative identity than an examination of Ricoeur's work alone. Schechtman, in her later work (2014), takes a relative distance from the notion of narrative identity and develops a broader notion of the self, known as the Personal Life View. I will deal with this later and show in which respects Ricoeur's notion of narrative identity turns out to be preferable.

Ricoeur and Schechtman share a critique of the prevailing debate over personal identity in which *idem*-identity or reidentification is central. The analytical debate over personal identity, they argue, aims at an account of personal identity in which one of its aspects is prioritized—sameness (*idem*) or reidentification—to the detriment of selfhood (*ipse*) or characterization.[6] Instead of focusing upon a criterion for sameness, Ricoeur and Schechtman aim at a notion of personal identity that is closer to everyday experience of the self, to who-ness, or self-characterization.

However, Ricoeur's and Schechtman's grounds for criticizing the dominant philosophical ideas about personal identity differ. Whereas Ricoeur thinks that there are two different aspects to permanence in time—*idem* and *ipse*—Schechtman claims that answers to reidentification questions do not account for the practical demands of a notion of personal identity.[7] Instead of seeking a metaphysical ground for identity, the latter's "narrative self-constitution view" allows for a person to characterize herself and to consider herself as continuous over time. Ricoeur's primary concern is not with practical demands but with accounting for mutability as well as constancy. He considers the self's permanence in time under the aspect of sameness as well as change: in the case of *idem*-identity the constancy of the self is central, but in the case of *ipse*-identity, we hold on to our promise even when everything around us changes (1992: 124).

There is another respect in which Schechtman and Ricoeur hold different interpretations of narrative identity. They both consider personal identity as having two sides—self-constancy (*idem*) and characterization of the self (who-ness, *ipse*)—but differ in their accounts of how these sides are combined. Narrative self-constitution for Schechtman implies that individuals come to understand themselves as persons by coming to think of themselves as persisting subjects who have had experiences in the past, who will continue to have experiences in the future, and who take these experiences as theirs (1996: 94). Individuals become "persons" through self-narratives, and personhood means the adoption of a reflexive attitude toward oneself. For Schechtman, not all individuals are persons, and not all accounts of oneself are "self-narratives," especially not those that do not coincide with the stories of others about oneself. A life story should be shared with others, or, as she writes, should be "objective" (1996: 95). She further claims that her perspective on personal identity as narrative self-constitution does not have the aim of substituting the answers to the reidentification question, but that characterization and reidentification should be seen as two different perspectives that interact (1996: 68). Precisely how they interact, and are dependent on each other, is not clarified in *The Constitution of Selves*.

Ricoeur, in contrast, does consider how these two can be combined. He understands narrative identity as dialectical: it has two poles, a pole of reidentification (*idem*) and a pole of selfhood (*ipse*). Narrative identity is always a combination of these two, but the amount of sameness or selfhood can differ. Ricoeur's preferred examples in this case are taken from classical literature: the characters in fairy tales are illustrative for those who are clearly identifiable and re-identifiable (1992: 148), and the protagonist Ulrich in Robert Musil's *Man Without Qualities* represents selfhood without the support of sameness (1992: 149). In real life, narrative identity is situated in between the relative constancy of one's character on the one hand (where *idem* and *ipse* coincide almost entirely), and the promise on the other hand, that one holds on to, even in the case everything around one has changed (here *ipse* is not supported by *idem*) (1992: 122).

Apart from this dialectic between *idem* and *ipse*, narrative identity for Ricoeur is also characterized in terms of a dialectic between self and other (Ricoeur 1992: 3). This dialectic implies that my identity is not only based upon my own concerns about what makes life valuable ("the good life"), but also includes concern for others and treating them well (1992: 169–202). Narrative and ethical identity are closely related for Ricoeur—as they are for Schechtman. On the one hand, ethical identity implies that one needs to be capable of giving narrative accounts of one's actions by reflecting upon and giving reasons for them. On the other hand, narrating already implies ethical evaluation. The relationship between narrative and ethical identity, for Ricoeur, implies that self-esteem and self-respect are important components of selfhood. Schechtman's theory does not explicitly relate narrative and ethical identity in this way, instead she understands narrative self-constitution to be crucial for practical questions concerning moral responsibility.

Notwithstanding these differences between Schechtman and Ricoeur, the similarities between their views are large enough to extract the main characteristics of their ontological narrative conception of the self:

1. The self-narrative implies that one's life story has a coherent configuration, in which narrated events are situated in the plot. Ricoeur in this respect speaks of "the synthesis of the heterogeneous" (1992: 141); Schechtman thinks that a certain amount of coherence is necessary for personhood, although she allows for a high degree of incohesion (1996: 97–100; 2007: 159–60).
2. The self-narrative is an organizing principle of one's life. It forms a particular kind of orientation that supports one's actions and decisions in life (Schechtman 1996: 95, 113); Ricoeur considers this dimension in terms

of "life plans" that are changeable and that take shape in a "back and forth" between ideals and "the weighing of advantages and disadvantages of the choice of a particular life plan on the level of practices" (Ricoeur 1992: 157–58).
3. The self-narrative has a temporal dimension: it integrates one's past and future. Ricoeur develops this idea in terms of "permanence in time," and considers *idem* and *ipse* as the two forms of permanence in time (1992: 113–18), while Schechtman claims that a present event is embedded in a narrative (2007: 162).
4. The self-narrative is not necessarily fully expressed, and it is not a singular life story: it can be told more than once (Ricoeur 1992: 161). Schechtman even writes that the telling of an explicit story is usually an inappropriate way of expressing one's self-conception (1996: 113). The self-narrative instead should be seen as a lens, a perspective, that contains the stories of others as well, for instance, the stories of my parents about my birth (Ricoeur 1992: 160). The narrator hence is not the creator or author, but merely the coauthor of her life, and her narrative identity only stops being constituted at the moment people stop talking about her.

Ricoeur and Schechtman (1996) consider narrative identity to provide an exhaustive notion of the self that integrates present, past, and future and that in itself forms a more or less coherent configuration. Other current theories suggest that it is merely one of the manifestations of the self. In the next section, I will explain why this is the case and then formulate the questions that motivate a return to *Fallible Man*.

NARRATIVE IDENTITY CONTESTED

Since its conceptualization by Ricoeur and Schechtman, the notion of narrative identity has been debated at large.[8] This debate can be summarized in terms of a few main problems: (1) the question of narrative coherence; (2) the question of the explicitness or implicitness of the narrative; and (3) the question of whether it offers a complete notion of the self.

First of all, narratives are generally considered more or less coherent unities with a beginning, middle, and end. Ricoeur and Schechtman both refer to the notion of plot in this respect (Ricoeur 1983: 65–71; 1992: 141–47; Schechtman 1996: 96).[9] But how much coherence should a life story contain in order to count as a narrative? And does the notion of plot not imply an overly coherent, well-ordered, and harmonious life-story?

Ricoeur conceives of the plot as a discordant concordance, in which the principle of order (concordance) presides over the reversals of fortune (discordances) that threaten its unity up to the close of the story (1992: 141). The plot mediates heterogeneous elements: various events are connected by the temporal unity of the story, disparate components of the action (intentions, causes, chance occurrences) gain a sequence because of the story. For Schechtman, likewise, "in order to be self-constituting" a narrative "must have a high degree of coherence" (1996: 98). She thinks of the coherence of the narrative in terms of a lens, through which we filter our plans and experiences, or also in terms of an organizing principle of our lives (1996: 113).

Both philosophers do allow for a certain amount of incoherence, however. Ricoeur discusses incoherence in terms of discordances that threaten the unity of the plot, but in the end are taken up into the configuration of the narrative. He carefully distinguishes narrative from life and conceives of emplotment as inverting the effects of contingency and turning them into necessity or probability by the act of configuration (1992: 142). Action in life and the act of narrating are distinguished, just like "physical" contingency and necessity. He argues, however, that in the end (literary) narratives and life histories are complementary (1992: 163) and that characters—the ones who perform the action in a narrative—are plots (1992: 143). Also, at first sight there seems to be a tension in his thinking between the notion of plot which implies that we compose our own life story in a singular way and the idea that others contribute to our life-story. How can a life story remain coherent if others contribute to it? Ricoeur solves this problem by distinguishing between the narrator, character, and author of a life story (1992: 159–60). He claims that the first two overlap, which implies that one's life story constitutes one's identity, but that the narrator is not considered the author of her life, but merely a coauthor (1992: 160). On the level of authors, he admits others as well (such as one's parents who recount the story of one's birth). The stories of these others thus can become a part of the life story of the narrator.

Schechtman, in her response to Strawson's critique (2007),[10] differentiates between weak, strong, and middle-range versions of narrative self-constitution and situates her view in line with the middle-range ones. For the coherence of the narrative this implies that "it employs [. . .] more than a mere chronology of events in one's history, but there is no requirement that an identity-constituting narrative have a unifying theme, or represent a quest or have a well-defined plot arc that fits a distinct literary genera" (2007: 163). Schechtman, in other words, allows for various forms of coherence. A self-narrative can vary from being fully integrated (1996: 98) to a simple answer to a question about oneself (1996: 114). In her recent book, *Staying Alive*, she expands her view to also include the stories of others (Schechtman 2014: 103),[11] thereby expanding the notion of coherence.

To conclude, Ricoeur and Schechtman allow for disintegrating elements to be included in the self-narrative and take into account the fact that the stories of others contribute to one's self-narrative. Coherence thus is perhaps not a strong requirement for self-narratives, but for both philosophers it still operates as a normative demand. Schechtman claims that the coherence of a narrative is critical for a narrative to be identity-constituting (1996: 98). Ricoeur claims that "[i]f my life cannot be grasped as a singular totality, I could never hope it to be successful, complete" (1992: 160).

A second major problem in the debate over narrative identity is the relationship between explicit and implicit narratives (Zahavi 2014: 57–58). Does a narrative need to be fully articulated in order to count as a narrative? Or can it contain implicit and even unconscious elements, as Schechtman contends (1996: 114–19)? This problem is closely related to the sort of self-construction at stake in narrative identity. Most accounts hold a view on narrative self-shaping which includes implicit narratives. As Dan Hutto explains, narrative self-shaping boils down to the idea that humans are reflective beings and that self-reflection involves active shaping of oneself and taking responsibility for who we are.[12] Narrative capacities are critical in this respect because the reasons for actions are considered as elements of a possible storyline (2016: 25).[13] Hutto shows in detail that Schechtman differentiates between different accounts of narrative self-shaping. In her response to Strawson's critique (2007), she distinguishes between "person" and "self." Constituting oneself as a person involves implicitly organizing one's experience according to a narrative that recognizes past and future experiences as one's own (2007: 171). Apart from this full-blown conception of narrative self-shaping, she distinguishes a minimal account of selfhood that includes narrativity, but only in the sense that I experience "the present as part of the whole narrative" (Schechtman 2007: 171). This sense of the self is concerned with the identification of actions and experiences as belonging to *myself* (2007: 169). In her later Person Life View, Schechtman leaves behind the notion of narrative self-shaping (or as she writes: self-constitution) altogether and claims that the lives of persons share the structure of a diachronically structured unit, which is not necessarily narrative but could just as well be conceived as a sonata or a sonnet (2014: 108–09). For Schechtman, therefore, it is not linguistic expression that is critical to narrative self-constitution, but rather the idea of a "structural unity of a person's life" (2014: 108).

Ricoeur's account of narrative identity implies that narratives are constitutive for self-experience as well. In this respect, he refers to Socrates's saying that an unexamined life is not worth living (1992: 178). It is self-reflection that makes life valuable. Narrating, values, and the evaluation of one's actions are all closely connected for Ricoeur. Narratives are ways of gathering one's life, constituting it into a whole, which is also relevant for giving it an ethical character (1992: 158). Narratives can be considered as first-order sense-making of events that happened to someone, in which the diverse elements of a situation are brought into an order (see Halsema and Slatman 2017). Ricoeur explains this process of capturing the heterogeneous elements of a situation, by means of his threefold mimesis in *Time and Narrative I* (1984). It is on the basis of the narrative structure of actions, and on the ability of narratives to resume and gather our actions and the events that happened to us, that we are capable of ethics at all. As Ricoeur explains, the very notion of "imputability" implies "the capacity of a subject to designate himself, or herself as the actual author of its, his, or her own acts" (2007b: 47). Narrative identity, and the self's capacities of speaking and acting, are the precursors to imputability. Together, these four capacities (speaking, acting, narrating, being capable of imputation) constitute what he calls his philosophical anthropology of "the capable human being." To conclude, Ricoeur perhaps does not consider the problem of whether narratives are explicit or implicit, but he clearly identifies narrative identity with self-shaping and responsibility. The self's identity is constituted by narrating about itself, and this narrative self-shaping plays a crucial role in taking responsibility for one's actions.

The third problem mentioned in the debate over narrative identity concerns the question whether personal identity can be reduced to narrative accounts; in other words, can narrative identity be seen as a complete notion of personal identity? This problem is well formulated by Dan Zahavi, who argues that narrative accounts are not sufficient but presuppose a phenomenal self-consciousness or "pre-reflective self-intimacy" (2007: 186) or also "a first-person perspective" (2014: 59). The notion of narrative identity for Zahavi means that who I am is not a given, but evolving and realized through my projects (2007: 179). Selfhood in the case of narrative accounts is mediated by language, and therefore part of a social process, depending upon one's values, ideals, and goals. In narrating about ourselves, we use concepts from the tradition and culture to which we belong, but others are called upon to hear and accept our narrative accounts of ourselves as well (Zahavi 2007: 181). Underlying this higher order and conceptually mediated form of self-consciousness, he claims, there is a sort of nonconceptual "mine-ness" that accompanies bodily sensations, emotional states, and cognitive contents (2007: 186). It is always there, although it will frequently recede into the background. One must already be in possession of this experiential ownership before any narrative practice, according to Zahavi: it precedes active storytelling (2014: 59).

Zahavi also shows that in phenomenology, this experiential dimension of selfhood is far from new, and that many different thinkers, from Sartre to Henry, have developed ideas close to this. They refer to this self-givenness or self-referentiality as *ipseity* (2007: 187). For these phenomenologists, the self is an integral part of the structure of conscious life (2007: 188); it is not merely a construction, but the self possesses experiential reality itself. It is identified with the first-personal givenness of experiential phenomena. It is this givenness which makes experiences subjective (Ibid.), in other words the experiences of things (the taste of a tomato, the smell of a flower) are not experienced as neutral, but as mine. It is together with the experience of the taste of the tomato, that I am given to myself as the one who tastes. "The self is conceived as the invariant dimension of first-personal givenness in the multitude of changing experiences," Zahavi writes (2007: 189). It is important to note that this experiential sense of self is not something apart from the experience of things in the world, but that it is "the self-experience of a world-immersed self" (Ibid.).

Another point that Zahavi makes is that narrativity cannot be the basis for intersubjectivity and the otherness of other persons. He shows that children, who do not yet have speaking capacities, already have a sense of self and respond to and interact with others. What is more, he argues that in order to hold on to the difference between self and other, narrative accounts are not sufficient, because they might lead to reducing the other to narratives. We need to accept the other as having subjective self-experience in order to conceive of her as other than me (Zahavi 2007: 199). Zahavi, in short, suggests that his phenomenological approach of selfhood complements the hermeneutical, narrative one (2007: 200).

The rest of this chapter aims to show that Ricoeur's philosophical anthropology in *Fallible Man* provides a form of selfhood that is able to integrate Zahavi's phenomenal self-consciousness with narrative identity, or rather, that includes phenomenal self-consciousness in narrative identity. In *Fallible Man* Ricoeur considers the human[14] self as fragile: humans do not coincide with themselves (Ricoeur 1986: 1). He claims that humans are mixtures and bring about mediations (Ricoeur 1986: 3).[15] The mixture his philosophical anthropology starts from is the one between human's finite embodied perspective versus the infinity of language. The conception of the self in this book is not yet the narrative one of *Oneself as Another*, but my hypothesis is that the notion of the self in this book provides a background to Ricoeur's later narrative conception of identity. As a result, Zahavi's understanding of narrative identity, as merely pertaining to the conceptual and social aspects of selfhood, will turn out to be too narrow. In the next section, I will study this notion of the self in *Fallible Man* through a close reading of the text that explores how Ricoeur conceives of its relation to the body and language. In the final section, I will discuss how this self relates to Zahavi's phenomenal self and draw the implications for Ricoeur's narrative self-conception.[16]

BODY, SELF, AND LANGUAGE IN *FALLIBLE MAN*

My aim in this section is not to overview the broader themes that Ricoeur addresses in *Fallible Man*, namely the possibility of fault and human evil, instead I will focus upon the interrelation between the concepts of body, self, and language. As mentioned, for Ricoeur the human self is torn between finitude and infinitude: "the self is conflict," he writes. The ontological locus of the human consists in the disproportionate relation of finitude and infinitude (Ricoeur 1986: 134). By "finitude" Ricoeur refers to a perspective, a limited nature, being consigned to death, and captivated by desire, whereas "infinitude" refers to a demand for totality, rationality, discourse, and love (Ricoeur 1986: 3–4). Finitude is related to the self's embodiment, and infinitude to the self's linguistic capabilities. In this section, by following the trajectory of Ricoeur's text, I will develop the relationship of the self to its body and to language in order to explore the notion of the self that underlies Ricoeur's later theory of narrative identity.

Ricoeur analyzes human disproportion on three levels: knowing, acting, and feeling, the three powers that characterize human beings. He starts with knowing, not because he considers humans primarily as cognitive beings, but because his aim is to develop a *philosophical* anthropology.[17] In my analysis of the relationship between the body, self, and language, I will follow Ricoeur, and will therefore start with the level of knowing, which is guided by the disproportion between perspective and transcendence.

On the level of knowing, the finite human perspective is not simply founded by the fact that we are embodied (Ricoeur 1986: 19). Ricoeur instead understands humans primarily as directed toward the world: "the first meaning I read in my body, insofar as the body is a mediation of appearance, is . . . precisely that it is open onto . . . . It is this openness onto . . . which makes my body an originating mediator 'between' myself and the world" (19). My body does not enclose me and is not the "sign" of my finitude, instead it opens me onto the world. Ricoeur does not confine the body's openness to the perception of objects; the body also opens me to others insofar "as it expresses, that is to say, displays the interior upon the exterior and becomes a sign for others, decipherable and offered to the reciprocity of consciousnesses" (19). The body, in other words, is "always *upon* the world."

At the same time, it is embodiment that reveals my finitude. How does this appear to me? In the form of the perspectival limitation of perception (Ricoeur 1986: 20). Every view is a point of view on something. However, I only become aware of it in reflection and not in the act of perceiving itself. It is "upon the object that I apprehend the perspectival nature of perception" (21), because my sense of it may be other than I at first presumed. It is only in discovering the perspectival nature of my embodiment that I discover the "here from where" character of my perceiving the object. Besides its openness to the world, the body is conceived of as the zero origin, the center of orientation from which I perceive. In this sense it narrows my openness to the world, but this is not a fate imposed upon me from the outside: "from the moment 'I am brought into the world' I perceive this world as a series of changes and re-establishments starting from this place which I did not choose and which I cannot find in my memory" (23). It is as a result of being born, which is an event for others and not for myself, that my point of view becomes detached from me, and is considered a fate that governs my life from the outside.

The knowing self, in other words, is thrown into the world, open to it, perceiving, intentional, and discovers its finite perspective in a reflexive act. This reflexive act arises as a consequence of the perception of things itself. Ricoeur describes it as "the perceived object's insurmountable and invincible property of presenting itself from a certain angle" (Ricoeur 1986: 21). In other words, it is "upon the object" that the self discovers its perspectival nature, and the body as center of orientation, the zero origin. It is upon discovering its embodiment as openness, that is at once limitation, that the self turns back upon itself. The free mobility of the body, that makes it possible to change one's position toward objects, contributes to this awareness of the body's perspectival nature.

Infinitude for Ricoeur is related to the verb and the process of signifying.[18] In order to transgress my limited perspective, I need to signify it as *one* perspective that relates to other possible perspectives. The intention to signify is transgression (Ricoeur 1986: 26). Ricoeur relates transgressing to expressing one-sidedness, to knowing, and to signifying (26). In short, the one-sidedness of a perspective on a thing needs to be acknowledged, which already happens in kinesthetic experience (22), but to which signification is added by means of the verb. This implies that it is not *because* of the language that we become aware of the perspectival nature that embodiment confines us to, but that language *supports* transcending our own perspective. In speaking, we communicate about things in their absence and in terms of their non-perceived sides (27). We convert our "here" into an "any-place-whatever" (31). In naming things, we transcend them. The point is not that we take a superior point of view upon the thing named, but that in using language we invert the point of view on the thing into "the universal of all points of view" (26). Using language, in other words, implies a shift from perspectivism to universality.

For Ricoeur human beings are born into a world of language that precedes and envelops them (Ricoeur 1986: 27). They therefore combine the situatedness of their perspective with the universality of language.[19] By means of their perspectival relation to things, humans come to realize the finitude of embodiment; by means of language, their capability of universalizing. Ricoeur writes: "I am not merely a situated onlooker, but a being who intends and expresses as an intentional transgression of the situation" (26–27). At the level of knowing, there is consciousness of objects, but the person has not gathered herself to one person yet and is not yet self-conscious (45–46). Self-consciousness implies the second level, "the practical synthesis," in which the perceiving body becomes a projecting body (53).

At the level of knowing, the perspective upon the things was a disinterested one, but embodiment for Ricoeur does not only include perspective but also affect. He conceives of affect not as something that is added to a perspectival point of view, but as projective: things appear interesting to me out of affect. I grasp the lovable, attractive, hateful upon the things I find lovable, attractive, hateful (Ricoeur 1986: 51). Similar to the case of knowing, the starting point of acting is not the subject, but its relation to the things and other people in the world. Affectivity or desire does not shut me up in my desiring self, rather in desire "I am outside myself" (53). It is openness and not closing that is revealed to me in affect. This "light of affectivity or clarity of desire" (54) is accompanied by an opacity, however, that defines human finitude on this level. Analogous to the body as a center of perspective, at the level of acting we find a total experience of the body as coenesthesis. Feeling, "finding oneself in a certain mood," reveals the "here" of the body at the same time as it reveals the sensed object. The body is not only a mediator. Besides "letting the world in," the body is immediately for itself: "affective closing," Ricoeur calls it (55). We sense the body's inexpressible presence to itself, and the primal difference between myself and all others: "to find oneself in a certain mood is to feel one's individuality as inexpressible and incommunicable" (55). We find ourselves and feel that this experience cannot be exchanged. It is at this affective level that, according to Ricoeur, the subject-pole of all perceptions thickens into self-love, that the zero origin of looking becomes self-attachment (Ibid.). Returning intermediately to Zahavi's problem with narrative identity (its lack of a conception of phenomenal nonconceptual mineness), it can be seen that for Ricoeur at the level of affect a sense of self comes into existence. This self is not yet conceptual, but it is an experiential self, that comes to itself by becoming aware of the distinction between itself and others. This awareness arises from the self's embodiment: in affect I sense the mineness of my perspective upon things, as well as being different from others.

Because my purpose is not the consideration of fallibility, I will not proceed to summarize the rest of this analysis. Instead, I will turn to the section in which Ricoeur further develops feeling as "the fragile moment par excellence" (Ricoeur 1986: 82). Feeling is what binds us to things and to other beings: "it connects what knowledge divides" (131). Feeling is beyond the duality of subject and object that is introduced on the level of knowledge. Feeling unites and throws us out of ourselves, while at the same time we sense ourselves existing in affection. Ricoeur, in this section of *Fallible Man* ("affective fragility") is concerned with the cleavage within the self in terms of being torn between *epithumia* and *eros*, happiness and pleasure, *logos* and *bios*, the spiritual and vital. The self is *thumos* for Ricoeur, which means that it is not situated between the aforementioned opposites, but it wants them both at the same time. This section shows again that feeling reveals a "both at once" structure: "an intention toward the world and an affection of the self" (89). Ricoeur phrases it picturesquely: "Feeling expresses my belonging to this landscape that, in turn, is the sign and cipher of my inwardness" (89). Instead of objectifying, feeling brings closer: objects touch me and I make contact with things, while at the same time realizing that it is me that experiences them.

In *Fallible Man*, we thus find a notion of the self that is immersed in the world, open to the things and others; upon finding itself as an affective being, the self comes to the awareness that its perspective differs from the perspective of others. Its affectivity colors its perception of things and other people, leading it to realize the singularity (and therefore finitude) of its own perspective. Self-awareness hence is secondary to the relation to the world and includes an act of reflection. The self's ability to speak, furthermore, introduces the ability to transcend its perspectival nature and to take a universal point of view.

In Ricoeur's philosophical anthropology in *Fallible Man*, in other words, we have found a notion of the self that is both embodied and discursive. It is on the basis of its embodiment that the self discovers its perspectival, finite nature that it is capable of transcending and universalizing because of its capacity for language. It is important to note that it is not language alone that leads to self-reflection or to the constitution of the self. The role of language in *Fallible Man* is rather to support the transcendence of the self's perspectival nature. Kinesthetic movement already makes one aware of one's perspective. Language rather is the self's further possibility to universalize, while its embodiment confines it to a specific perspective. The self is precisely this mixture of infinitude and finitude, transcendence, and the body as zero origin.

THE HERMENEUTICAL SELF INCLUDES
THE PHENOMENAL SELF

Earlier we saw that Zahavi criticizes narrative accounts of the self as insufficient and argues that we need an account of "experiential ownership," or "pre-reflective subjectivity" that precedes active storytelling. On the basis of Ricoeur's phenomenological analysis of the relationship between the body, self, and language in *Fallible Man*, my aim in this section is to develop the relationship between this phenomenal self in Ricoeur's early work and the hermeneutical self in Ricoeur's later work, and to formulate an answer to Zahavi's critique.

In *Fallible Man* Ricoeur's starting point for considering the human relationship to the world is the body. Also in *Freedom and Nature*, the book preceding *Fallible Man*, the body has an important role to play. In his later work,

Ricoeur does not consider embodiment extensively anymore. Yet, narrative identity is clearly embodied for him. Instead of working out his notion of the body, in *Oneself as Another* he refers to the phenomenological tradition from Maine de Biran to Husserl and Heidegger in order to explain the body (or better: the flesh) as the first passivity that constitutes the ontological basis of narrative identity (Ricoeur 1992: 321–28). The body appears as an *I can* (1992: 111–12, 323) and as a passivity, that is, as the first encounter with otherness that opens the self to other forms of otherness, such as the otherness of other people.[20] *Fallible Man* helps to understand what Ricoeur means with this notion of the body as intermediate between self and world and self and others. We have seen that in this book, Ricoeur understood the body as at once opening onto the world and as an intimacy to the self: being embodied allows me to relate to and be open to things and other people, but it also makes me realize my perspectival and affective nature. It is in realizing its perspectival nature that selfhood first comes into existence. In *Oneself as Another*, Ricoeur explains this dual aspect of embodiment in terms of the body's activity (wanting, moving, doing) as well as resistance: the body mediates between the intimacy of the self and the externality of the world (1992: 322).

The second important source for his notion of embodiment in *Oneself as Another* is Husserl's *Cartesian Meditations* (1931). Ricoeur's aim in his dialogue with Husserl is to articulate the body's "otherness." Instead of conceiving the body as primordially mine, which is central in an Husserlian account of the body, he understands the body as at once open to the world and as the self's first encounter with its perspectival nature, which leads to self-awareness and differentiation from others. He, therefore, claims that his aims are closer to Heidegger's "thrownness" than to Husserl's idealistic notion of the body (Ricoeur 1992: 326–27). Heidegger, however, did not develop an ontology of the flesh, while Husserl does. Therefore Ricoeur turns to Husserl. The main point of Ricoeur's debate with Husserl is that the body should not only be conceived of as "mine," but that it is also and at the same time a body among other bodies. While developing an ontological notion of the flesh that is primordial and makes the world accessible to us, Husserl has difficulties in thinking the body as part of the world, as objective *Körper*, he claims. Husserl has no answer to the question: "How am I to understand that *my* flesh is *also* a body?" (1992: 326, emphasis added). Here phenomenology finds its limit, Ricoeur adds. Husserl's "solution" to this problem is to make the flesh part of the world (*mondaneiser*), that is, to identify oneself with one of the things of nature, a physical body. Ricoeur claims that the body can only function as such when it is flesh *and* body, and when it is perceived in this way *both* by myself and the other (1992: 326). In other words, the body's being one among others should be considered as no less primordial than its being flesh.

Earlier, we have seen that for Zahavi narrativity cannot be the basis for intersubjectivity and the otherness of other persons, because children who are not yet capable of speech do have a sense of self, and because there is a danger of "reducing others to narratives," instead of accepting them as persons with subjective self-experience (Zahavi 2007: 199). Based on Ricoeur's analysis in *Fallible Man*, however, we can contend that it is not the case that the self "constitutes" others as having self-experience, but that it is the other way around: the self at first understands itself as part of the world, and then differentiates itself from others. The self in *Fallible Man* starts to realize that it is distinct, because of what Ricoeur calls "affective closing." Upon finding out that my affective perception of things and other people is different from yours, I not only discover that there is something incommunicable about my experiences, but also that you and I differ. It is here that self-consciousness starts and that the self differentiates itself from others. Language supports this process, but is not crucial for it, as we have seen.

Ricoeur's self is not closed-in upon itself, but ontologically open to others and otherness, as his critique of Husserl above shows. In his ontology of the narrative self in *Oneself as Another*, the body forms the first passivity that opens the self to otherness (Ricoeur 1992: 319–29). On the basis of *Fallible Man*, we now can explain that the body plays this role, because it has the twofold role of situating the self in the world and opening it to this world, while at the same time being the ground of the self's limitation. In this sense, the body intermediates between self and world, and on an ontological plane forms the self's first encounter with finitude and otherness, that opens it to the otherness of other people (the second ontological passivity).

Zahavi's other argument is that children do not yet have speaking capacities but do already have a sense of self and respond to and interact with others. Ricoeur's analysis helps in understanding children's preconceptual sense of self not as something that is given with embodiment, but as the gradual result of a process of distinguishing themselves from things and other persons.

Zahavi distinguishes the phenomenal self from the hermeneutical self and understands the first as preceding narrativity. For Ricoeur, the self is an embodied being born in a world of language. Self-reflection for him is for a large part conceptual, as his notion of narrative identity shows, but that does not mean that "self-shaping" or self-constitution is merely linguistic. On the basis of his philosophical anthropology in *Fallible Man*, we have found that it is in relation to things and other persons that the self develops self-awareness, and that language strengthens and supports this. In contrast to Zahavi, who separates narrative identity from phenomenal self-experience, on the basis of Ricoeur's philosophical anthropology we can now claim that both coincide. Ricoeur's *Fallible Man* therefore gives rise to a broader notion of narrative identity that includes phenomenal self-experience.[21]

AN INCLUSIVE NOTION OF NARRATIVE IDENTITY

The relationship between body, language, and self in *Fallible Man* offers a philosophical anthropology that supports Ricoeur's notion of narrative identity. The self in *Fallible Man* is embodied and complements its perspectival nature with the universality of language. Its self-consciousness starts from distinguishing itself from the things in the world and from others, who relate to the world differently. With this philosophical anthropology in mind, narrative identity can no longer be seen as the expressed aspect of personal identity, instead it pertains to a self that comes to understand itself in a linguistic, and therefore cultural, historical, and social context. This self can understand itself as numerically one (cf. Baker 2016), because it contains *idem*-identity, but it can also identify with various narratives about itself, because it combines *idem*- with *ipse*-identity. This self furthermore is capable of taking responsibility for its actions, because of its capacity for self-reflection and self-evaluation of its acts.[22] Important to note, at the end of this chapter, is that the narrative self does not have another identity or sense of self than this inclusive narrative one, but that it also never completely coincides with it.[23] For a person's narrative identity is open and never-ending, continuing even after death. It only stops when people stop talking about her.

NOTES

1. To mention a few: Ricoeur is an important source in Rita Charon's *Narrative Medicine* (2006); in Dan Zahavi's conception of narrative identity (2007, 2008, 2014); Galen Stawson refers to Ricoeur in his critique of narrative identity (2004).

2. Note that Ricoeur speaks of "personal identity" as narrative; "the self" for him is a fuller notion that is reflexive (1992: 1–2) and that relates narrative and ethical identity.

3. Gallagher's pattern theory does not imply that the self has multiple aspects, but rather that each pattern in itself forms a self. "The self" is thus not something that has its own independent existence, with various aspects, but he conceives of "self" as "a cluster concept which includes a sufficient number of characteristic features. Taken together, a certain pattern of characteristic features constitute an individual self" (2013).

4. Daniel Dennett (1991) is also an important voice in this debate, but his notion of narrative identity as fiction in important respects differs from Schechtman's and Ricoeur's, therefore I do not consider it in this chapter.

5. Schechtman in later work (2014) distances herself from her earlier work and considers narrative identity to be one of the aspects of her Person Life View.

6. In this chapter I consider Ricoeur's *idem*-identity to be close to Schechtman's identity as reidentification, and *ipse*-identity to be close to "characterization."

Schechtman claims that considering personal identity merely in terms of reidentification does not provide answers to the practical demands ("the four features": moral responsibility, self-interested concern, compensation, and survival, 1996: 14–15) of personal identity, and that a notion of self-characterization will do so. Ricoeur considers narrative identity a dialectics between the poles of sameness or *idem* (that what remains the same in a numerical sense, in a qualitative sense, or as continuity between the first and the last stages of its development) and *ipse*, selfhood, that he works out in terms of keeping one's promise, denying change, and holding firm (1992: 123–124).

7. In the case of "the four features" mentioned in the last endnote, we need a concern of personal identity that "includes a sense of oneself as a persisting individual whose actions cohere with one's beliefs, values, and desires (. . .) and whose current actions have implications for the future" (Schechtman 1996: 159).

8. To name only a few sources: Strawson 2004; Hutto 2007; Zahavi 2014; De Mul 2015.

9. Ricoeur and Schechtman both also refer to MacIntyre's notion of "narrative unity of a life," in *After Virtue* (1981). I will not discuss MacIntyre here, because Ricoeur and Schechtman both deviate from his notion in important respects.

10. Strawson (2004) argues that the narrative self-conception implies diachronic self-experience and claims that not all people consider themselves as such. Instead he claims that his self-experience is episodic, which implies not figuring oneself as something that was there in the past and will be there in the future.

11. The reason for doing so, for Schechtman, is that in this way, narrative self-constitution can be seen to apply to the personhood of people with dementia and to infants as well.

12. Hutto cites Christine Korsgaard's "problem of the normative" (1996) as exemplary in this respect.

13. Hutto (2016) defends a modest version of narrative self-shaping, which includes that the competence needed for making sense of ourselves and others in terms of reasons occurs through engaging in sociocultural practices that are considered as storytelling practices (Hutto 2016: 39).

14. Ricoeur uses the masculine form, but I instead use the feminine form or plural.

15. Ricoeur hereby distinguishes his philosophical anthropology from the ones popular in the 1960s, such as Sartre's: he does not consider finitude the central characteristic of human reality, and human's transcendence transcendence *of* finitude, but takes a different starting point in human's being both, perspective and discourse, demand for totality and limited nature (1986: 3).

16. From this moment onward, I will concentrate on Ricoeur and leave Schechtman's account of narrative identity behind. The reason is that Schechtman in her recent work (2014) is not concerned with narrative identity because of its linguistic characteristics, but mainly because narratives create life as a structural whole (2014: 107–109). It is not the expression of the self in language that is critical for her; she thinks that the structural unity of a person's life can also be expressed in other ways. It is not clear how to understand this "structural unity": does Schechtman aim at something similar to Zahavi's phenomenal self-experience or does she consider the self as constructing itself reflexively? I also have difficulties with the integration of her PLV

that consists of physical and psychological capacities; activities and social interactions, and the social and cultural infrastructure of personhood (2014: 112–113), but this is not the place to elaborate these problems.

17. If a ranking would need to be suggested for knowing, acting, and feeling, it would be acting that is primary for Ricoeur.

18. Note that at this stage of his intellectual trajectory, Ricoeur did not yet take "a linguistic turn." His reinterpretation of the Cartesian opposition between human's finiteness and infinity, however, already includes perceiving human's capacity for transcending because of language.

19. Note that this combination has various implications. It also includes the possibility of giving absurd significations, which has to do with the power to signify emptily, a power to speak in the absence of the this-here (28).

20. See Derksen and Halsema 2011: 212–216 for an extensive account of Ricoeur's body notion in *Oneself as Another*. Part of my analysis here is derived from this chapter.

21. An important objection against narrative identity that should be dealt with is that it presumes the capacity for speech. Also in *Fallible Man* Ricoeur understands humans as speaking beings. Does this imply that children and demented persons do not have a sense of self? In *Oneself as Another*, Ricoeur includes the stories of others about the self, and therewith extends the notion of narrative identity to the narratives of others about the self. However, self-experience in the sense of having the capacity to reflect upon oneself *as self* is not present in children and people with dementia. This does not imply that they do not have first-person experience, but it does mean that they do not have the capacity to refer to it as "self."

22. Persons who are not capable of self-reflection as a consequence cannot be held responsible for their actions in the same way as persons who can. Children and demented people do have a sense of self, which can be understood as narrative in the sense of *idem*-identity, but because of their limited capabilities to reflect upon their actions, they cannot be held fully accountable for them.

23. Ricoeur carefully distinguishes life from narrative (see Ricoeur 1991a, 1992: 159–163).

REFERENCES

Atkins, Kim. 2004. Narrative Identity, Practical Identity and Ethical Subjectivity. *Continental Philosophy Review* 37: 341–366.

Baker, Lynne Rudder. 2016. Making Sense of Ourselves: Self-narratives and Personal Identity. *Phenomenology and the Cognitive Sciences* 15 (1): 7–15.

Charon, Rita. 2006. *Narrative Medicine. Honoring the Stories of Illness*. Oxford University Press.

Dennett, Daniel. 1991. *Consciousness Explained*. Back Bay Books.

Derksen, Louise D. and Annemie Halsema. 2011. Understanding the Body. The Relevance of Gadamer's and Ricoeur's View of the Body for Feminist Theory. In *Gadamer and Ricoeur. Critical Horizons for Contemporary Hermeneutics*. Eds. Francis J. Mootz III and George H. Taylor. Continuum: 203–225.

Gallagher, Sean. 2013. A Pattern Theory of the Self. *Frontiers in Human Neuroscience* 7: 443.
Halsema, Annemie and Jenny Slatman. 2017. The Second-Person Perspective in Narrative Phenomenology. In *Feminist Phenomenology Futures*. Eds. Helen A. Fielding and Dorothea E. Olkowski. Indiana University Press: 242–256.
Husserl, Edmund. 1931. *Cartesianische Meditationen*. Elisabeth Ströker (Hrsg.), Felix Meiner Verlag, 1995.
Hutto, Dan. 2007. *Narrative and Understanding Persons*. Cambridge University Press.
———. 2016. Narrative Self-shaping: A Modest Proposal. *Phenomenology and the Cognitive Sciences* 15: 21–41.
Korsgaard, Christine M. 1996. *The Sources of Normativity*. Ed. Onora O'Neill. Cambridge University Press.
Kyselo, Miriam. 2014. The Body Social: An Enactive Approach to the Self. *Frontiers in Psychology* 5: 1–16.
MacIntyre, Alisdair. 1981. *After Virtue*. University of Notre Dame Press.
Mul, Jos de. 2015. The Game of Life: Narrative and Ludic Identity Formation in Computer Games. In *Representations of Internarrative Identity*. Ed. L. Way. Palgrave Macmillan: 251–266.
Ricoeur, Paul. 1978. From Existentialism to the Philosophy of Language. In *The Philosophy of Paul Ricoeur: An Anthology of His Work*. Eds. Charles E. Reagan and David Stewart. Beacon Press: 20–35.
———. 1984. *Time and Narrative*. Vol. I. Trans. Kathleen Blamey and David Pellauer. University of Chicago Press.
———. 1986. *Fallible Man*. Revised trans. Charles A. Kelbley. Fordham University Press.
———. 1991a. Life in Quest of Narrative. In *On Paul Ricoeur: Narrative and Interpretation*. Ed. David Wood. Routledge: 20–33.
———. 1991b. Narrative Identity. In *On Paul Ricoeur: Narrative and Interpretation*. Ed. David Wood. Routledge: 188–199.
———. 1992. *Oneself as Another*. Trans. Kathleen Blamey. Chicago University Press.
———. 1995. Intellectual Autobiography. In *The Philosophy of Paul Ricoeur*. Ed. Lewis Edwin Hahn. Open Court, 3–53.
———. 2007a. *Freedom and Nature*. Trans. Erazim V. Kohák. Northwestern University Press.
———. 2007b. *Reflections on the Just*. Trans. David Pellauer. University of Chicago Press.
Schaafsma, Petruschka. 2014. Philosophical Anthropology against Objectification. Reconsidering Ricoeur's *Fallible Man*. *International Journal of Philosophy and Theology* 75 (2): 152–168.
Schechtman, Marya. 1996. *The Constitution of Selves*. Cornell University Press.
———. 2007. Stories, Lives, and Basic Survival: A Refinement and Defense of the Narrative View. *Royal Institute of Philosophy Supplement* 60: 155–178.
———. 2014. *Staying Alive. Personal Identity, Practical Concerns, and the Unity of a Life*. Cambridge University Press.

Strawson, Galen. 2004. Against Narrativity. *Ratio* XVII: 428–452.
Zahavi, Dan. 2007. Self and Other: The Limits of Narrative Understanding. In *Narrative and Understanding Persons*. Ed. Dan Hutto. Cambridge University Press: 179–201.
———. 2008. *Subjectivity and Selfhood. Investigating the First-Person Perspective*. MIT Press.
———. 2014. *Self & Other. Exploring Subjectivity, Empathy, and Shame*. Oxford University Press.

Chapter 8

From Fallibility to Fragility

How the Theory of Narrative Transformed the Notion of Character of Fallible Man

Pol Vandevelde

Even those who are familiar with Ricoeur's work may wonder how the notion of character, which was approached in the psychological sense of personal traits in *Fallible Man*, could be transformed into that of a "narrative character" in his later works, such that "life" could be spoken of as being "in search of narratives" (Ricoeur 1991b) or that "the narrative category of character" could "contribute . . . to the discussion of personal identity" (1992: 143; 1960a: 170). This is what I want to examine in this chapter.

Tracing the transformation that took place between Ricoeur's early work, *Fallible Man* and his later works, such as *Oneself as Another*, has two hermeneutic advantages. Prospectively, it shows that the transformation from the phenomenological and psychological notion of character in *Fallible Man* to the narrativist account in his later works resorbs the tensions that Ricoeur only names in *Fallible Man*—what he calls the "disproportion" between the finitude of human beings (as manifested by their character) and their aspiration to infinity or "happiness." Retrospectively, tracing this transformation, first, accounts for the fact that, despite the changes, there is a consistency to Ricoeur's position and, second, shows how radical the theory of narratives is when it comes to the notion of character: by giving precedence to the "who" question of those who give the account over the question of "what" an individual is, precedence is given to ethics over ontology. I will draw out these two hermeneutic advantages in two sections. First I will examine the notion of character in *Fallible Man,* and second I will examine how the theory of narrative transforms this notion.

THE ONTOLOGY OF "DISPROPORTION" IN *FALLIBLE MAN*

The "philosophy of the will" addresses a theme that remains constant in Ricoeur's thought, up to one of his last works, *Memory, History, Forgetting* (2000; 2004a): the tensions in human life and human activities. In *Fallible Man* he borrows Pascal's notion of "disproportion" to name these tensions (between our finitude and the infinity of our aspirations). In *Time and Narrative* he calls it a "heterogeneity" (as the diversity of facts and events happening in the past or in our life). In *Oneself as Another* he speaks of a "passivity" of the self (as body, conscience, and other people). Throughout Ricoeur's work, these tensions do not stand outside human reach, as if they were forces oppressing human beings and shaping their existence outside their consciousness. Already in *Freedom and Nature,* despite the fact that the will cannot recover what makes it possible, the involuntary was not an autonomous force beyond the reach of the will. The same is true in *Fallible Man,* where a disproportion is only such from the perspective of a "synthesis," and in *Oneself as Another*, where there is passivity only from the perspective of an "activity." That is to say that the involuntary, disproportion, and passivity are discovered by the subject and thus recovered as an other in the subject, as an alterity that preceded the subject, and as having an efficacy that needs the subject to take its force.

In *Fallible Man* Ricoeur uses Cartesian terms and speaks of "the Cartesian paradox of the finite-infinite human being" (1960a: 22; 1986a: 4; trans. mod.). Everything human is of a finite sort and yet human beings have aspirations or strivings for something that transcends their finitude. This "disproportion" is the experience of an excess, of that which transcends their limitations. They experience a "noncoincidence" with themselves (1960a: 21; 1986a: 4).

As with *Freedom and Nature*, where the "*in*voluntary" is what challenges or unsettles the voluntary, likewise in *Fallible Man* Ricoeur presents the noncoincidence with oneself in negative terms. As the title of the book makes clear, fallibility is intrinsic to the constitution of human beings who are characterized negatively as capable of failing.[1] This negative dimension of the disproportion at the ontological level calls for a "restoration" of unity in the form of reconciliation, which Ricoeur calls a "synthesis." As he writes in *Freedom and Nature*, "the theory of the voluntary and the involuntary not only describes and understands, but also restores" (1950: 21; 1966: 18).

The "synthesis" that can resorb the disproportion is what is problematic in Ricoeur's view and what, I argue, motivates him to abandon his "psychological" views in *Fallible Man* and take a narrative turn in his later work. As I will show, the synthesis cannot work for structural reasons because it is performed by the subject—what Ricoeur calls the "cogito"—and it will have to take place at the level of consciousness and thus in the form of a judgment. Yet, the synthesis "synthesizes" precisely that which allegedly cannot be subsumed under a judgment—the involuntary or fallibility. As we will see, the theory of narrative displaces the experience of disproportion from the ontological structure of the human being and shifts it to the ethical stance they take. Let us see the way in which fallibility manifests this tension that needs reconciliation.

By fallibility, Ricoeur means the ontological possibility of falling and doing evil, of having a "bad will." It is part of the human condition to have the "capacity [*pouvoir*] of failing" (1960a: 161; 1986a: 223, trans. mod.), to be "capable of failing" (1960a: 161; 1986a: 223), or to "'find oneself' exposed to failure [*se "trouve exposé" à faillir*]" (1960a: 21; 1986a: 4, trans. mod.). Through this capacity to fail moral evil is possible: "What do we mean when we call human beings fallible? Essentially this: that the *possibility* of moral evil is inscribed in their constitution" (1960a: 149; 1986a: 204; trans. mod.).[2] *Fallible Man* thus complements the phenomenology of the will of *Freedom and Nature*—an eidetics of the will—and represents for Ricoeur an "outline of philosophical anthropology" (1960a: 11; 1986a: xix)—in the form of an "empirics" of the will.

Ricoeur examines three forms of the disproportion that is constitutive of human beings, thus three forms of their "noncoincidence" with themselves with regard to knowledge at the theoretical level, action at the practical level, and feeling at the affective level. These three "disproportions" also represent three levels of human "fragility" in the sense that they are fallible in each of these three domains: theoretical, practical, and affective. For each disproportion there is a corresponding "synthesis." At the first level of knowledge, the disproportion is between reason and sensibility, to the extent that we have a finite perspective on objects and yet claim objectivity. Ricoeur sees Kant's notion of transcendental imagination as performing a "synthesis" of the finite perspective in order to provide objectivity. At the second level of action, there is a disproportion between character and happiness to the extent that my character gives me my limited situation and my dispositions but I strive for happiness as the completion of all my limited strivings. The "practical synthesis," which Ricoeur borrows from Kant again, is performed by the respect for persons, as that which mediates my character and my striving for happiness. At the third level of feeling there is a disproportion between my desires that bind me to the organic aspect of life—*bios*—and those that lead me to pursue the *logos* and strive for being rational. The affective synthesis mediating desires and aspirations is performed by "feeling" or "heart" (Plato's *thumos*). I will not discuss the first and third disproportions here, but instead will focus on the second, practical one, involving character.

Character as a Set of Psychological Traits

Against the Sartrean position, Ricoeur maintains that freedom is not absolute, but rather it is "lived" at the practical level through my character, which represents "the finite manner of freedom" (1960a: 77; 1986a: 93).[3] My psychological dispositions and inclinations determine my way of being situated in the world and my limited projects and goals determine how I envisage my place in it. Yet, I aspire to happiness, which would be the fulfillment of my aspirations. Such is the disproportion between my character and happiness. Character is described in terms of that which limits human beings. As "the finite openness of my existence taken as a whole" (1960a: 75; 1986: 89), character is on the side of "finitude" (1960a: 85; 1986: 103) or "contingency" (1960a: 155; 1986a: 212). Ricoeur qualifies this finite and contingent way of being as a "narrowness": "Character is nothing but the narrowness of my access to all values of all human beings across all cultures" (1960a: 87; 1986a: 108, trans. modi.). While on the side of contingency, character is not fate in the strong sense of a force "which governs me from the outside" (1960a: 78; 1986a: 94, trans. mod.) but it is fate "in a certain way," as Ricoeur says, and in two respects: "as unalterable [*immutable*]" and as "received, as inherited" (1960a: 78–79; 1986a: 94).

Character is "unalterable" or "immutable" in the sense that it is not subjected to the will as what, for example, I can choose to have. Rather, it is "the radically non-chosen origin of all my choices" (1960a: 79; 1986a: 95). Besides being unalterable, it is also "inherited" as that which I received at birth and gave me my situation in the world. In other words, it is the facticity of my existence in the chronological and existential sense. Chronologically, my birth is "the already-there [*le déjà là*] of my character" (1960a: 80; 1986a: 96, trans. mod.) to the extent that my birth gives my character a precedence over my will. Existentially, my birth is "nothing other than my character" (1960a: 80; 1986a: 96). Yet, because this character was mine from the start and made me the subject I am, character is both donation (as gift) and empowerment (as taking as my own). It is a "gift [*donation*] which makes me heir to my own life [*héritier de ma propre vie*]" (1960a: 80; 1986a: 97) in the sense that it is from the retrospective move of taking it as my own—in the position of heir—that the gift is such. In Ricoeur's words, "the fate of character and heredity discloses its meaning: it is the given, factual narrowness of my free openness to the totality of the possibilities of the being-human [*l'être-homme*]" (1960a: 81; 1986a: 98).

To the finitude (narrowness, contingence) of character, Ricoeur opposes the infinite counterpart of happiness, which is the totality of the aspirations we have. He takes from Aristotle the view that the good is that toward which all things, actions, and choices strive. Ricoeur then adds to this Aristotelian notion the Kantian sense of a "totality": all these goods toward which we strive are subsumed under happiness.[4]

In the first disproportion at the theoretical level, the notion of totality was applied to the objectivity to which knowledge aspires. The transcendental claim to knowledge (in a Kantian sense) goes beyond the limited perspectives we can ever have on an object (e.g., in perception) and presents a form of totality of perspectives as the objectivity of knowledge. In a similar way, Ricoeur argues that at the practical level of action, regardless of the fact that we are situated and disposed in specific ways by our character, "we are 'directed toward' happiness" as the totality of sense and contentment. "Happiness . . . must be to the totality of human aims what the world is to the aims of perception. Just as the world is the horizon of *the thing*, happiness is the horizon in all respects" (1960a: 82; 1986a: 100, trans. mod.). Ricoeur characterizes happiness as "the excess of meaning, the overflow [*le trop*], the immense" (1960a: 86; 1986a: 105) or as a "feeling of the 'immense.'" Through excess, "the horizon is clear, unlimited possibilities open up before me" (1960a: 85; 1986a: 104).

Because of the excess of happiness or disproportion between happiness and character, a "mediation" analogous to Kant's transcendental imagination at the theoretical level is needed. Just as the transcendental imagination mediates sensibility and reason in a way that allows for the finite perspective of the knower to be transcended into objective knowledge, Ricoeur claims that Kant's notion of "respect" is the practical mediation between character, as what is specific to me, and happiness, which opens me to the whole of humanity (1960a: 67; 1986a: 77).

With regard to this notion of respect, I will only point out the role of "synthesis" that Ricoeur ascribes to it and I will programmatically raise the question of where the synthesis is exercised. Ricoeur does not really answer this question in *Fallible Man* other than by appealing to the Kantian "ideal" of the person, which Ricoeur calls "humanity." Using this ideal, Ricoeur considers an individual to be one instantiation of humanity and as such a person worthy of "respect." In this way, the person as representative of humanity is precisely "a synthesis of happiness and character" (1960a: 86; 1986a: 105). However, this only names the problem of reconciling finite perspectives and infinite totality. It does not solve it. Ricoeur tells us that the "disproportion" between that which anchors me in a finite perspective (my character) and that which attracts me to go beyond my own finitude (happiness) is not external to me, but "inhabits the human will" (1960a: 84; 1986a: 103, trans. mod.). Yet, he can only describe the effect of disproportion: it distends or tears apart— "in themselves and for themselves, human beings remain torn" (1960a: 157; 1986a: 216, trans. mod.). The synthesis is just the suffering of the discord.

The theory of narrative that he develops later in *Time and Narrative* (1983; 1984) and *Oneself as Another* offers a more convincing "synthesis."

FROM THE PSYCHOLOGY OF CHARACTER TO THE CHARACTER IN A NARRATIVE

The English word "character," in its dual meaning as psychological and narrativist, is fitting for characterizing Ricoeur's narrative turn away from the psychological consideration of character in *Fallible Man*—*caractère* in French—toward a narrativist approach in which the self becomes a character in a plot—*un personnage* in French. Ricoeur came to realize that the self comes to a self-understanding through narratives and thus by being embedded in plots. "Understood in narrative terms, identity can be called, by linguistic convention, the identity of the character [*personnage*] . . . the identity of the character is constructed in connection with that of the plot" (1990: 168; 1992: 141).

This narrative turn has three major consequences. First, it causes the transformation of brute experiences, actions, and events into "sense" or "meaning"; second, it dissociates fallibility (or guilt) from fragility, an association that was central in *Fallible Man*; and, third, it inverts the relation between ontology and ethics. While in *Fallible Man* ethics presupposed an "ontology of disproportion," "ethics" takes precedence over any ontology of the self in *Oneself as Another*.

Narrative Transformation of Brute Reality into Sense

Fallible Man was an exercise in philosophical anthropology, focusing on that which a human being is (essentially *"faillible"*). Later on, Ricoeur came to see that, because human beings manifest themselves through what they do, action, for example, is not only where human beings can fail, but it is also where they manifest who they are. Action thus reveals the field in which the human "essence" unfolds, as it were, and thereby decenters whatever essence a human being may have by exporting it to the public realm of interactions with others. Action thus exposes who we are as human beings but not as a secondary moment originating from a preexisting self. Rather, the decentering of the human beings through what they do means that they are not just an internal structure made of voluntary and involuntary or a disproportion, but, more fundamentally, they are a connection between "what" they do and "who" they are.

With this externalization, a new tension arises between the action and its meaning. The meaning escapes agents because the action can be interpreted by others or by agents themselves at a later time, and the meaning includes the consequences of the action, which may not have been intended or anticipated. "The meaning of action separates itself from the event of acting [*la signification de l'action se détache de l'événement de l'action*]" (1986: 191). This new tension cannot be resorbed by a "synthesis" that would take place in existence in the static and psychological sense as in *Fallible Man* (through respect, for example). The synthesis is itself a task to be accomplished or a "work" to be done, one that is of a narrative nature. The narrative will perform the synthesis.

This narrative performance of a synthesis involves a combination of first-person and third-person perspectives, and consequently a combination of the two temporalities pertaining to these perspectives. On the one hand, the narrative is *post factum* as a retrospective look, which synthesizes by giving actions, experiences, or events a representation in the form of a story told "of" those actions, experiences, or events. This preposition "of" does not name a relation of mirror image, copy, or duplication but a transformation from the order of physical movements into meaning. Narratives give the "meaning" of the action, experience, or event. On the other hand, this movement of articulation by a narrative inserts the voice of the narrator (e.g., historians) into the "reality" of what is recounted. Historical narratives, for example, bring what took place back into a narrative presence but the meaning of the past is "for" historians. The narrative voice is thus a conflation of the temporality of the third-person and first-person perspectives. Let us see how this works.

A narrative provides a "synthesis of the heterogeneous" or a "discordant concordance," in which either self, actions, or events are brought to a form of unity. By "synthesis of the heterogenous," Ricoeur explains, "I am attempting to account for the diverse mediations performed by the plot: between the manifold of events and the temporal unity of the story recounted; between the disparate components of the action—intentions, causes, and chance occurrences—and the sequence of the story; and finally, between pure succession and the unity of the temporal form" (1992: 141). At the level of action, for example, an agent is not a self-contained subject. When acting we also "read," literally, what others are doing or going to do, and we ourselves follow some basic scripts, whether we are aware of them or not, so that our goals and movements are intelligible. Think of how harmonious the behavior of people in a restaurant is, roughly, abiding by some scenarios belonging to this kind of environment, which would be very different in a church or lecture hall. As Ricoeur shows, action has a "semantics," a "symbolics," and a temporal structure.

The semantics of action is what transforms a set of gestures and movements into a "meaningful" whole that is recognizable as an action. Whenever we change jobs, for example, we have to become familiar with the way other people work and what they expect us to do. We need to learn the implicit conceptual network that gives interactions their meaning, or their "semantics." As Ricoeur writes, "our familiarity with the conceptual network of human acting is of the same order as the familiarity we have with the plots of stories that are known to us" (1991b: 28). There is also a "symbolics" of action. In Ricoeur's example, raising one's arm is used symbolically by a person to draw attention, raise a question, stop a taxi, or vote, depending on the context. "Symbols are the internal interpreters of action" (1991b: 29). This holds true not just for observers who will find a "readability" to action (1991b: 29) but also for agents, who can then act "meaningfully." Action also has a temporal structure and temporal features—beginning, end, transition between the two—that give it a "pre-narrative quality" (1991b: 29) so that we can connect gestures and movements in a specific sequence of what becomes an "accident" of two people bumping into each other, or an "attack," or a "reunion."

Because of the semantic, symbolic, and temporal structure of action, there is a "connaturality" between the narrative of action and the action itself. By making explicit the "network" already inherent in action (its goal, circumstances, and protagonists), the narrative neither does violence to the "texture" of action nor is redundant of the action but gives its "meaning." It is thus no exaggeration to say that action is a "quasi-text" (1991b: 29) or a "potential story" (1986: 142). One can even say of one's life that it is "a story in its nascent state," or that it is "in search of a narrative" (1991b: 29).[5]

As a result of this narrativization, experiences and actions are no longer merely products of a subject—a *cogito*, as Ricoeur calls it in the *Philosophy of the Will*. Rather, they are also a public manifestation of a person's character, of "who" that person is. Because my character in the psychological sense is manifested in my deeds and actions, it is also manifested as the character in the narratives I and others tell of myself. This conflation of character in terms of psychological traits and character as the narrativist protagonist in actions and events gives me a readability so that people will decipher me in my deeds and actions—from a third-person perspective—and say that I "remained true" to myself or that I did something "out of character." This readability represents the constancy I have despite the variations at the level of sameness as identity (*idem*) in age, appearance, and activities. In this sense, character becomes for Ricoeur one model of "permanence in time" (besides keeping one's word) (1992: 118). This permanence in time is not merely what others say about me but lies in part in my own hands through my ability to account for myself—from a first-person perspective—so that "the permanence of character expresses the almost complete mutual overlapping of the problematic of *idem* and *ipse*" (1992: 118). Narratives thus serve as a mediation between the third-person and first-person perspectives or, as Ricoeur puts it, "between the pole of character, where *idem* and *ipse* tend to coincide, and the pole of self-maintenance, where selfhood frees itself from sameness" (1992: 118–19).

Ricoeur describes this mediation as the fact that "character has a history," which it "contracted" "in the twofold sense of the word 'contraction': abbreviation and affection. It is then comprehensible that the stable pole of character can contain a narrative dimension, as we see in the uses of the term 'character' identifying it with the protagonist in a story. What sedimentation has contracted, narration can redeploy" (1992: 122). That which sedimentation has contracted is a "what": the subjects as narrated from a third-person perspective (by themselves and others). Narration can re-deploy a "who" in the sense that subjects can be narrators of their own experiences and actions from their first-person perspective or readers of narratives involving them, and usually both. "The subject then appears both as a reader and the writer [*scripteur*] of its own life, as Proust would have it. As the literary analysis of autobiography confirms, the story of a life continues to be refigured by all the truthful or fictive stories a subject tells about himself or herself. This refiguration makes this life itself a cloth woven of stories told" (1988: 246).

In other words, our self-understanding is itself narrative-like in the sense that we understand ourselves through the narratives we have read.[6] This combination of first-person and third-person perspectives explains that permanence in time, which we have through our character, is itself a narrative work of self-understanding and, as such, evolving. This is quite different from *Freedom and Nature* where Ricoeur had placed character under the "absolute involuntary," along with the unconscious and life. At that time, as Ricoeur says retrospectively, character belonged "to that level of our existence which we cannot change but to which we must consent" (1992: 119). In *Fallible Man*, as we saw, character is also immutable and inherited. But this is precisely what Ricoeur rejects in *Oneself as Another*:

> Instead of conceiving of character, in the framework of perspective and of opening, as the finite pole of existence [in *Fallible Man*], I am interpreting it here in terms of its place in the problematic of identity. This shift of emphasis has as its principal advantage the fact of putting into question the immutable status of character, taken for granted in the earlier analyses . . . Character, I would say today, designates the set of lasting dispositions by which a person is recognized. (1992: 120–21)[7]

Narrativization accounts for the way in which we can be the co-authors of our own lives on the model of Aristotle's notion of *sunaition* as a co-cause (1992: 160). We cannot be the sole author because we do not have a direct or intuitive access to our self. Rather, the self is manifested in the heterogeneous (facts, events, and so forth, which we cannot change). Yet, we are not merely a story because we perform the synthesis of the heterogeneous and thereby bring concordance to what is discordant. As Ricoeur says, "we learn to become the *narrator* and the hero *of our own story,* without actually becoming the *author of our own life*" (1991b: 32). This is how narrativization reconciles the third-person perspective (from which we are a character in the narratives told about ourselves) and the first-person perspective (from which we are the author of those narratives).

What was an "ontology of disproportion" in *Freedom and Nature* in the sense of a noncoincidence of human beings with themselves, which they "suffer," becomes a narrative task for human beings of making this "discordance" "concordant," and this means narrating it as a synthesis of the heterogenous both on the side of experiences (actions and events) and on the side of selfhood. "Gathering all these factors into a single story makes the plot a totality which can be said to be at once concordant and discordant (this is why I shall speak of discordant concordance or of concordant discordance)" (1991b: 21).

The narrative transformation of, first, actions into meanings and, second, character in the psychological sense into both a protagonist in actions or events and the author of narratives conflates the "what" we are with the "who" we are, so that "character is truly the 'what' of the 'who'" (1992: 122). Because the question of "who" we are always involves our first-person perspective, this question cannot only pertain to a philosophical anthropology as in *Fallible Man*. This brings us to the second consequence of the narrative turn, for example, that there cannot be a strictly third-person perspective from which fallibility can be said to be "constitutive" of human beings.

Narrative Transformation of Fallibility into Fragility

We saw in the previous section that the "'disproportion' of self to self" was understood negatively in *Fallible Man* as a "primordial discord" (1960a: 148; 1986: 202) or as "the *ratio* of fallibility" (1960a: 21; 1986: 4). Ricoeur speaks alternatively of fallibility and fragility, and seems to equate them most of the time as the susceptibility or inclination to have a bad will or doing evil.[8] In his "Intellectual Autobiography" (1995) he criticizes this unilaterality in *Fallible Man* and recognizes the need to differentiate fallibility (or guilt) and fragility (or vulnerability).

> I had to work out the ontology of finite will implicit in the dialectic of acting and suffering. To this ontology, I gave the very Pascalian name of an ontology of disproportion. Human frailty, our vulnerability to moral evil, would be nothing other than a constitutive disproportion between a pole of the infinite and a pole of the finite. To my mind, the most original feature of this meditation was not so much the idea of disproportion as the character of frailty attaching to the mediations interspersed between the opposing roles. (1995: 15)

The significant difference between fallibility and fragility (or vulnerability), in my view, lies in the focus of the approach. Fallibility is what a static third-person approach finds in describing human beings by "faulting" them, literally, for what they lack. Fragility (or vulnerability) is what a dynamic approach finds in accounting for the first-person perspective of what human beings live and experience. In other words, once the manifestation of human existence is seen as belonging to existence itself, once "being" is extended to "acting and suffering among others," the "what"-question—"what are human beings?"—cannot be separated from the "who"-question—"Who am I in my deeds and actions?" The recognition that human beings manifest themselves in what they do brings the negative side of a "capacity to fail" back into a positive condition of being fragile and vulnerable. As a consequence, the "disproportion" can no longer be just a fact that is "constitutive" of being human, that is, an ontological fact or a facticity and, accordingly, our vulnerability can no longer be a *factum* as fallibility. Rather, this fragility and vulnerability lie in the fact that we are not the masters of the meaning of what is experienced and done but are open and exposed to being narrated, embedded in plots, or, alternatively, unable to bring to concordance what happened to us.

What provides the positive aspect of fragility and vulnerability is the narrative voice of the first-person perspective. It is no longer facts and events that confront us but their sense or meaning (this was the first transformation operated by the narrative turn). Rather, actions and events are looked at retrospectively, and in this retrospective look a voice is also lent to those actions and events. For example, the "past," which in one sense "was" before me, is such only because I give it a voice. Once I tell a narrative about myself, I am split. We already mentioned the split between author and character. The new split here is between the present of the performance of telling the story and the past of what is narrated—for example, my past. The narrative voice integrates these two dimensions of temporality into one: the present of the narration. It may be that actions were performed in the past, but it is in the present of the narration that the past of those actions gains its meaning.

While the "voice" comes *after* the experiences, facts, or events, and is mine, I lent this voice to those experiences, facts, and events so that they gain presence.[9] The present of my voice is also a gift to the past, offering it retrospectively a new present. The narrative voice is the very manifestation of my fragility, precisely because through my narratives I recognize the antecedent voice of what escapes my power—in the form of past experiences, facts, and events. Thus "the narrative voice," Ricoeur says, "is neither that of memory nor that of historiography," which would be from a third-person perspective, "but that which results from the relation of the posteriority of the narrative voice in relation to the story it tells" (1985a: 98–99), that is from a first-person perspective. The presence of my voice in giving a present to what happened means that narratives have an ethical valence because they include the existential attitude of those who give the narratives and this attitude is one of response. If historians give us new accounts it is because, in some sense, they "respond" to that which called upon them to be told. This leads to the third transformation caused by the theory of narrative.

Narrative Transformation of Ontology into Ethics

The anthropology of human beings in *Fallible Man* could start with a traditional ontology of substance even if it were amended to include the "involuntary," as that which challenges the will from within, or if it were amended to include the possibility for the will to become "bad will." People are ontologically—in their "constitution"—fallible. They are first and foremost those who have "missed the mark" (1960a: 159; 1986a: 218), as Ricoeur evocatively says. This expression "missing the mark" is what the Greek term *hamartia* means, as a term of archery. It is a "mistake," but the term was used to name the terrible "mistake" at the heart of a tragedy, such as Oedipus's deed. It was then used later in the Gospels to name that which has been translated as "sin" in English.[10] The "mistake" in question is thus not merely of a psychological order but an ontological disorder or a tear in the fabric of the world. Such was Ricoeur's starting point in *Fallible Man* where human beings are fallen, "bewildered and lost," and have "forgotten the origin" (1960a: 159; 1986a: 219). In such a world, Ricoeur ominously said, "ethics arrives too late" (1960a: 159; 1986a: 219).

Once narrative transforms subjects into characters, narrators, or interpreters, the relation of priority between ontology and ethics shifts. As we have seen, reality (actions, events, self) has been transformed into meaning so that agents (or subjects in general) have the role of interpreters of actions, events, and their own life. Because we cannot go back to what "really" happened and confront reality "face to face," as it were, experiences, actions, or events receive their ontological weight retrospectively: through their "readability" or "interpretability" and thus from their presentations and descriptions in narratives.

This readability of action has a liberating effect against the brutality of actions or events in the sense that they can be recounted—"presented," "described," that is, "narrated"—in different ways. As Ricoeur notes, "it is always possible . . . to narrate differently" (2004b: 157; 2004c: 104). The "sense" or "meaning" can be modified or changed. This is what allows Ricoeur to say in *Memory, History, Forgetting* that, despite the brutality of events in the past, there remains the possibility of a "happy memory." Yet, besides the liberating effect of a transformation into meaning, there is the correlative danger of narrative idealism, which would de-realize actions and events, and merely dramatize them. Ricoeur is keenly aware of this danger of heterogeneity between the sense or meaning of the action or the event, on one side, and its "reality," on the other. "If the 'sense-content' is what makes possible the 'inscription' of the action-event [*l'événemnt d'action*], what makes it real? In other words, what corresponds to writing in the field of action?" (1986: 193; 1991c: 152). We need a guarantee that the narrative is truth-telling and not a fabrication.

Narratives have two valences, one with regard to their object and one with regard to their author. In their first valence, narratives claim to render the articulation and thus the meaning of the action itself so that narratives reach a level of "representation" that can claim to be a re-presentation of the action itself. This is what historians do. Although they tell us stories, these stories are "true" and any competitor to a historical narrative will be another historical narrative. The second valence of narratives is on the side of their authors. The guarantee that narratives are "of" experiences, actions, and events, and not merely fabricated, lies in the existential attitude of those who provide the narrative. This existential attitude keeps the meaning connected to the actions or events recounted and avoids a narrative idealism that would dispense with the "reality" of what "really happened."

Ricoeur has described this existential attitude of those who give the narratives in two ways. The first one is a "debt" that we have to "render" what took place because the past or what happened is demanding to be recounted. Historians, Ricoeur says, "are all moved by the desire to do justice to the past" because they as well as their readers have "an unpaid debt" (1985b: 273; 1988: 152). Ricoeur acknowledges that this notion of debt is "strange" but he finds it implied in the expression used by historians and painters: "They seek to 'render' something, a landscape or a course of events. In this term 'to render,' I see the desire to 'render its due' to what is and to what once was" (1985b: 273; 1988: 152). The debt that is felt results from a duty to respond to a call coming from what asked to be narrated. "We tell stories because in the last analysis human lives need and merit being narrated. This remark takes on its full force when we refer to the necessity to save the history of the defeated and the lost. The whole history of suffering cries out for vengeance and calls for narrative [*appelle récit*]" (1983: 143; 1984: 75). This makes historians "insolvent debtors" (1985b: 253; 1988: 143).

The second way Ricoeur describes the existential attitude of those who give narratives is attestation. He applied this notion first to the self. Attestation is linked to the "I can" and is a confirmation or an endorsement of this "being capable": "Attestation is the sort of confidence or assurance (nondoxic epistemological status) that each of us has of existing (ontological status) on the mode of self (phenomenological status)" (1991a: 382. My translation).[11]

In *Memory, History, Forgetting* Ricoeur extends the notion of attestation to that which I am capable of and connects it to the narratives historians give. By giving a narrative, historians "attest" to their own ethical stance. The belief *in* historians—the trust we have in them—redoubles the truth of the statement—we believe *that* their historical narratives are true.[12] Attestation is thus productive of truth at two levels and at the same time. As endorsing my own capability it is an "alethic mode" (*mode aléthique* [*ou véritatif*])—here I am, as a truth-teller—and as accompanying my statements it is an "epistemic mode of assertions" (2004b: 140; 2004c: 91) that makes the historical account an "attestation to reality" (*attestation de réalité*) (2000: 363; 2004a: 278).

Far from being extrinsic to the narrative, the existential attitude of historians belongs to the narrative "voice" that retrospectively gives an ontological status to what is recounted, and it can perform this remarkable feat through the voice's credence and, thus, through its ethical status. By presenting a narrative of what took place, authors, such as historians, attest to their moral status as truthful and trustworthy storytellers. Ethics, which arrived too late according to *Fallible Man*, becomes prominent after the narrative turn insofar as ethics gives narratives their valence as "true representations" of what has taken place.

The different transformations performed by the theory of narrative (of reality into meaning, fallibility into fragility, ontology into ethics) find a remarkable outcome in making it possible for memory—for example, the memory of a horrific past—to become a "happy memory." This is the title of the "Epilogue" of *Memory, History, Forgetting*. I cannot discuss this here except to point out the extent to which the notion of happiness from *Fallible Man* has also changed along with that of character. In the early work, happiness is a "disproportion" at the practical level as the totality that regulates (in a Kantian sense) the way in which an individual, with limited access to the world (through character), is a person open to humanity (with its aims and possibilities). Happiness was not a feeling. It belonged to a transcendental framework as an ideal although it was an ideal that kept human beings "torn" and in "discord." By contrast, in *Memory, History, Forgetting,* happiness is no longer the opposite pole of character but, in fact, the success of the narrative work once we have accepted, first, that the past matters in the meaning it has for the present—this is what the narrative voice accomplishes; second, that our psychological traits are manifested and presented in narratives so that we are, even as historians, protagonists in our narratives; and, third, that any ontology depends on our ethical attitude.

Ricoeur himself draws an analogy between *Memory, History, Forgetting* and *Freedom and Nature* with regard to the treatment of guilt. His last work is a phenomenology of memory in the same way that his first major work, *Freedom and Nature*, was a phenomenology of the will. In both works, the question of guilt or fault had to be provisionally bracketed. Just as *Fallible Man* examined this question of guilt that had been "bracketed" in *Freedom and Nature*, likewise the "Epilogue" to *Memory, History, Forgetting* is about guilt, which had been bracketed in the main part of the work. Guilt is approached in the "epilogue" from the perspective of its cleansing or "forgetting," which is forgiveness. Forgiveness is not a forgetting of what happened, but rather a transformation of the sense or meaning of what happened, especially with regard to victims and perpetrators. This transformation through forgetting and forgiveness is precisely what narratives can do. Of necessity, narratives are selective, and of necessity other ways of narrating the "same" event are possible. This possibility of re-articulating painful events, of bringing into discussions different perspectives does not delete what happened but provides a broader readability of what happened. This broader readability can bring past enemies or descendants of perpetrators into the discussion. If forgiveness can play a role in history—Ricoeur is ambivalent about it—it would not be merely a private psychological event that might allow victims and perpetrators (or their descendants) to move on. In Ricoeur's narrative framework, forgiveness has the power to change the meaning of the past so that human beings may be reconciled with what took place and find peace with themselves and former perpetrators in a happy memory.

> If indeed facts are indelible [*ineffaçables*], if what has been done cannot be undone and if we cannot make it the case that what has happened has not, by contrast, the sense of what has happened is not fixed once and for all. Besides the fact that the events of the past can be interpreted otherwise, the moral burden associated with the debt toward the past can be increased or alleviated depending on whether the accusation confines the guilty individual in the painful feeling of the irreversible or whether forgiveness opens the perspective of a deliverance from the debt, which amounts to a conversion of the very sense of the event. (Ricoeur 1998: 29)

Such a "happy memory" as the result of a narrative work could resorb the "disproportion" left jarring in *Fallible Man* and "restore" the integrity of the human being, which was the elusive goal of the *Philosophy of the Will*.

NOTES

1. As Ricoeur insists, "guilt is not synonymous with fault" (1960b: 99; 1967: 100). Culpability or fallibility name an ontological component of human existence or of the human condition whereas fault is an instantiation of such a capacity to fail.

2. Fallibility is thus "the constitutional weakness which makes evil possible" (1960a: 11; 1986a: xix).

3. In *Freedom and Nature* he speaks of "my freedom's mode of being [*la manière d'être de ma liberté*]" (1950: 345; 1966: 368).

4. Happiness is thus not simply pleasure, and remarkably not a "feeling," as Ricoeur understands feeling in *Fallible Man*. Rather, it is *eudaimonia* or beatitude, as the life of a person, which can be said retrospectively to have been a good life.

5. Narrative is thus "the text *par excellence*" (1995: 29).

In *Time and Narrative* Ricoeur speaks of a triple mimesis in order to show the interactions between (1) the world of experiences as a pre-figuration in the sense of having a pre-narrative nature (Mimesis1); (2) the actual narratives as a configuration of the world of experience (Mimesis2); and (3) the effect actual narratives have on the world of experience when subjects and agents use what they have read and "re-figure" the world of experience and action (Mimesis3). On this, see Vandevelde 2008, 2013.

6. As Ricoeur explains, "it therefore seems plausible to take the following chain of assertions as valid: self-understanding is an interpretation; interpretation of the self, in turn, finds in the narrative, among other signs and symbols, a privileged form of mediation; the latter borrows from history as well as from fiction, making a life story a fictional history or, if one prefers, a historical fiction, interweaving the historiographic style of biographies with the novelistic style of imaginary autobiographies" (1992: 114).

See also: "My thesis is here that the process of composition, of configuration, is not completed in the text but in the reader and, under this condition, makes possible the reconfiguration of life by narrative. I should say, more precisely: the sense or the significance of a narrative stems from the *intersection of the world of the text and the world of the reader*. The act of reading thus becomes the critical moment of the entire analysis. On it rests the narrative's capacity to transfigure the experience of the reader" (1991b: 26).

7. In footnote, he says: "Character, I would say today, is sameness in mineness" (1992: 120).

8. Ricoeur says: "The 'disproportion' whose exegesis we have been pursuing through knowing, acting and feeling, takes on the name of fragility in the affective order" (1960a: 142; 1986a: 191).

9. As Ricoeur asks, "could we not say that the preterite [of the narration] preserves its grammatical form and its privilege because the present of narration is understood by the reader as *posterior* to the narrated story, hence that the told story is the *past of the narrative voice*? Is not every story in the past for the voice that tells it?" (1985a: 98).

10. See also Ricoeur 1960b: 74; 1967: 72.

11. As Ricoeur describes it in *Oneself as Another*, "attestation can be identified with the assurance that each person has of existing as the same in the sense of ipseity, selfhood" (1990: 346; 1992: 298). We find analogous formulation in *Memory, History, Forgetting*: "What I expect from my close relations is that they approve of what I attest: that I am able to speak, act, recount, impute to myself the responsibility for my actions" (2000: 162; 2004a: 132).

12. If challenged, historians will attest to their ethical stance and the truth of what they say by exhibiting the documents used and presenting the explanatory procedures employed. "It is together that scripturality, comprehensive explanation, and

documentary proof are capable of accrediting the truth claim of historical discourse. Only the movement that moves back from the art of writing to the 'research techniques' and 'critical procedures' is capable of raising the protest to the rank of what has become a critical attestation" (2000: 363–64; 2004a: 278).

REFERENCES

Ricoeur, Paul. 1950. *Philosophie de la volonté. Le volontaire et l'involontaire.* Paris: Aubier Montaigne.
———. 1960a. *Finitude et culpabilité, Vol. I L'homme faillible.* Paris: Aubier Montaigne.
———. 1960b. *Finitude et culpabilité, Vol. II La symbolique du mal.* Paris: Aubier Montaigne.
———. 1966. *Freedom and Nature: The Voluntary and the Involuntary.* Trans. Erazin Kohák. Evanston, IL: Northwestern University Press.
———. 1967. *The Symbolism of Evil.* Trans. Emerson Buchanan. New York: Harper & Row.
———. 1983. *Temps et récit, vol. 1.* Collection Points. Paris: Les Éditions du Seuil.
———. 1984. *Time and Narrative, vol. 1.* Trans. Kathleen McLaughlin and David Pellauer. Chicago: University of Chicago Press.
———. 1985a. *Time and Narrative, vol. 2.* Trans. Kathleen McLaughlin and David Pellauer. Chicago: University of Chicago Press.
———. 1985b. *Temps et récit 3, Le temps raconté.* Collection Points. Paris: Les Éditions du Seuil.
———. 1986a. *Philosophy of the Will: Fallible Man.* Trans. Charles Kelbley. New York: Fordham University Press.
———. 1986b. *Du texte à l'action.* Paris: Les Éditions du Seuil.
———. 1988. *Time and Narrative, vol. 3.* Trans. Kathleen Blamey and David Pellauer. Chicago: The University of Chicago Press.
———. 1990. *Soi-même conune un autre.* Collection Points. Paris: Les Éditions du Seuil.
———. 1991a. "L'attestation: entre phénoménologie et ontologie." In *Paul Ricoeur. Les métamorphoses de la raison herméneutique,* eds. Jean Greisch and Richard Kearney. Paris: Éditions du Cerf, 381–403.
———. 1991b. "Life in Quest of Narrative." In *On Paul Ricoeur. Narrative and Interpretation,* ed. David Wood. London: Routledge, 20–33.
———. 1991c. *From Text to Action: Essays in Hermeneutics II.* Trans. Kathleen Blamey and John Thompson. Evanston, IL: Northwestern University Press.
———. 1992. *Oneself as Another.* Trans. Kathleen Blamey. Chicago: The University of Chicago Press.
———. 1995. "Intellectual Autobiography." In *The Philosophy of Paul Ricoeur,* ed. Lewis Edwin Hahn. Chicago, IL: Open Court, 3–53.
———. 1998. La marque du passé. *Revue de Métaphysique et de Morale* 1: 7–31.

———. 2000. *La mémoire, l'histoire, l'oubli*. Collection Points. Paris: Éditions du Seuil.

———. 2004a. *Memory, History, Forgetting*. Trans. Kathleen Blamey and David Pellauer. Chicago: The University of Chicago Press.

———. 2004b. *Parcours de la reconnaissance. Trois études*. Paris: Éditions Stock.

———. 2004c. *The Course of Recognition*. Trans. David Pellauer. Cambridge, MA: Harvard University Press.

Vandevelde, Pol. 2008. "The Challenge of the "such as it was": Ricoeur's Theory of Narratives." In *Reading Ricoeur*, ed. David Kaplan. Albany, NY: State University of New York Press, 2008, 141–62.

———. 2013. Le fondement ontologique du récit selon Ricoeur: mimesis, dette et attestation. *Studia Phaenomenologica* XIII: 244–59.

Chapter 9

The Quest of Recognizing One's Self

Timo Helenius

Ricoeur argues, in *Fallible Man*, that human existence is a continuous transition that repeatedly reinstitutes the frailty of the human being. In Ricoeur's view, such fragility—by which he ultimately means that the self is always mediated and does not coincide with itself (Ricoeur 1986: 5–6)—provides a grounding for a capable self. The human disproportion or de-centeredness should therefore be understood as "a power to fail (*pouvoir de faillir*), in the sense that it makes human being capable of failing (*capable de faillir*)" (Ricoeur 1986: 145). In this light, this chapter will analyze Ricoeur's theory of being a capable person only through a process that admits being not capable. I will explore this reciprocity of power (*puissance*) and powerlessness (*impuissance*) by drawing connections between Ricoeur's early phenomenological anthropology and his later discussion of recognition especially as it pertains to the work of recognition. While keeping its material focus in recognition—an important theory Ricoeur opens up in *Fallible Man*—this essay will ultimately discuss a key tenet of Ricoeur's philosophical anthropology, that is, human existence as capable fallenness.

While pursuing the task of this essay, I will also propose an alternative to frame Ricoeur's account of the human being. In contrast with interpretations that distinguish between Ricoeur's early and late anthropology (i.e., between "being fallible" and "being capable"), I argue for the continuity of Ricoeur's anthropology of "capable of falling." Jean-Luc Amalric, for example, has noted that in contrast to his earlier anthropology of "fallible human" (*l'homme faillible*), Ricoeur proposes a later anthropology that focuses on the "capable human" (*l'homme capable*) through "different modalities of the experience of 'I can'" (Amalric 2011: 13). The terminological shift from *l'homme faillible* to *l'homme capable* seems to propose that, in spite of his continued anthropological interest, Ricoeur's argument changed over time and adopted a more positive outlook on human potentiality. The stance that this chapter will take, however, is that Ricoeur's anthropology does not necessitate such a shift of emphasis. Even though there appears to be shift on the surface between the earlier and later works, the thesis that this essay will put forward is that we do not have to fully agree with such estimations.

In spite of his examination of fallibility, or the conditions of fallenness, Ricoeur does not set aside the idea that the myth of fall might not only function negatively—as pointing out the human incapabilities resulting in from the fall, and particularly after it—but also positively. "A myth of fall," Ricoeur argues, "is possible only within the context of a myth of creation and innocence" (Ricoeur 1986: 145). Leaving aside his explanation of the necessity of this framing, Ricoeur's next move introduces an idea that should be taken into account when his overall anthropology of the "I can" is evaluated. It is the reciprocity between being fallen and being capable that is Ricoeur's anthropological thesis from the very beginning, instead of any firm distinction between the two. An extended citation from *Fallible Man*—that situates our opening lines—clarifies the issue well enough:

> But the concept of fallibility includes the possibility of evil in a still more positive sense: man's disproportion is a *power* to fail (*pouvoir de faillir*), in the sense that it makes man *capable* of failing (*capable de faillir*). [. . .] Thus evil, in the very moment when "I admit" that I posit it, seems to arise from man's very limitation through the continuous transition of the vertigo [leading from weakness to temptation and from temptation to fall]. It is this transition from innocence to fault, discovered in the very positing of evil, that gives the concept of fallibility all its equivocal profundity. Fragility is not merely the "locus," the point of insertion of evil, not even the "origin" starting from which man falls; it is the "capacity" for evil. (1986: 145–46)

In passages like this, *Fallible Man* already introduces the framework for Ricoeur's later analyses in *Oneself as Another* and *The Course of Recognition*. It is only in contrast with one's limits and incapacities that the understanding of being capable, or the "I can," can be formulated.

Drawing support from Ricoeur's *Freedom and Nature*, this chapter will begin by discussing the two-sided phenomenon of being both capable and bound (*situé*). In this early work Ricoeur stresses the idea that a capable human being, *l'homme capable*, is situated within the inescapable dialectics of necessity and freedom. Following the early Ricoeur, I will conclude that the self is "a product of separation" (Ricoeur 1966: 29), that is, a human subject is not posited by himself or herself but ultimately by his necessary sociocultural situation (namely *l'homme situé*) that stands over and against the self but also—in the mode of being among—recognizes the subject as capable of falling, that is, with his or her powers and lack of powers. A human being recognizes, or understands, himself or herself as capable/fallible only through this sociocultural process of mediation—or the orders of recognition—he or she is not capable of avoiding and into which he or she would always have to "fall" in order to gain a notion of being a self. In its later parts, the essay will deepen this notion of finding oneself capable in the presence of being not capable by alluding to the idea of the mediated self Ricoeur further develops in his later works such as *Oneself as Another* (1990) and *The Course of Recognition* (2004). In sum, Ricoeur's very carefully elaborated notion of *l'homme capable de faillir*, or the "human being capable of falling," is more informative of his anthropological understanding than the assumed distinction between the early theorization concerning *l'homme faillible* and the later focus on *l'homme capable*.

BEING CAPABLE AND BOUND: THE RECIPROCITY OF THE VOLUNTARY AND THE INVOLUNTARY

The anthropology presented in *Fallible Man* relies on the phenomenological analyses of *Freedom and Nature*. The earlier work explores the two-sided phenomenon or experience of being both capable and bound (*situé*)—the human condition of "a general reciprocity of the voluntary and the involuntary," as Ricoeur calls it (1966: 276). Put differently, Ricoeur strives to examine a subject's fundamental possibilities, that is, those possibilities that are available for a situated, reflecting subject. These possibilities, *les possibilités fondamentales de l'homme*, are also reflected in *Fallible Man* through the reciprocity of *puissance et impuissance*, or being capable and not capable. Overall, it is not wrong to claim that *Freedom and Nature* prefigures and grounds the theories of human being that Ricoeur elaborates in many of his works later up to *The Course of Recognition*. Summarizing his main point here at the outset of this discussion, Ricoeur maintains that self-understanding is not immediate but reflective. More precisely, Ricoeur insists explicitly that the Self (*le Soi*) is "a product of separation," or, that the self is figurable only as a self that first fails to have a notion of itself and can only have one by acquiring it as a self fallen away from itself. In brief, "the Self is an alienated I" (1966: 29), and the only way to overcome this alienation is through the other—by which the self will have to be recognized as a situated, social, ethico-political, and historical self. My self, my personhood, is available to me only reflectively in a situation, that is, that the self finds itself as capable only from the ruins of an "I" that has bound itself at a very basic level of being active and in relation to other(s).

Let me make two crucial observations by restating the point in a more theoretical manner. First, the duality of the pre-reflective relation between the

"I" and the object of its intention enables the whole intentional, or projecting action. Second, a self-affirmative subject, a self, is achieved only indirectly by this intentional objectification, that is, by those intentional acts which objectify the "I" and facilitate the reappropriation of those acts as manifestations of the self. To achieve a notion of the self, my endeavors, including the practical ones, will have to be taken into account as Ricoeur also later argues in the essays of *From Text to Action*. "I affirm myself in my acts," the early Ricoeur stressed, "I project my own self into the action to be done" (1966: 59). In short, the self finds the "I" as the locus of personal identity that in itself is not directly achievable or accessible, instead it is available only through a reappropriation. Such reappropriation, however, implies that the "I" commits itself—*il s'engage*—as well as binds itself (*il se lie*) to the object that results from the action to be done: "[The 'I'] throws itself ahead of itself in posing itself as the object, as a direct complement of the project. In projecting myself thus, I objectify myself in a way, as I objectify myself in a signature which I will be able to recognize (*je pourrai reconnaître*), identify as mine, as my sign" (1966: 59). Phrased differently, my subjectivity is available for me only through its objectification or a certain losing of the self in order for it to be regained—this is the duality of being capable through having fallen or the basic "evil" that I commit unceasingly: the betrayal of the most intimate experience of being an "I." In short, there is a connection between losing oneself and recovering oneself, between failing and reconciliation.

The question of the pre-reflective nexus of the self, however, may lead to a slight confusion. Is not the "I" a logical necessity for any self and thereby the needed core that does not submit to any kind of fallenness? Ricoeur himself asserts, in reference to Nabert's philosophy, the importance of such an "I" in *Freedom and Nature* and repeats this point later in *Oneself as Another* under the duality of the *idem* and *ipse* self. Even though I recognize myself reflectively—or as a narrative *ipse* self—that is, in making a notion of myself in my acts which objectify my subjective being-here, the pre-reflective "I" remains as the unchangeable core of my identity, or, in other words, as the unreflected precondition of my self. As the self's condition, the "I" cannot be detached from it; self-identification requires this connection. Ricoeur acknowledges that the projected self can take over the projecting "I"—that there is the risk of "exiling my self into the margins of its acts" (1966: 60)—but argues that this separation from being a subject to an objectified subject is prevented by the "voiceless consciousness" (*la conscience sourde*) that all acts spring forth from their subject-pole, from the "I," that is, from the primordial locus of identity. This voiceless "I," however, remains completely mute as a projecting self if the subject does not view it through the projected self.

Here, then, the theme of fallenness needs to be reintroduced in a manner that also acknowledges the condition of the unreflected "I." What I want to emphasize is that the apparent duality and dynamic tension between the "I" and the self actually reaffirms the notion of the fallen self that, in its fallenness, is a capable self at the same time. The interplay between being bound ("projected") and being capable ("projecting") implies that a self never achieves a total notion of itself, also because of always being "in a corporeal, historical situation, because he stands neither at the beginning nor at the end but always in the middle, *in medias res*" (1966: 175). *Freedom and Nature* calls this state of incompleteness the "genuine condition" of human beings, "*la condition véritable*," or the authentic state of being a human (1966: 174). In short, Ricoeur maintains that "to exist is to act" (1966: 334), meaning that a meaningful existence is available only through action that stands for and is appropriable as the acting self. It is in this situation of never-ending acts that a person attempts at self-identification through reflection, reliant on the unreflected that yet provides the impetus for projecting a self.

This excursion into *Freedom and Nature* should be concluded with one last expansion of the argument. Self-identification is an unending task, as a subject is always already contested by all impulses, perceptions, and stimuli, including those coming from the social sphere of life. As is well known, for Ricoeur a subject is never a solipsistic one but always concerns with-being and being-among—his later "little ethics" put this as "to live a good life with and for others in just institutions" (Ricoeur 1992: 172). Human history and the contemporary social topography that reflects it add to the challenge of indeterminacy already implicit in being incarnated in the world. Ricoeur maintains that daring and risking are inseparable from the process of individualization that gathers the notion of my self, my personhood:

> Social topography projects itself in contradictory affective signs and painful alternatives [or choices]. Familial, professional, cultural, sporting, artistic, religious, and all such associations, tear us apart so that a person has to create his own unity, his independence, his originality, and to dare his own style of life. The person is born (*naît*) from this distortion among the conflicts of duties. (1966: 148)

Ricoeur argues, in other words, that being-with and being-among disperse a subject by throwing himself or herself in an unavoidable state of unwittingly making choices that are always existential ones; this necessity to choose while at the same time being torn apart is a fundamental trait of the voluntary and the involuntary. The unity of one's life, one's own personal self, is not given but gradually formed in an unceasing process of being a self that is capable only because of being bound; this is why in Ricoeur's anthropology of "capable of falling" it is fallibility that is the capability.

FAULT: AN EVENT WITH IMMENSE POSSIBILITIES

Ricoeur's phenomenological description of human existence leads us to think that at its basic level human experience bears a scar or a wound and that its persistent yearning always portrays for us some paradise lost; this is also what both theology and psychoanalysis teach us. This train of thought is not foreign to other philosophers either. Take Aristotle, for example, who, in contrast with humanly achievable, defines ultimate happiness as pure contemplation, and for that reason as "the activity of gods" (Aristotle 2004: 1178b). In spite of its rational capacity, human life can be called happy insofar as it carries an aspiration toward a harmony that, however, will never be fully achieved; "human nature is not self-sufficient for the purpose of contemplation." Human lives are hylomorphic, embodied, in need of external goods, and influenced by animal and social desires that pull a person out and apart from himself. As Ricoeur claims in *Fallible Man*, this "was expressed by Aristotle in his celebrated formula, *'the will moves by desire'*" (1966: 327; 1986: 51–52). This is why, Aristotle argued, it is already a difficult task to determine the proper manner of comportment. Whoever is capable of sufficiently, albeit constantly so, navigating through the rocky waters of human life can be called a virtuous and happy person, while admitting that the same person is still subject to human imperfection as well as vulnerable to misfortune or bad luck. Human being, in other words, cannot be defined by perfection but by that activity that manages to competently achieve the mark in spite of the ramifications of this human mode of being.

A similar tone can be heard in Ricoeur's early exploration of the basic structures of human experience. *Freedom and Nature* already addresses the bodily and the linguistic activities of a human subject trying to understand his or her "fundamental possibilities" (1966: 3, 15). Put differently, Ricoeur seeks to describe the peculiarly human experience from the viewpoint of its "possibilities" in spite of the fault that introduces "the drama of divided human being (*l'homme divisé*)" (1966: 21). To describe this condition without imposing metaphysical assumptions or ethical evaluations of it, however, Ricoeur bracketed the question of the fault in this earlier work. Still, it did not escape him that "the fault is an event with immense possibilities" (1966: 22). Fault, too, explains what is humanly possible: "At its outer limits it is a discovery of the infinite, an experience of the holy in reverse, of the holy in the demonic; it is sin in the strongest sense of the word" (1966: 22). Even though not capitalizing on the notion—which he later did in *Fallible Man* and *The Symbolism of Evil*—Ricoeur's *Freedom and Nature* was already gesturing toward the thought that perhaps the human being is absurdly flawed.

As to the question of what this fault might more fundamentally be, Ricoeur's early work provided a tentative proposal that signaled his wider and long-lasting interest in this matter. Here we need to touch upon the notion of productive imagination. "The essences of willing," Ricoeur argues, "are what I understand in terms of a single model, specifically an imaginary model, when I say 'project,' 'motive,' 'need,' 'effort,' 'character,' and so on" (1966: 4). This Kantian approach is thereby grounded in the premise that "a schematic understanding of these key functions precedes any empirical, inductive study undertaken according to experimental methods borrowed from natural sciences" (1966: 4). The immense possibilities of the productive imagination—or schematization—are, however, discussed in a manner that carries a certain Sartrean undertone in the form of a reaction to his phenomenology. First, there is an evident onto-existential deprivation or a displacement that results in from these possibilities:

> Even though conceptual thought is not necessarily a naturalistic reduction, it always starts with a definite loss of being. I appropriate what I understand, I lay a claim to it, I encompass it by a definite power of thought which sooner or later comes to regard itself as positing, forming, and constitutive with respect to objectivity. This loss of being which, with respect to the object, is a loss of presence, is with respect to the subject who articulates the knowledge of conceptual deincarnation: I exile myself into the void as the nondimensional subject. Thus on the one hand I appropriate reality, and on the other I cut myself off from its presence. (1966: 16)

This reductive displacement, in other words, can also be put in terms of an accidental, albeit passionately pursued, movement toward not-being that correlates with "a certain bondage which the soul imposes on itself" by "binding itself" (1966: 23). Such tyranny or enslavement is *un esclavage par le Rien* or "a bondage to *Nothing*" (1966: 23) that, in Ricoeur's thought, is the realm of the imaginary that entices and excites—and which we *passionately* pursue in order to make ourselves be. The presence of the fall, however, is evident in this:

> All passion is vanity. Reproach, suspicion, concupiscence, envy, hurt, and grief are various names for chasing after the wind. This fiction, this lie, reveals the decisive role of imagination in the genesis of passion. Here again we shall not forget to note the points of least resistance where imagination might insinuate its myths and make the soul succumb to the charm of Nothing. (1966: 23)

In brief, Ricoeur argues that the fault is linked with the imaginary, or the universe of vain passions bound to the imagined or nothingness, and thereby absurd in its face. Yet, as the uncanny, it brings forth this permeating aspect of human experience, the sense of a "lost paradise" or the deprivation of control over oneself, and thereby proposes to take seriously and to explore this experience of self-inflicted alienation that "seizes the *whole* human being" (1966: 26). Whatever we humans do, Ricoeur thereby argued, we do it in the light of a *paradis perdu*, or the struggle to fulfill ourselves through our actions, even if we never fully achieved what is imagined.

For Ricoeur, the self remains a frustrating enigma and aporia up to the very end, both in itself and with others. The pursuit of a harmonious balance both within and with others is as endless as it is upsetting. This frustration is not to be understood in the sense of petty everyday annoyance, but as a grievance that goes all the way down and shapes the whole of human existence. Echoing Hegel's stance, later affirmed by Kierkegaard, that "human beings are inwardly conscious that in their innermost being they are a contradiction, and have therefore an infinite *anguish* concerning themselves" (Hegel 1985: 305), Ricoeur states—also echoing Augustine's *Confessions*—that human being is "a fullness of true anguish" because it is bound to a fiction of the self that drives it in its endless pursuit of trying to make the illusory real: "starting with the fault, freedom, fascinated by a dream of self-positing, exiles itself" (1966: 23). This is the human "fall" since the fault begins with original and subsequently limited—if not altogether lost—freedom. "*It is I who* makes myself a slave: I *impose* on myself the fault which *deprives* me of control over myself" (1966: 26). In other words, Ricoeur stressed that the self *is* the fault because it is fundamentally "a product of separation," or nothing but "an alienated I" (1966: 29). The self exists always only in unison with this fault that should be understood as a kind of double collapse away from the imagined pure "I" into the profound distress of living as a self in need of ultimately unachievable self-affirmation.

Though flawed, the human being is also free. The imaginary illusion of the radical autonomy of the self uproots human being from its conditions and establishes a sense of subjective freedom that is ultimately recognized through guilt and remorse. At first glance, it may be an awkward—and very Kierkegaardian—thought that "a person receives himself through remorse at the center of his freedom" (1966: 28). Ricoeur nevertheless clarifies that the guilty consciousness points out a necessary duality that is constitutive of self-consciousness. The human freedom is nothing but *la liberté serve*, or a "freedom in bondage" (1966: 27) that ignites the dual experience of betrayal and responsibility of the self as well as of the others. Ethical considerations aside, most fundamentally I am responsible of recognizing that my actions are my own, and that the "I" can only be found as "the subject pole of my acts" (1966: 57). I exile my self to the acts that I do, and in return gain a notion of being the subject or the "I" who has done "all this." This is the "paradoxical coexistence of freedom and fault" that "poses most difficult problems"; it sums up as "the paradox of choice" (1966: 26–27, 149). I acknowledge my self only as an agent that is active in its desiring will and, thereby, free. Yet I do this by first betraying my self in its intimate immediacy in casting the self to my actions that bespeak of the acting subject that I am. For this rupture, expulsion, or ejection, Ricoeur explains, "I accuse myself, and in accusing myself retrace the vestiges of my signature on the act" (1966: 58). Such self is always a fallen consciousness that is wounded by nothing but itself; it is a guilty consciousness because of its freedom that betrays itself. Being free, human being is miserably free.

THE QUEST FOR ESTEEM

As we now shift toward the textual evidence in *Fallible Man* for an anthropology of being "capable of falling," it may be necessary to express some reservations regarding the reading that is about to follow. As is already clear in the general suspension or bracketing of the fault that Ricoeur executes in *Freedom and Nature* and the subsequent "removing the parentheses" in *Fallible Man* (1986: xli), the two works do not propose their respective arguments at the same level. *Freedom and Nature* provides a "pure description" regarding certain ontological limitations, whereas *Fallible Man* discusses the transcendental conditions that in some of Ricoeur's later texts concern moral limitations or failures. In spite of these differences, the two works nevertheless keep the same phenomenological anthropology in sight and also probe into the question of existential (self)recognition that—already according to the early Ricoeur—remains a perpetual task or a *quest*. This theme runs through many of his works, but here we will focus on the discussion concerning esteem as it will ultimately lead us to see how the affirmative "I can" emerges on the grounds of the *l'homme capable de faillir*.

To emphasize the importance of Ricoeur's analysis of esteem in *Fallible Man*, I will point out Ricoeur's crucial statement in his last published work of his lifetime, *The Course of Recognition*. There Ricoeur focuses on Hegel's concept of *Sittlichkeit* from the point of view of social esteem and argues that this sense of esteem "sums up all the modes of mutual recognition that exceed the mere recognition of the equality of right among subjects" (2005: 202). Pushing the point even deeper, Ricoeur goes on to argue that socioeconomic, sociopolitical (including juridical), and (institutionalized) sociocultural complexes can be understood as different "orders of recognition" (2005: 203–04). According to Ricoeur's explication of Axel Honneth's three patterns of intersubjective recognition—love (or the economics of filiation), law or rights, and social esteem or solidarity—each of these various "organized mediations" indirectly recognizes a subject by granting a status or standing as a social agent. The triad of these "orders of recognition" is not unique insofar as it continues the discussion formerly carried out by Jean-Marc Ferry, from whom Ricoeur derives his terminology, and Axel Honneth, whom Ricoeur criticizes in his work.

In addition, and importantly for us, Ricoeur's triad echoes an earlier triad that can already be found in his earlier work that also focused on the idea of being recognized, albeit from the viewpoint of cultural objectivity as positive facilitation. *Fallible Man*, under the title "Affective Fragility," presents a triad that follows the same arrangement as that of *The Course of Recognition*; the economics of having, politico-juridical power, and culturally gained esteem are all social in nature. In addition, in its general progression from consciousness to ideal self-consciousness, and furthermore to mutual recognition in cultural objectivity, *Fallible Man* prefigures the line of Ricoeur's argument in *The Course of Recognition*. This earlier triad that grounds and explains the later "orders" is the focus of my interest in this section. Despite these similarities between Ricoeur's early and later work, I have argued that *Fallible Man* brings forth more explicitly the necessity of cultural philosophy than *The Course of Recognition*, which implies but does not elaborate on this topic.

An important sidenote may be warranted here. In spite of Ricoeur's professedly unorthodox reading of Kant, *Fallible Man* is saturated with Kant's philosophy beyond the critical works: it turns against the critical works with the help of Kant's *Anthropology*. Ricoeur's engagement with Kant's philosophy amounts to, I maintain, not only an anthropology of a capable/fallible human being, but also to a corresponding philosophy of culture which concretizes the notion of object in *Fallible Man*. According to Ricoeur, a subject becomes recognized and gains an understanding of being a capable human being—*l'homme capable de faillir*—only in the light of cultural objectivity.

To begin with our reading of the notion of esteem, then, it should be made very clear that Ricoeur's analysis is based on Kant's concept of the three cultural passions or "manias" (*die Leidenschaften*) as laid out in *Anthropology from a Pragmatic Point of View*: ambition (*Ehrsucht*), dominion (*Herrschsucht*), and avarice (*Habsucht*). This analysis of the perverted manias for honor, authority, and possession focuses on these desires, which hinder or distort the use of reason. Passions as hidden human dispositions, or desires, are always in affiliation with those purposes that reason sets, but as perverted inclinations they are, according to Kant, "without exception evil" (Kant 1999: VII.267). Kant's understanding is that passion, as a weakness leading to servile submission, collides with the concept of freedom, which is established by reason alone: "Ambition is a weakness of people, which allows them to be influenced through their opinions; dominion allows them to be influenced through their fear; and avarice allows them to be influenced through their own interest" (VII.272). These three acquired passions, which arise "from the culture of humankind" (VII.267), are in Kant's view possible only for human beings and concern interhuman relations.

Ricoeur's discussion—or, perhaps, his application—of these cultural passions makes evident the necessity of cultural objectivity in a search for the human constitution. *Fallible Man* argues that the three perverted inclinations (*-sucht*) indicate an authentic *Suchen*, that is, a fundamental human quest (*requête*) that takes the threefold cultural form of a search for having (*avoir*), power (*pouvoir*), and esteem (*valoir*). Put differently, Ricoeur maintains that the specifically human quests for having, power, and esteem connect to a primordial search for an authentic mode of being. In itself, this primordial search, which Ricoeur calls an "imagination of the essential," remains an assumption of an unperverted primordial condition, or "an innocent kingdom," which precedes the empirical state of "having fallen" (1986: 112, 144). The self, insofar as it is available to itself, is always already "fallen." Consequently, the most concrete notion of the self is achievable only within the same context of analysis, that is, in the realm of cultural passions that indicate of this "fall."

To restate, Ricoeur insists in *Fallible Man* that both distinguishing an individual self and articulating the relationship between individual selves require the support of the "objectivity that is built on the themes of having, power, and esteem"; this is why he also calls these aspects of human experience "roots of self-affirmation" (1986: 113, 116). Again, then, Ricoeur emphasizes in the concepts of having, power, and esteem the fundamentally indirect character of achieving the notion of a self; there is no immediate intuition of one's own being. The human subject "is constituted only in connection with things that themselves belong to the economic, political, and cultural dimensions" (1986: 113). The objectivity of these "things" and quasi-things allows intelligibility without completely distorting the existential level of experienced subjectivity. A human subject, a self capable of reflection, is found only in this redefined objectivity, that is, through the cultural objectivity of these three Kantian cultural passions.

The leading idea for Ricoeur in the threefold analysis of having, power, and esteem is that a human subject recognizes himself or herself only in and through the various cultural forms his or her being assumes and the "monuments" he or she has produced, and which stand over and against himself or herself by objectifying the experience of his or her own being. Ricoeur's analysis of the third human quest in *Fallible Man*, esteem, thereby fully opens the realm of cultural recognition—or, in the language of *History and Truth*, "the cultural sphere of mutual recognition" (1965: 113–14). Neither the reciprocally exclusive relations of having, nor the hierarchical and asymmetrical relations of power reach the level of the quest for worth, or "the quest for esteem in another's opinion" as Ricoeur defines it in *Fallible Man* (1986: 120). This most primordial quest is also the constitutive one for a human subject who, according to Ricoeur, becomes for the first time recognized as an individual self: "It is there [in the realm of interpersonal relations] that I pursue the aim of being esteemed, approved, and recognized. My existence for myself is dependent on this constitution in another's opinion" (1986: 121).

To reiterate, Ricoeur defines the quest for esteem as the desire to exist and to be acknowledged, that is, to be recognized as a self. The quest for esteem is not, however, only a subject's mere desire to be recognized, but also includes a fundamental mutuality that establishes the ground for the fulfillment of gained esteem. For this reason, Ricoeur characterizes the quest for esteem as "the true passage from consciousness to self-consciousness" (1986: 121). The key moment, I should stress, in this analysis of esteem is thereby Ricoeur's emphasis on the *received* recognition from others upon which human subjects are founded. Ricoeur summarizes his conviction clearly: "My 'Self,' it may be said, is received from the opinion of others that establishes it. The constitution of subjects is thus a mutual constitution through opinion" (1986: 121). Once again, as later in *The Course of Recognition*, receiving is "the pivotal category" on which a subject's self-consciousness depends (2005: 243). The quest for esteem, as *Fallible Man* defines it, is, in other words, "the quest of recognition" (1986: 122).

RECEIVED RECOGNITION

Some further clarifying remarks may be in order. Even though he distances himself from Kant's initial analysis of the three passions in his *Anthropology*, Ricoeur's *Fallible Man* maintains a Kantian tone by holding on to the idea of "objectivity" from the *Critique of Pure Reason*. With regard to this particular quest for esteem/recognition, however, Ricoeur resorts to Kant's *Groundwork*, in which a rational being is defined as an objective end in himself. "Kant gives the name of humanity to this objectivity," Ricoeur argues; "the proper object of esteem is the idea of man in my person and in the person of another" (1986: 122–23). In other words, by expanding the notion of objectivity Ricoeur stretches the register of his analysis to recognition, while still claiming to follow the trail of Kantian philosophy. More importantly, by using this mixed notion of objectivity, Ricoeur is able to join together the diverse elements of his analysis of the quest for esteem:

> I expect another person to convey the image of my humanity to me, to esteem me by making my humanity known to me. This fragile reflection of myself in another's opinion has the consistency of an object; it conceals the objectivity of an existing end that draws a limit to any pretension to make use of me. It is in and through this objectivity that I can be recognized. (1986: 123)

As Kant's categorical imperative denies using other rational subjects merely as means, Ricoeur reasons, everyone must treat others as ends in themselves. They will have to "esteem me" and "make my humanity known to me," that is, make my being-an-end-in-myself known to me. In this esteem the others offer to me in their opinions or statements with regard to my personhood, and I can then "read" the objective truth that I truly am an existing being and an end in myself. This objective recognition—which is fragile only because I infer it in my subjectivity—gives me therefore the notion of being a self or a person, that is, a human being with self-consciousness.

This "formal objectivity," however, would render a living subject's experience insignificant, if it were not supplemented with a correlating notion of "material objectivity," or cultural objects which *mediate* the notion of esteem. Here we approach again the notion of the self as *capable de faillir*. Again, Ricoeur's insistence on not suspending the subject's concrete experience necessitates this "materializing" of esteem and recognition. These objects differ from the economic and political ones in the sense that they can be seen as media for self-expression in general, and therefore as proper cultural works. Ricoeur's definition of the "works of the mind" pushes him then to the no-man's land between philosophical anthropology and cultural philosophy:

> "Works" of art and literature, and, in general, works of the mind (*l'esprit*), insofar as they not merely mirror an environment and an epoch but search out human possibilities, are the true "objects" that manifest the abstract universality of the idea of humanity through their concrete universality. (1986: 123)

Ricoeur, in other words, argues that the notion of humanity—a subject's being-an-end-in-himself—is manifested in those "highly expressive" works (1986: 59–60) that pertain to a human being's fundamental quest or *Suchen* of expressing himself or herself most accurately and most authentically. This, ultimately, is the cultural institution of which Ricoeur is interested in; *History and Truth* maintains that even though "it is not very common to speak of 'institutions' in respect to culture, such as with regard to political, social, or economic life, yet the profound meaning of the institution appears only when it is extended to the images of human being in culture, literature, and the arts" (1965: 126). These works that institute the tensional idea of humanity are concrete and yet universal because as works of imagination they always remain in the mode of the "possible"—they explore human possibilities—as art and literature demonstrate.

The "material objectivity" of genuinely "true works," which reveal a subject to himself and mediate the idea of humanity to others, is, therefore, cultural. The "I can" is achieved culturally, as a capable self in its cultural fallenness. In brief, therefore, the "material objectivity" *is* culture, as also

History and Truth argues: "The struggle for recognition is pursued by means of cultural realities. [. . .] This quest for mutual esteem (*d'estime mutuelle*) is pursued through images of human being (*images de l'homme*); and these images [which are embodied in cultural works] constitute the reality that is culture" (1965: 118–19). The formal objectivity of a subject's being-an-end-in-himself is quasi-materialized in cultural works which bear witness to my being-an-end-in-myself, and by which I can be recognized, although indirectly, in others' opinions concerning them.

THE SELF CAPABLE OF ETHICO-CULTURAL RECOGNITION

The thesis that a person understands himself or herself as capable only in the reciprocity of not being able can also be analyzed under the notion of recognition. Personal abilities point to a capable subject, a subject perhaps even capable of self-recognition. In that case recognition by others would not be necessary at all. For Ricoeur, however, even the primal self-assertion rests on the anticipation of mutuality, that is, it implies the notion of an "other" that is not the self-same self anymore. In brief, echoing his earlier comments on social topography in *Freedom and Nature* and on the threefold existential search (*Suchen*) analyzed in *Fallible Man*, in *The Course of Recognition* Ricoeur maintains that "self-assertion does not signify solipsism" (Ricoeur 2005: 252, 255). Not only reflective self-assertion must be distinguished from all the attempts to ground a solitary subject, but "each modality of the 'I can'" implies an "alterity" (2005: 252). Reduced to the theoretical level of the "I," the notion of being a capable person is still formed, at least, in the anticipation of mutuality, that is, under the mode of "being recognized" by others rather than recognizing one's self in its immediacy.

This extension to Ricoeur's "phenomenology of being capable" in the reciprocity of being able and not able has, therefore, also its social, ethical, and political dimensions. The "ones close by" are those to whom I have already related at birth and before I was given my name, and also those to whom I will relate after my death in their memories of me—and who, between birth and death, acknowledge my being in the mode of being-with. Ricoeur very clearly argues in *Memory, History, Forgetting* that the "I can" rests on this mutual recognition of a person's capabilities in the relations with those "close by":

> My close ones are those who approve of my existence and whose existence I approve of in the reciprocity and equality of esteem. This mutual approbation expresses the shared assertion that each one makes regarding his or her powers and lack of powers (*ses pouvoirs et ses non-pouvoirs*), what I termed attestation

in *Oneself as Another*. What I expect from my close ones is that they approve of what I attest: that I am able to speak, act, recount, impute to myself the responsibility of my actions. (Ricoeur 2004: 132)

Put differently, my personal "I can," or the moment of self-recognition, is ultimately possible only among others, that is, among beings inhabiting the external reality that are not the same as I am. It is only in the mode of "being among" that I am recognized as being capable or as having "powers" and also lacking them.

The notion of being related and thereby made capable by the process of mutual affirmation of being capable and not capable leads us to take a further step in this exploration of Ricoeur's anthropology. In connection with the idea of necessary sociality, recognition of being capable is set on the path of mutuality as contextuality. The moral selfhood, or ethical ipseity, is a task that emerges in the conflicts of actual socio-practical, that is, cultural life; it is best manifested "in interpersonal relations governed by the principle of respect owed to persons and in institutions governed by the rule of justice" (1992: 285). Put differently, an ethico-politico-practical self, capable of mutual recognition, is born in the unavoidable concrete contestations of a situated living together, that is, when facing the condition of being conditioned. As I have lengthily argued elsewhere (see Helenius 2016)—in reference to *Fallible Man* and *Oneself as Another*—this cultural condition of contextual mediations in instituted human praxis is the universal condition of becoming *l'homme capable de faillir*. A human being understands himself or herself as capable only through a culturally conditioned process he or she is not capable of avoiding. The objectification discussed above, in other words, becomes manifest in cultural productivity that enables the self fallen-away-from-itself to read itself as capable.

In sum, Ricoeur's notion of *l'homme capable de faillir*, or the "human being capable of falling," is therefore more informative of his anthropological understanding than the assumed distinction between the early *l'homme faillible* and the later *l'homme capable*. This point becomes evident especially with regard to the question of esteem, which, in my reading, forms the hard core of Ricoeur's anthropology well beyond *Fallible Man* in which it is first presented. In form of a brief conclusion we are thereby able to state that *Fallible Man* leads an attentive reader to gather that the culturally enabled "becoming what you are," or the figuring of oneself as a human being capable of falling (meaning: being capable of being a mediated self—but always and only a mediated self) is *the* course of recognizing the fundamental human possibilities. This is the human path that we are all on, living our lives by executing the quest of (self)understanding in light of the occasionally dawning sense of a "clearing" or the possibility for a repair and reconciliation.

REFERENCES

Amalric, Jean-Luc. 2011. "Affirmation originaire, attestation, reconnaissance: Le cheminement de l'anthropologie philosophique ricoeurienne." *Études Ricoeuriennes / Ricoeur Studies*, 2(1), 12–34.

Aristotle. 2004. *The Nicomachean Ethics*. Trans. J. A. K. Thomson & H. Tredennick. London and New York: Penguin Books.

Gadamer, Hans-Georg. 1989. *Truth and Method*. Trans. J. Weinsheimer & D. G. Marshall. New York: Crossroad.

Hegel, Georg Wilhelm Friedrich. 1985. *Lectures on the Philosophy of Religion. Vol. III: The Consummate Religion*. Trans. R. F. Brown, P. C. Hodgson, & J. M. Stewart. Berkeley, Los Angeles, CA; London: University of California Press.

Helenius, Timo. 2016. *Ricoeur, Culture, and Recognition: A Hermeneutic of Cultural Subjectivity*. Lanham, Boulder, New York, London: Lexington Books.

Honneth, Axel. 1995. *The Struggle for Recognition: The Moral Grammar of Social Conflicts*. Trans. J. Anderson. Cambridge, MA: Polity Press/Blackwell Publishers.

Kant, Immanuel. 1999. *Gesammelte Schriften* (Akademie-Ausgabe) (Past masters electronic edition ed.). Charlottesville, VA: InteLex Corporation.

Ricoeur, Paul. 1965. *History and Truth*. Trans. Charles A. Kelbley. Evanston, IL: Northwestern University Press.

———. 1966. *Freedom and Nature: The Voluntary and the Involuntary*. Trans. E. V. Kohák. Evanston, IL: Northwestern University Press.

———. 1969. *The Symbolism of Evil*. Trans. E. Buchanan. Boston: Beacon Press.

———. 1984. *Time and Narrative 1*. Trans. Kathleen Blamey & David Pellauer. Chicago: The University of Chicago Press.

———. 1986. *Fallible Man*. Trans. Charles A. Kelbley. New York: Fordham University Press.

———. 1991. *From Text to Action: Essays in Hermeneutics II*. Trans. Kathleen Blamey & John B. Thompson. Evanston, IL: Northwestern University Press.

———. 1992. *Oneself as Another*. Trans. Kathleen Blamey. Chicago and London: The University of Chicago Press.

———. 2004. *Memory, History, Forgetting*. Trans. Kathleen Blamey & David Pellauer. Chicago: The University of Chicago Press.

———. 2005. *The Course of Recognition*. Trans. David Pellauer. Cambridge, MA: Harvard University Press.

———. 2007. *Reflections on the Just*. Trans. David Pellauer. Chicago and London: The University of Chicago Press.

Chapter 10

Finitude, Culpability, and Suffering
The Question of Evil in Ricoeur

Jean-Luc Amalric

No one will deny that the question of evil occupies an absolutely central place within the *Philosophy of the Will*. As the "Introduction" of *Freedom and Nature* clearly attests, the complex and ambitious project of Ricoeur's first major work is fully governed by this question in the development of its methodology. Not only is it the question of evil that motivates "the epoche of the fault and Transcendence" employed in *Freedom and Nature* as well as *Fallible Man*, but it is also the question that leads—in *The Symbolism of Evil*—to the famous "graft of hermeneutics onto phenomenology" which will later become the most representative trademark of Ricoeurian hermeneutics.

The essence of Ricoeur's reflection on evil and the methodological decisions that accompany it therefore seems to be summed up in the central opposition between *Finitude and Guilt*, which is the title of the second volume of the *Philosophy of the Will*. Undoubtedly, the originality of this work resides in its decision to develop an approach to evil and the bad will which categorically rejects any reduction of evil to finitude. In contrast with a dominant philosophical tradition that continually reduces evil to finitude in order to be able to integrate it into the rationality of its discourse, Ricoeur will instead defend the audacious idea of an *irreducible difference between finitude and guilt*. Why, then, would we not limit ourselves here to an examination of the meaning and scope of this fundamental distinction between finitude and guilt?

By associating the notion of *suffering* with the central notions of finitude and guilt in the title of this chapter, my intention is to try to arrive at a more complete understanding of Ricoeur's treatment of the question of evil—not only, of course, in the *Philosophy of the Will* where it is a center of focus but also in the philosopher's later works where this question, though present, does not necessarily occupy a central place. With *The Symbolism of Evil*, Ricoeur provides an extremely rich and thorough exegesis of the experience of guilt, but the whole problem is to understand how he interprets suffering. What exactly is the relationship as well as the difference between guilt and suffering in Ricoeurian thought? And how should these two dimensions of evil be connected with the question of finitude?

At the time of the *Philosophy of the Will*, Ricoeur locates the core of the experience of evil in guilt and that is why the analysis of suffering recedes into the background. In this context, his refusal to reduce evil to finitude can also be read as a refusal to reduce guilt to finitude. As I will try to show, however, one can already find in the three works of the *Philosophy of the Will* scattered elements of a thinking of evil as suffering that exceeds the mere analysis of evil as fault. For, it is precisely this question of suffering—in its character as both suffered and undeserved—that will have increased importance in the philosopher's later works. This is the case, first, in a number of important essays and articles that Ricoeur dedicates directly to the issue of evil in the 1980s–90s. Two of these texts date originally from 1986—"Evil: A Challenge to Philosophy and Theology" (Ricoeur 1995) and "The Scandal of Evil" (Ricoeur 1988)—while the third, published in 1992, is titled "Suffering is not Pain" (Ricoeur 1992a).

Apart from these texts, it also seems to me that the development of the central theme of "the human being who acts *and* suffers"—which governs Ricoeur's philosophical anthropology from *Oneself as Another* to *The Course of Recognition*, while passing through some essential texts in *The Just* and *Reflections on the Just* (for example, "Autonomy and Vulnerability")—corresponds to a progressive deepening of the question of suffering in the Ricoeurian philosophy of human action.

This chapter will begin by asking about the close connection uniting the Ricoeurian reflection on the question of evil with the reflection on questions of methodology. Everything happens as if, for Ricoeur, the question of evil actually required a certain conception of philosophy, its method and its limits. In the second step, my reflection will focus on what is undoubtedly the most remarkable feature of Ricoeur's conception of evil in the *Philosophy of the Will*, namely his refusal to reduce evil to finitude—a refusal itself underpinned by the major distinction between *finitude and guilt*. While focusing on the sense of the methodological "epoche" of the fault and Transcendence implemented in *Freedom and Nature* and *Fallible Man*, which makes this major distinction possible, I will try to assess its scope by connecting the sophisticated analyses that Ricoeur dedicates to the question of finitude and guilt with those, rarer, but less essential, analyses that he dedicates to the question of suffering. Finally, this examination of the complex relationships between finitude, guilt, and suffering in the *Philosophy of the Will* leads me to sketch an analysis of the evolution of Ricoeur's thinking on evil in his later works. As is well known, Ricoeur himself characterized this evolution by emphasizing how he had come to pay increasing attention to the question of evil undergone and suffering in relation to the issue of moral evil and guilt. But the whole problem, then, is to know exactly what the distinction between finitude and guilt becomes in this new context.

PHILOSOPHY AND EVIL, OR THE NECESSITY OF METHOD

What is the close link that connects the question of evil with the question of philosophical method for Ricoeur? And in what sense can it be said that the centrality of the issue of evil has proved to be decisive for the major methodological decisions of Ricoeur's philosophy?

The starting point of a philosophical thought or, more precisely, the problem through which it articulates its initial developments is often decisive for its orientation and its future direction. For this reason, the fact that a philosophy begins with a reflection on desire and human freedom rather than a reflection on perception or knowledge is far from indifferent. To start with perception, knowledge, or more broadly a theory of representative acts is for philosophical reflection to posit itself as rational knowledge or as a science and to settle from the outset into the comfort of a theoretical position that is supposedly autonomous. Conversely, a philosophical reflection that starts from human action, from the will and human freedom, runs the risk of colliding very quickly with an opaque, contingent, and absurd experience—the experience of evil, the bad will and of servile freedom—whose irrational nature directly threatens its project of a rational understanding of the world. Because it understands that it may be defeated by this confrontation with the experience of evil, philosophical reflection is then forced to ask itself the question concerning its theoretical limits as well as that of its method.

In the *Philosophy of the Will*, it is precisely this discomfort and this *challenge* of the experience of evil that motivates the whole development of Ricoeur's philosophy of the will. Even though Ricoeur often draws a parallel between his project of a phenomenology of the will and the project of the *Phenomenology of Perception* that Merleau-Ponty published five years earlier, we must assess—beyond their shared use of the phenomenological method—everything that separates the two philosophers. In a sense, the philosophy of Merleau-Ponty could be interpreted as a growing radicalization of the Greek definition of philosophy as *wonder*.[1] In other words, it is the mystery of the pure presence of the world, the mystery of the "there is," which is at the heart of Merleau-Ponty's philosophy and which thereby defines it fundamentally as a philosophy of perception. For Ricoeur, on the contrary, it is no longer the "there is" of the world but the "there is" of evil that provokes the philosopher's *feeling of indignation and revolt* and that sets philosophical questioning in motion. In other words, the shock produced by the absurd and tragic experience of evil leads philosophy to try to deal with this scandal of evil by orienting itself primarily toward a philosophy of action.

In the *Philosophy of the Will*, it has been said that the experience of fault and guilt governs the Ricoeurian approach to evil, and logically it is in the religious experience of sin and in the confession of evil in the religious consciousness of evil that the philosopher finds one of the fundamental *sources* of philosophical reflection. Ricoeur writes:

> Sin as an alienation from oneself is perhaps an experience more astonishing, disconcerting, scandalous than the experience of nature, and for this reason it is the richest source of interrogative thought [. . .] Sin is perhaps the most important opportunity to question, but also to reason incorrectly through premature answers. But just as the transcendental illusion, according to Kant, attests by its own embarrassment that reason is the power of the unconditional, so too the untimely responses of Gnosis and of the etiological myths attest that the most moving human experience, that of being lost as a sinner, communicates with the need to understand and arouses the awareness of its very character as a scandal. (Ricoeur 1967b: 8)

As the closing lines of this passage attest, Ricoeur sees the scandal of evil as the true origin of the "philosopher," and for this reason he stands apart from the dominant philosophical tradition which usually locates the origin of philosophy in the astonishment that accompanies our experience of the perception of the world. What does such an interpretation of the source of philosophy mean? Not that the theoretical task of philosophy should be renounced, nor that it should be entirely subordinated to a practical and ethical approach, but rather—something quite different—*that it is impossible to separate the problems of science from the problems of wisdom.*[2] The task of philosophy, in this sense, is to think theoretical and ethical questions together or, if you will, to always connect epistemological and ontological questions with ethical questions.

This elucidation of Ricoeur's definition of philosophy as a mixture of *"theoria"* and *"sophia"* is absolutely essential. For it allows us to understand why, in Ricoeur's philosophy, questions of method can never be reduced to mere epistemological questions, but always at the same time have an ethical scope.

It is indeed very striking to observe that the methodical arrangement which conditions the unfolding of the work, namely "the epoche of the fault and Transcendence" implemented in *Freedom and Nature* and in *Fallible Man*, has a scope that is both theoretical and ethical. Not only does this "bracketing" of the fault and Transcendence condition the very possibility of an eidetic description of the will which, without it, would end up with the irrational and unintelligible fact of servile freedom. As we will see in the second part, this is precisely what makes possible a certain way of thinking about human *finitude* in its irreducibility to *guilt*. But it is also what invites us to an ethical questioning about the being of appearing—that is to say, in this case, about the being of the will beyond the phenomenon of the bad will which is imposed on the empirical level. The epoche of the fault and Transcendence indeed works as an ethical and critical interrogation addressed to philosophy's theoretical claims. To be more precise, it has the role of challenging the "naive" or spontaneous claim of philosophical discourse to constitute itself as an autonomous science or self-knowledge, by foregoing any ethical questioning about what this discourse *does* in taking this or that theoretical or methodical stance.

That is a real application of the question of evil to the very status of philosophical reflection. *Because evil is an issue which cannot be approached from a purely theoretical and speculative point of view by philosophy, it is a question that reverberates on the act of philosophizing itself.* To the extent that philosophical reflection is the exercise of a freedom that thinks, it must wonder about the evil of which it is capable, when it plunges us into illusion, leads us to deny our finitude, or deceives us by putting forward unfounded and premature syntheses. In this sense, we can understand better why, if Ricoeur agrees with Husserl in criticizing the naivety of the "natural attitude," he also comes to denounce as a "second naivety," a "transcendental naivety,"[3] which consists—according to Husserl's idealistic interpretation of phenomenology in the *Ideas I* and in the *Cartesian Meditations*—of affirming the absolute constituting power of the transcendental ego and the correlative reduction of being to appearing. As Ricoeur writes: "Transcendental reflection gives rise to the illusion that philosophy could be a reflection without an *askesis*, without a purification of its own gaze [. . .]. The conquest of constituting subjectivity by philosophy is, strangely enough, a guilty cultural grandeur, like economic and political. Transcendental phenomenology is already the work of this ego that wills itself by itself and without ontological roots" (Ricoeur 1967: 232, tr. mod.).

It seems to me that what Ricoeur denounces here as a "transcendental naivety" is, going beyond Husserlian idealism, the theoretical naivety of a philosophy which believes that rational thought works spontaneously *in a realm of innocence*—as if the exercise of philosophical reason could escape from ethical questioning about the meaning and scope of its activity. From this perspective, one can ask whether the epoche of the fault and Transcendence that opens the *Philosophy of the Will*—as a methodological neutralization of ethics[4]—has, in Ricoeur's work, a scope that far exceeds the joint deployment of a phenomenology of the will and a reflexive anthropology of fallibility. Everything happens as if the question of evil, beyond the

Philosophy of the Will, haunted the whole of Ricoeur's work and continued in a more or less veiled or implicit manner to govern his method.

The most troubling thing about this issue is undoubtedly the "Epilogue" of *Memory, History, Forgetting*—a work originally published in 2000, forty years later than the second volume of the *Philosophy of the Will*. In the turn of a phrase, Ricoeur concedes that the phenomenology of memory he developed in the first part of the book has in fact been deployed—like his earlier phenomenology of the will—through an "epoche" of guilt. "As I put it in the *Freedom and Nature*, based upon the hypothesis of the *epoche* of guilt, it is within the eidetic indeterminacy of a description that as a consequence of its method does not recognize the distinction between innocence and guilt that the phenomenology of memory has been guided from start to finish" (Ricoeur 2004: 461).[5] This is to say that there is a continuity of Ricoeur's methodological position with regard to phenomenology and more broadly with regard to any philosophy that would purport to escape from a critical examination of its ethical implications. A few lines later, the philosopher even goes so far as to characterize his epoche of guilt as "a conscientious doubt as methodical as is Cartesian hyperbolic doubt" (Ricoeur 2004: 461) and he thereby reminds us of the decisive link which, in his philosophy, has constantly joined together the question of evil and the question of method. The epoche of the fault thus appears as this *inaugural methodological suspicion* that Ricoeur's critical hermeneutics exercises toward philosophical discourse and its pretensions in order to remind it of its unsurpassable ethical horizon.

It seems to me, for this reason, that the question of evil accompanies the whole of Ricoeur's work and that the epoche of guilt—whether it operates explicitly or implicitly—has precisely the function of *maintaining philosophical questioning within the horizon of the question of evil and of wisdom*, by preventing it from enclosing itself in a purely theoretical or theoretic stance.

GUILT, FINITUDE AND SUFFERING IN THE *PHILOSOPHY OF THE WILL*

Against the Philosophical Reduction of Evil to Finitude

What treatment, then, does the *Philosophy of the Will* give to the question of evil? As the introduction has already pointed out, the central thesis of the book is to affirm the existence of a fundamental discontinuity between *finitude and guilt*, that is, to make guilt a limit situation that is heterogeneous from the constitutive finitude of the human condition.

Before analyzing in more detail the meaning and scope of Ricoeur's thesis concerning evil, we must assess what makes it original. To defend, as Ricoeur does, the idea of an *irreducible difference between finitude and guilt* is to make a very bold decision that completely reverses the interpretation of evil within the dominant philosophical tradition. From Plotinus to Spinoza and from Leibniz to Jaspers and Heidegger, this dominant tradition has always tried to *reduce evil to finitude*. As Ricoeur points out in multiple passages of his work, there is an almost inherent tendency in the philosophical treatment of the problem of evil which consists of *reducing the "mythical" character of guilt* by referring evil to human finitude. Everything happens as if the philosopher had to *"demythologize" the fault* in order to be able to integrate it within the rationality of philosophical discourse.

What interests us, in this reduction of evil to finitude, is that it always includes at the same time a certain *thesis about the relationship between guilt and suffering*, that is, about what the philosophical tradition has referred to as *moral evil* and *physical evil*. To consider only one example in classical thought, the whole contribution of Leibniz's theodicy is to elaborate—beyond the notions of physical evil and moral evil—the new notion of "metaphysical evil" which refers specifically to an evil of finitude [*mal de finitude*] that is constitutive of the human. In other words, for Leibniz there is a natal imperfection of the created being, which makes it prone to suffering *and* to sin. In the context of a *metaphysics of creation,* one can then explain evil through the *finite ontological constitution of the human* not only because this constitution accounts for the existence of evil, but also because it allows *a unification of moral and physical evil* by referring them to a common origin in metaphysical evil.

In a completely different context, twentieth-century philosophies of existence—in particular, those of Jaspers and Heidegger—perform a similar gesture of reducing evil to finitude and it too functions as an attempt to unify evil by finitude. In volume II of his *Philosophy,* Jaspers equates the fault with a "limit situation"[6] and places this fact on the same plane as other "limit situations" such as death, suffering, and struggle. In so doing, Jaspers carries out a kind of *"secularization" of the fault* which gives it a "pseudo-homogeneity" with the other negative elements of human existence: it transforms the experience of the fault into a kind of general feeling freed from all mythical sense. So instead of thinking the fault on the basis of innocence, Jaspers pulls the fault over to the side of finitude, that is, to "the primitive, unfathomable, unchosen constitution of existence."[7]

For Ricoeur, the same goes for the approach to finitude and guilt that Heidegger develops in particular in § 58 of *Being and Time*. Because he seeks the original existential meaning of being-guilty, Heidegger is led to derive the guilty conscience from the *formal and finite structure* of existence. This existence, in its "being-thrown" and in its "being-toward-death," includes the fact that it is not the foundation of its being. And in the experience of anxiety, it discovers itself authentically as "being-in debt." Under such conditions, *Dasein* is neither more nor less guilty depending on actual circumstances; its being in debt does not result from the actuality of a fault committed but, "insofar as it exists every time factically," it is always already in debt, that is to say, guilty or indebted as long as it exists.

However, it is precisely this gesture of the "demoralization of conscience" in which the notion of debt is "too quickly ontologized at the expense of the ethical dimension of indebtedness"[8] that Ricoeur continually criticizes in Heidegger from his early works all the way up to *Oneself as Another*. For Ricoeur, even if Heidegger concedes in a note to § 62 of *Sein und Zeit* that the existential analytic of being in debt "does not 'know' fundamentally anything about sin" and that it only allows us to think about the ontological condition for the factical possibility of sin, nothing obliges the philosopher to leave it up to the theologian to think about sin and nothing obliges dispensing with the path that leads back from ontology to ethics, for it is this lack of a return from ontology to ethics that makes the existential analytic of being in debt ultimately equivalent to a reduction of evil to finitude.

As Ricoeur points out in the Introduction of *Freedom and Nature*, it is because Heidegger—undoubtedly under the influence of Kierkegaard—has missed the irreducible specificity of the experience of fault that he believes he can integrate it into the existential analytic and the unitary structure of "care"—and that the fundamental ontology thus turns out to be contaminated by a kind of general absurdity. For Ricoeur, everything happens as if the reduction of evil to finitude in contemporary philosophy found one of its main sources of inspiration in a certain interpretation of Kierkegaard's philosophy. In his book *Gabriel Marcel and Karl Jaspers: Philosophy of Mystery and Philosophy of Paradox*, Ricoeur in fact writes:

> Starting with Kierkegaard, the fault loses its *moral* character of forfeiture in order to assume an *ontological* meaning; sin is limitation itself, the narrowness of existence; but since existence deepens itself only by limiting itself, freedom and the fault become indistinguishable, at least if freedom seeks to be real "historically." But by becoming inevitable and constitutive, it seems to me that it is no longer, strictly speaking, what remorse reveals, that is, the double assurance that a value has been violated and that I could have acted and been otherwise; the ethical nuance introduced by value each time *violated* and the conviction of a possibility of innocence always *lost* constitute the meaning of guilt. It is this sense that is obliterated already in Kierkegaard, a little more in Jaspers, and completely in Heidegger. (Ricoeur 1948: 144)

Faced with this reduction of guilt to finitude that occurs in contemporary philosophy, what then is at stake in the Ricoeurian thesis regarding the irreducibility of guilt to finitude? And what follows in relation to suffering?

Starting from the moment when, in Jaspers or Heidegger, the fault acquires *the general sense of the misfortune of existence*, the important thing is to understand that it can no longer be understood as an *event that might not have been*. It can no longer, in other words, be apprehended against the background of innocence and hope, because it has become a *constitutive dimension of our finitude*. Even if the philosophies of existence seem to be at the antipodes of Leibnizian theodicy, they nevertheless develop along with it in a paradoxical complicity. By reabsorbing guilt into finitude, they come to *align the fault with suffering and death,* and their recourse to an *ontological concept of finitude* ultimately leads to what might be called a post-metaphysical conception of the unity of evil (both physical and moral).

Against this *constitutive guilt* which results from the reduction of evil to finitude, Ricoeur will defend both the idea of a *constitutive finitude* of the human and the idea of an *irreducible contingency* of the fault. It seems to me, in this sense, that Ricoeur's distinction between finitude and guilt should be interpreted primarily as a distinction between *structure* and *event*.[9] Indeed, to explain the fault through finitude would be to reduce evil to a necessary consequence of the *finitude of the structural constitution of the human* and correlatively to lose the *contingent dimension and irreducible event character of the fault*.

The whole methodical arrangement of the *Philosophy of the Will* can thus be construed as an attempt to dissociate finitude and guilt. It takes note of *the aporia of the inscrutable origin of evil* while preserving the irreducible event character of the fault. In this context, we have seen that it performs an epoche of the fault and Transcendence that allows—first in *Freedom and Nature* and then in *Fallible Man*—for the attainment of a conception of human finitude which is methodologically unbound from the question of evil and guilt. As is well known, *The Symbolism of Evil* will take up the burden of removing the abstraction of fault and of thinking the paradoxical and enigmatic experience of evil without distorting it. Between a phenomenological and reflexive approach that tells us about the *structural finitude of human-being* and the *anthropological possibility of evil*, but remains below its *actuality* and an ethical approach that always arrives too late, insofar as it starts from a concrete person who has already committed a fault, it will be, in the final work of the *Philosophy of the Will*, a matter of inventing another approach to the question of evil. This will involve precisely the deployment—from the confession that the religious consciousness makes of evil—of a *hermeneutics of the symbols and myths of evil* that is able to "save" the event of the fault. The philosopher will therefore appeal to *the religious experience of evil* recorded in the symbols and myths of evil, because it alone seems to protect against the philosophical reduction of guilt to finitude.

THE CONSTITUTIVE FINITUDE OF MAN ON THE THRESHOLD OF GUILT: "CONSTITUTIVE NOTHINGNESS" AND "EVENT-LIKE NOTHINGNESS"

What about this finitude, which in some way falls short of the ethical that is gained by way of the abstraction of the fault? To stick to the essentials, I would say that in *Freedom and Nature* it is probably the idea of *dependence* which best sums up the concept of finitude that is gradually disclosed through the phenomenological analysis of the will. "What we maintain," writes Ricoeur, "is that the Cogito is not entirely action, but action and passion" (Ricoeur 1966: 447). Indeed, the three constitutive moments of wanting: "to decide," "to move," and "to consent" all imply a form of *dependence* which translates into a *fundamental receptivity*, or if you will, a *fundamental dialectic between activity and passivity*. In a nutshell, deciding is "the act of the will which is based on motives"; moving is "the act of the will which activates abilities or powers"; consenting is "the act of the will which acquiesces to a necessity" (Ricoeur 1966: 341). The central thesis of the book, in fact, is that our will is *finite* because it depends on a *relative involuntary* of our motives and our powers, as well as an *absolute involuntary* which is located in the three figures of character, the unconscious and life. In this respect, if the limit idea of a reciprocity of *the voluntary and the involuntary* still describes a *relative finitude*, the notion of the absolute involuntary implies, on the other hand, a *passivity* and a *radical finitude* to which I must consent, if I aim to go beyond a freedom that is abstract and confined to a gesture of refusal, in order to arrive at an incarnate freedom.

The strength of this conception of finitude is that it allows us to think of the *necessity* of the absolute involuntary as a "sustained negation": that is to say as a "constitutive negation" that is not an evil, but only a *limit* to which I must consent. In other words, it provides access to a thinking of the *contingency* and the *facticity* of the human condition which, beyond the *sorrow* that accompanies it, is not contaminated by guilt or a general absurdity. Contingency is indeed the "sorrow of the finite" but it is not yet evil. For Ricoeur, our finitude is then summed up in the phrase "only human," by which he defines human freedom in the conclusion of *Freedom and Nature*. Our freedom is "only human" in the sense that "to will is not to create," that is, in the sense that it is a "receptive initiative" or a "dependent independence."

Faced with this first Ricoeurian conceptualization of a human finitude unbound from the concrete experience of guilt, the whole point of the complementary conceptualization developed in *Fallible Man* is to allow this time for a thinking of finitude within the broader framework of a *philosophical anthropology*. This means being able to think together human knowing, acting, and feeling. Truly speaking, here it is more than just a broadening of the analysis of the dialectic of activity and passivity developed in *Freedom and Nature*. In developing the concept of *fallibility*, *Fallible Man* gives rise to a conception of human finitude that goes to the encounter of evil; it now conceives finitude as *fragility* and this fragility, in turn, as the *ability to fail*. As such, even if this human capacity to fail does not yet explain *the event* of the fault, and if, in this sense, it fails to understand *the origin of evil*, it nevertheless has the merit of leading us to the very threshold of guilt by allowing us to understand its *possibility*.

The decisive contribution of *Fallible Man* is thus to propose a complete overhaul of the concept of finitude. Ricoeur writes: "To put it simply, I doubt that the concept of finitude is the central concept of philosophical anthropology; it is rather the triad of finitude-infinitude intermediary. One should not begin therefore with the simple, for example, the perception, but with the couple, the perception and the word; not with the limited, but with the antinomy of the limit and the unlimited" (Ricoeur 1978: 21). In this rejection of a philosophical anthropology centered solely on the concept of finitude, there is clear evidence of a direct critique of the Heideggerian ontology of finitude that is outlined, in particular, in his *Kantbuch*. For Ricoeur, indeed, human finitude is not merely a transcendence toward the world or an opening to the temporality of the transcendental imagination. According to him, finitude only makes sense on the basis of an *originary affirmation*[10] which constitutes the pole of the infinity of the human being. In this sense, human finitude is not what is *originary*, instead it is the "fragile mediation" that results from the relationship between the original affirmation that constitutes us and the "existential difference" which is its negation. It is, in other words, the *properly human limitation* which proceeds from our internalization of the *disproportion* between the finite and the infinite.

Everything that appears to us, in the human, as *finitude* or as "the negation of finitude" can only be revealed to us on the basis of an original and absolute affirmation which has always transcended or transgressed this finitude. The human is a *being of mediation* who can only understand itself through a continual synthesis of the finite and the infinite. As Ricoeur writes:

1) The situation of the human between being and nothingness, to speak like Descartes, is the situation of a being who itself is a *mediation* between being and nothingness, between the infinite and the finite.
2) This *mediation* is projected in the synthesis of the object, which is both discourse and existence, meaning and appearance.
3) This mediation is translated into *action* in the practical synthesis of the person who is both an end and existence, a value and presence.
4) This mediation is *reflected* internally in the feeling of a disproportion of the self to itself, of a noncoincidence or an internal "difference" which attests to the original fragility of human reality. (Reagan and Stewart 1978: 35)

Due to the epoche of the fault and Transcendence, the philosophical anthropology of *Fallible Man* thus brings to light a positive meaning of finitude as *limitation* which reveals the *fundamental possibilities of human-being* on this side of the Fault. Throughout the book, the emblematic notion that best sums up this positive meaning of finitude on this side of evil is the notion of "perspective," as a finite or "limited opening." For Ricoeur, the opening of "saying" (as a negation of "seeing") reveals the closure of my perceptual perspective; the opening of my practical destination (that is to the position of the existential-value of others as the "negative" of my faculty of desire) reveals the closure of my character; and finally the opening of *eros* (or intellectual love) reveals the closure of my vital feeling by performing a negation of pleasure as the affective horizon of my will to live. The closure of my theoretical, practical, and affective openness to the world, to others and to myself, is thus never identified with evil, even if it defines the narrowness of my freedom. This, of course, uncorks an "original discord" and a noncoincidence of the self to itself which defines the affective fragility of man, but this fragility and this fallibility remain below the fault and the actual experience of evil.

For Ricoeur, an abyss continues to separate the *possibility of evil* from its *actuality*, and that is the reason why only an interpretation of the myths of evil will allow for a symbolic thinking of the passage between the *finite structure* of the human and *the event* of the fault. Faced with the "constitutive nothingness" resulting from our finitude, the fault must remain an "event of nothingness"[11] whose origin is inscrutable. The enigma of evil, in fact, is not only the enigma of a *positing* of evil by human freedom but is also inextricably the enigma of a *passage* from fallibility (as a structure) to the fault (as an event) that reveals evil as an achievement of human weakness. In other words, the event of evil is not only the advent of a *guilty conscience*—that is to say of a conscience which has confessed evil and which judges itself to be free and responsible—it is also the advent of a conscience plagued by evil and which then appears as a *victim*. Between a *structural approach* to the fundamental possibilities of being human and its *finite freedom* and an *empirical approach of the historical human as always already guilty*—which is also to say as a human who is always already "disfigured" by the experience of evil—only a hermeneutic of the myths of evil, and in particular of the Adamic myth, thus seems able to allow us to think a passage from innocence to the fault in the immemorial time of the myth.

The Question of Suffering: Between Finitude and Guilt

If the central aim of the *Philosophy of the Will* is, as we have seen, to "save" the irreducibility of guilt to finitude, what then is the status of suffering? It seems to me that the richness of this work resides precisely in the fact that it proposes a *dual approach to suffering*. First, there is a somewhat "neutral" approach to suffering—it attempts to think a *"methodologically innocent" suffering* by way of an analysis of finitude made possible by the epoche of fault and Transcendence. Second, there is an approach to *"guilty suffering"* through a hermeneutic of the symbols and myths of evil. More precisely, the analysis of "guilty suffering" successively passes through an interpretation of *the symbolism of the stain in the archaic experience of the sacred* and then through a *dynamic interpretation of the Adamic myth* which consists in a recovery of the tragic theme of the Wicked God and the Hebraic theme of "just suffering" as presented in an exemplary manner in the *Book of Job*.

The first approach takes place in the third part of *Freedom and Nature* which is devoted to consent and necessity[12]; the second approach is located in Chapter 1 of the first part of *The Symbolism of Evil* which is devoted to the stain (Ricoeur 1967: 25–46); Chapter 2 of Part Two devoted to the "wicked God and the tragic vision of existence" (Ricoeur 1967: 161–174); and finally Chapter 5 of the same part, particularly § 2 which deals with the "reaffirmation of the tragic" (Ricoeur 1967: 306–346).

To sum things up, I would say first that *Freedom and Nature* develops a *philosophical interpretation of suffering* as a *decrease in being* in which suffering is *unbound from guilt and thought in terms of finitude* as an experience of our *fundamental contingency*. As Ricoeur writes: "Man born from woman (Job 14: 1) lacks being on its own" (Ricoeur 1967: 319); and it is precisely this inability to exist by oneself, this "sorrow of the finite" which is the source of suffering. In the context of the Ricoeurian phenomenology of the will, suffering thus flows from our facticity and our contingency: for humans, it is an experience of the *necessity of already being born* which is inextricably also an experience of the "nonnecessity of being." The abstraction of the fault performed in *Freedom and Nature* thus has the merit of bringing to light a "suffering of finitude" which is not yet identified with evil nor related to a generalized guilt.

The Symbolism of Evil is quite different precisely because it corresponds with a removal of this abstraction from the fault: through a hermeneutics of the primary symbolism of the stain and defilement, here Ricoeur tries to restore for us the most archaic *religious interpretation* of suffering. In this *archaic experience of the sacred* where "the ethical order of evildoing is not distinguished from the cosmological order of faring ill" (Ricoeur 1967: 27), evil and misfortune have not yet been dissociated and the suffering man feels vaguely guilty for the violation of an order. He must pay for this violation, and the fear of the impure, which is the anticipation of punishment and vengeance, continually consolidates this *fatal link between evil and misfortune*. Thus, just as punishment inevitably proceeds from defilement, *the "evil-undergone" of suffering turns out to be originally linked to the "evil-doing" of the fault*. The most remarkable feature of this analysis of the most primitive forms of "guilty suffering," is that it shows us that it is the archaic religious experience of defilement, instead of philosophical reflection, that is at the origin of the most tenacious schemas of the rationalization of the evil of suffering tied to the law of retribution.

Beyond this hermeneutics of the symbol of the stain, it is definitely in the final chapter (V. "The Cycle of Myths") of *The Symbolism of Evil* devoted to a *dynamic reading of the myths of evil* in light of the preeminence of the Adamic myth that Ricoeur outlines for the first time a *more personal interpretation of suffering* in relation with guilt. When he proposes the thesis of a *possible reappropriation of the tragic in the Adamic myth*—a myth that he considers to be the only truly anthropological myth—Ricoeur first emphasizes the "anti-tragic" character of this myth. In his eyes: "The fated aberration of man, the indivisibility of the guilt of the hero and the guilt of the wicked God are no longer conceivable according to the twofold confession, in the Augustinian sense of the word confession, of the holiness of God and the sin of man" (Ricoeur 1967: 311). Does this mean, then, that the Adamic myth is foreign to any form of tragic experience?

For Ricoeur, this is not the case. On the opposite side of an evil posited by freedom, there is the ineluctable character of the evil involved in the very exercise of freedom and in an evil that is always already there—as embodied by the figure of the serpent—elements which refer to a tragic anthropology. At the same time, it is necessary to recognize that the *ethical theology* of the Hebrews performs a critique of the initial chaos of the Theogony and of the wicked God of tragedy; it already offers a certain *revolution in the thought of suffering*. This revolution will be accomplished in the *Book of Job*.

In the *Book of Job*, by meditating on the *suffering of the innocent*, Jewish thought defeats the moral vision of the world and the theory of redistribution that accompanies the ethical theology that it itself has developed. According to Ricoeur, here there is a *return of ethical understanding to the tragic understanding of God* that, in the same gesture, leads us back from the prophetic accusation to tragic pity. We can then say that it is in this dichotomous vision of an Adam who is guilty and justly exiled and a Job who unjustly suffers that *suffering for the first time is thought on its own in its absolutely enigmatic, absurd, and scandalous character*. As Ricoeur writes: "Only a third figure could announce the transcending of the contradiction, and that would be the figure of the 'suffering servant' who would turn suffering, the evil that is undergone, into an *action* capable of redeeming the evil that is committed" (Ricoeur 1967: 324). But if the conclusions of *The Symbolism of Evil* allow us to see the *possibility of a reversal of the relationship between guilt and suffering*, it is necessary to acknowledge that this possibility remains a limit idea and does not ever take the form of an actual dialectical surpassing [*Aufhebung*].

Thus, unlike the *disconnection between suffering and guilt* that was allowed by the epoche of the fault in *Freedom and Nature*, it seems that the hermeneutical analyses of *The Symbolism of Evil* always lead us back to the idea of an *unsurpassable relationship between the evil of suffering and the evil of guilt*. In this sense, even the inverted relationship between suffering and guilt that emerges with the figure of the "suffering servant" still remains a *relationship*. If, as Ricoeur attempts to show, the dynamic history of the confrontation with the symbols and myths of evil carries within itself an *iconoclastic and critical movement*, it is necessary to admit that this movement fails to get us out of this relationship between guilt and suffering that was disclosed by the archaic symbolism of defilement. Whatever their dynamic evolution may be, the symbols and myths of evil continue to point toward the idea of an obscure *"common root" of suffering and guilt*.

In this context, the "Ricoeurian reaffirmation of the tragic" at the heart of the Adamic myth seems to me to have a dual function in *The Symbolism of Evil*. First, it prevents any reading of the cycle of myths in terms of a surpassing or *Aufhebung*. Second, through the exemplary figure of Job, it prevents any closing of the *enigmatic and insistent question of innocent suffering*.

The Evolution of Ricoeur's Thought on Evil and the Question of Suffering

In this third and final part of my reflection, I would like to confront the early analyses of finitude, guilt, and suffering in the *Philosophy of the Will* with the main lines of *the evolution of Ricoeur's thought on evil* in his later works. It seems to me that this evolution gives rise to a series of delicate questions that I would like to bring up now. These questions, as we will see, concern both a general interpretation of the *methodological sense of the hermeneutic turn* of Ricoeurian philosophy and a question about the *specific status of suffering in relation to guilt*.

Let me begin by citing two very illuminating passages from Ricoeur's "Intellectual Autobiography" which will serve as the starting point for my investigations.

The first quotation concerns *the retrospective interpretation that Ricoeur provides of the "hermeneutic turn"* carried out in *The Symbolism of Evil*. When, in this autobiographical text, Ricoeur returns to the meaning and scope of *The Symbolism of Evil*, he writes: "Beyond the *regional* problematic of the entry of evil in the world, it was also the *general* status of self-understanding that was questioned by *The Symbolism of Evil*. By accepting the mediation of symbols and myths, self-understanding incorporated into reflection a slice of the history of culture" (Ricoeur 1995: 17).

What is striking to me, in this first passage, is the use of the adjectives "*regional*" and "*general*." The problem of the origin of the evil which was absolutely central and inaugural for all of the *Philosophy of the Will* is now presented as "regional," while the question of self-understanding—in other words, a hermeneutics of the self mediated by myths, symbols, and texts—now becomes the central and general question for Ricoeurian philosophy.

Hence my first question is: what still justifies the Ricoeurian *grafting* of hermeneutics on phenomenology, if the latter is no longer directly legitimized by the concern to preserve the irreducible event of the fault? In *The Symbolism of Evil*, it is precisely the recognition of this *irreducibility of the event of the fault to finitude* which in turn is the basis for the idea of an *irreducibility of symbols and myths* to philosophical rationality. In other words, it led to the *"saving" of both the myth and the symbol* by showing the impossibility of philosophical thinking to do away with symbols and myths. It compelled the philosopher to accept the long detour of the interpretation of symbols and to abandon the idea of a presuppositionless philosophy, which would be absolutely autonomous and self-founding. As the exemplary analysis of the Adamic myth showed, the mythical *story* alone is able to account for the *contingent event of evil* "by stretching out in the form of a succession of events the paradox of the superimpression of the historical (the evil already in human history) upon the original (that is, the original goodness of being created)" (Ricoeur 1995: 17).

This question, expressed as an objection, is formidable, and I will limit myself here to suggesting only a path of reflection. It seems to me that the grafting of hermeneutics onto phenomenology, in Ricoeurian philosophy, can only be found legitimate, beyond *The Symbolism of Evil*, if one accepts a shift of emphasis from the event *of evil* to the event as such. Let me explain: in the works after the *Philosophy of the Will*, it seems that the event of the fault becomes only a *paradigmatic event*, or if you will, the paradigm for every event, in its character as a contingent occurrence. So if, after *The Symbolism of Evil*, one can continue to support the thesis of the irreducibility of symbols and myths to philosophical rationality, this would be due more fundamentally to an *irreducibility of the contingency of the event to any reflection on structure*—a structure that we have seen is linked to the philosophical concept of finitude (which was approached in a phenomenological or reflexive manner). We will then perhaps be able to understand why Ricoeur came to shift his attention from the *mythic story* to *historical* and *fictional stories*. And this is also why he was led to grant the notion of *narrative identity* a central place within self-understanding.

The second quotation from Ricoeur's "Intellectual Autobiography" concerns *the evolution of Ricoeur's thinking on evil* and the decisive role played by *Freud and Philosophy* within this evolution. "For me," writes Ricoeur, "the passage through Freud was of critical importance; besides the decreased concentration I owe him to him on the problem of guilt, and a greater attention to undeserved suffering, I owe to the preparation of my book on Freud the acknowledgement of the speculative constraints tied to what I have called the conflict of interpretations" (Ricoeur 1995: 21).

Setting aside the question of the conflict of interpretations and *Freud and Philosophy* which exceed the scope of my project, I will focus on this *passage from evil committed to evil undergone* in Ricoeur's reflection on evil. How should we interpret this evolution? What is its meaning and scope?

First, this evolution marks an increasing attention to the importance of *question of affectivity* which now leads the philosopher to associate his analysis of evil as a *practical category*—that is, as a category of doing or acting—with an analysis of evil as an *affective category*—that is, as a *category of feeling and suffering*. I think this evolution explains Ricoeur's increased attention to the problem of suffering: suffering is first *what affects us* and in this sense it might well be our most original experience of evil. The accusation and blame that are directed at a *guilty freedom* are then replaced by the complaint and lamentation of the *victim*.

Second, in the quotation that served as my starting point, Ricoeur speaks about an "undeserved suffering," which means that—under the impetus of his reading of Job and the tragic—he is increasingly operating with a *disconnection of suffering and the fault* that invites us to escape from the cycle of retribution, all the while pointing to the *irreducibility of suffering to the fault*. In this sense, one can read the evolution of Ricoeurian thought on evil as a continuous critical effort to deconstruct the *non-distinction of suffering and guilt* that is conveyed by the archaic religious experience of the sacred. Does this mean that Ricoeur abandons the question of guilt along the way? The answer is negative. For Ricoeur, the fact that we still experience suffering as an evil testifies to the "extraordinary intertwining"[13] of the phenomena of suffering and guilt. And it also remains true that the portion of suffering that results from the action of humans on each other is enormous. It seems to me, as such, that the theme of "the human being who acts and suffers"—which becomes central in *Oneself as Another*—corresponds precisely to the taking into account of this *profound entanglement of action and suffering* at the core of human plurality.

Third, insofar as the later developments of Ricoeur's thought on evil contribute to a disconnection of suffering from guilt at least partially, what interpretation of the *relationship between suffering and finitude* does he offer? I have insisted that the distinction between finitude and guilt in the *Philosophy of the Will* can be interpreted as a *distinction between structure and event*. Now, what strikes me in the later writings of Ricoeur—whether it is *Oneself as Another* or *The Just I and II*—is precisely the refusal to reduce suffering to what could be called a "purely structural" finitude.

How should this refusal be translated? It seems to me that it gives suffering mostly the status of *a contingent event*. Suffering—as a *decrease of our power to act*[14] in relationship with ourselves and in our relationship with others—then becomes synonymous with *vulnerability* and, more precisely still, *vulnerability to the event*. This is a thesis that appears very clearly in the article entitled "Autonomy and Vulnerability" (1995) which is published in *Reflections on the Just*. In this text, Ricoeur continues to insist that the "historical figures of fragility" and vulnerability are more significant than "the basic, fundamental figures, having to do with finitude in general" (Ricoeur 2007: 76). What exactly does that mean, however? It means that the dimension of the *passivity of the evil undergone* is interpreted by Ricoeur as a *vulnerability to the contingency of the event*. I cannot develop this hypothesis here, but I think the *three figures of alterity-passivity* in *Oneself as Another*—my own body and the flesh, the alterity of the other, and conscience—can be interpreted as three figures of an *affection by the event*. In short, there would be a dialectic that is "structural" between *ipse-identity* and *idem-identity*, as well as a dialectic of the "event" between ipseity and alterity. But it is in this latter dialectic that the essence of suffering as a diminution of our power to act will unfold.

I will end with a final question concerning the methodological order. If, as *The Symbolism of Evil* shows, only a hermeneutics of the symbols and myths of evil seems able to take up a reflection on guilt, then what type of philosophical discourse is suited to an analysis of suffering? And first of all, is such a discourse even possible? In the introduction of his 1986 article entitled "The Scandal of Evil," Ricoeur writes: "while we have some well-established traditions concerning moral evil and sin, we do not have any such traditions with regard to evil suffered and suffering, in other words, the figure of the human victim rather than the human sinner. The sinner gives much to talk about, the human victim, much to be silent about" (Ricoeur 1988: 57).

If *non-guilty suffering* is truly a scandal for thought, it also threatens to lead us to silence more than to the word by producing in the suffering person a real *crisis of symbolization*.[15] One might even wonder whether the myth that was an indispensable mediation for a thought concerned with preserving the *"transhistoric contingency"* of guilt does not become an obstacle for a thought that tries to think the *specific scandal of non-guilty suffering*. Can a thought of suffering still remain in the lineage of "demythologization"—that is, in the line of a thought that liberates the symbolic function of myth by relinquishing its explanatory function concerning the origin of evil? Should it not, on the contrary, think "against" myth or at least bracket myth? This is the very powerful thesis of Jérôme Porée's book *La Philosophie à l'épreuve du mal: Pour une phénoménologie de la souffrance* (1993).[16] According to the author, suffering must be the topic of an approach that is, above all, *phenomenological* because it is a phenomenon and an ordeal whose radicality fundamentally escapes from a hermeneutics of the symbols and myths of evil.

What about Ricoeur's position with regard to this topic? My interpretation, which I will only outline as a conclusion, is the following. I would say that by gradually passing from guilt to suffering, Ricoeur radicalizes a certain gesture of thought which is *already* determinant in *The Symbolism of Evil*. What is this gesture of thought? It seems to me that we can summarize the meaning of the demythologizing and dynamic reading of the Adamic myth proposed at the end of the book as a *critical gesture* that pulls the myth to the side of a *story of wisdom* rather than a *story of origins*. These are precisely the terms by which it is described in Ricoeur's "Intellectual Autobiography": "I was therefore able to interpret the biblical narrative, improperly called the narrative of the Fall, as a narrative of wisdom, which casts in the form of a narrative of the beginning the unthinkable event of the passage from the original goodness of created being to the wickedness that has occurred and been acquired by historical humanity" (Ricoeur 1995: 17). In this respect, the choice of the Adamic myth as the only truly "anthropological" myth seems to me to be clearly announcing Ricoeur's intention to move from myth to wisdom. It signifies unambiguously the choice to develop an *anthropological approach to evil* and the correlative refusal to follow the path of a *metaphysical speculation about evil*.

As early as *The Symbolism of Evil*, one can therefore find that Ricoeur's hermeneutics of guilt sketches a critical gesture leading it away from *myth* and in the direction of *wisdom*. In later works that will increasingly focus on the question of suffering, this very same gesture will be radicalized, to the point of turning against myth itself by carrying out an *escape from the mythical imaginary*. This passage to the limit is accomplished precisely by the *wisdom of the Book of Job* which refuses any *mythical consolation*. To the extent that this wisdom unfolds like a thought experiment which, assuming the hypothesis of the excess of an absolutely unjust suffering, ruins the mythical thesis of retribution, Ricoeur now insists on the fact that this wisdom represents "*an inverse line of thought from that of myth*" (Ricoeur 1988: 60). On the other hand, it can also be said that if the tragic theology of the wicked God is *unspeakable*, this is because *tragic wisdom* performs a critical gesture analogous to the wisdom of Job.

So can there be a *hermeneutics of suffering* just as there was a *hermeneutics of guilt*? It seems to me one of the headings in Ricoeur's essay "Suffering is not Pain"—"What suffering gives to thought"—is an echo of the conclusion to *The Symbolism of Evil*, and it allows an affirmative answer to this question. Even if suffering initially silences us and compels us to *deconstruct the symbolic and mythical imaginary* which obscures it,[17] as an event it also forces us to think, to interpret, and thereby to re-symbolize our existence. "The whole history of suffering," Ricoeur writes in *Time and Narrative*, "cries out for vengeance and calls for narrative" (Ricoeur 1984: 75). To create a narrative, in spite of the enormous opacity of suffering, is to attempt to symbolize or re-symbolize an experience. It is, in other words, to initiate a certain *imaginative work on suffering*. In my opinion, such a task may be the responsibility of the writer or poet who wants to express the powerful shaking of the experience of suffering, but it is also the responsibility of the historian or philosopher who is concerned, as Benjamin was, to preserve the history of the vanquished.

Translated by Scott Davidson

NOTES

1. This Greek definition of philosophy as "wonder" is, as is known, described by Aristotle's *Metaphysics A.2*.

2. It is interesting to note that this idea of the inseparable nature of the problems of science and of the problems of wisdom already appears in *Freedom and Nature*, in a critique that Ricoeur addresses to Husserl—not certainly about the question of evil, but about the problem of the unity of man and the union of the soul and the body. In the closing chapter of the book ("From Refusal to Consent"), Ricoeur writes: "Husserl believed he could separate the problems of rigorous science from the problems of wisdom, but once we reintroduce the existence of the body into the Cogito, the problems of wisdom communicate with those of knowledge" (Ricoeur 1966: 467, tr. mod.). It should be recalled that in *Philosophy as a Rigorous Science*, Husserl was defending the thesis that philosophy should be conceived as a science and not as a wisdom—adding that it should therefore opt for clarity as opposed to depth. What link can then be drawn between the problem of the union of mind and body and the question of evil? If one remembers that the entire *Philosophy of the Will* is animated by the search for an "integral Cogito," it will then be recalled that this search is inextricably ontological *and* ethical, since it aims at an experience of the unity of the human who has an experience of a "regained integrity," beyond the tragic experience of evil.

3. These expressions of "naturalistic naivety" and "transcendental naivety" are employed in Ricoeur's 1952 article: "Methods and Tasks of a Phenomenology of the Will" (Ricoeur 1967: 232).

4. Up to this point, we have talked about bracketing or neutralizing ethics when we talked about the method of the first two works of the *Philosophy of the Will*: *Freedom and Nature* and *Fallible Man*. Both of these works unfold under the abstraction of the fault and allow us to access the fundamental possibilities of being human below the level of the fault. But if we are to follow the "Introduction" of *Freedom*

and Nature, it should be added that this abstraction of the fault is also an abstraction of Transcendence, that is, an abstraction of the notion of salvation with which Ricoeur associates transcendence. What, then, about the removal of this double epoche of the fault and Transcendence? Due to the incompleteness of the *Philosophy of the Will*, this double abstraction will only be partially lifted. By developing a hermeneutic of the symbols and myths of evil, *The Symbolism of Evil* is indeed an actual removal of the epoche of the fault, but Ricoeur will never write the "poetics of the will" which purportedly would remove the abstraction of Transcendence by allowing us to conceive the active creativity of a regenerated and delivered freedom.

5. In this late work by Ricoeur, only the "Epilogue" devoted to "difficult forgiveness" is thus supposed to remove the epoche of guilt implemented in the phenomenology of memory.

6. Jaspers's term "limit situation" refers to situations—death, suffering, struggle, and fault—all of which are, in various ways, lesions of our empirical being and modalities of the failure of our human condition. Because they make our empirical condition untenable, they are a kind of "pedagogy of anxiety" that inspires us to transcend this condition by revealing our freedom.

7. This last formulation is borrowed from Dufrenne and Ricoeur (1947: 191).

8. These expressions are taken from Ricoeur's interpretation of the Heideggerian analysis of conscience [*Gewissen*] in the tenth study of *Oneself as Another* (Ricoeur 1992: 348–350).

9. For a more detailed analysis of this distinction between structure and event, see Amalric 2018.

10. For a detailed analysis of Ricoeur's retrieval of Nabert's concept of the "originary affirmation" in the conclusion of *Fallible Man*, see Chapter II ("Negativity and Originary Affirmation") of Amalric 2013: 225–280.

11. Ricoeur uses these two expressions of "constitutive nothingness" and "event-like nothingness" in "Methods and Tasks of a Phenomenology of the Will" (Reagan and Stewart 1978: 231).

12. See "The Sorrow of Contingency" in Ricoeur (1966: 450–456).

13. Ricoeur uses this phrase in his essay: "Evil: A Challenge to Philosophy and Theology" in Ricoeur (1995b: 250).

14. In "Suffering Is not Pain," Ricoeur explicitly acknowledges the "Spinozist accents" of this definition of suffering as a "decrease in the power to act," emphasizing the fact that "only acting can also be suffering." He is thus led to seek the signs of this decrease in the registers of speech, action, narrative and self-esteem.

15. This expression of the "crisis of symbolization" is borrowed from Porée (2000: 145). In this admirable book, Jérôme Porée borrows this expression himself from André Jacob: *L'Homme et le mal*, while commenting on the latter's thesis.

16. See Porée 1993. In his article "Suffering is not Pain," Ricoeur underscores his own debt to the then unpublished work of Jérôme Porée, and there is no doubt that Ricoeur's thought on suffering in the 1990s is nourished by this important book.

17. I am thinking in particular here of the deconstruction of the imaginary of death which *Living up to Death* carries out (Ricoeur 2009). Indeed, in these fragmentary notes, Ricoeur carries out a critical work on our representations of death which,

through a form of ascetic wisdom, aims to unbind death from evil, all the while liberating an affirmation of life in "the cheerfulness joined to a hoped-for grace to exist living up to death" (Ricoeur 2009: 7).

REFERENCES

Amalric, Jean-Luc. 2013. *Paul Ricoeur, l'imagination vive*. Paris: Hermann.
Amalric, Jean-Luc. 2018. La médiation vulnérable. Puissance, acte et passivité chez Ricoeur. Etudes Ricoeuriennes/Ricoeur studies, 9(2): 44–59.
Dufrenne, Mikel and Paul Ricoeur. 1947. *Karl Jaspers et la philosophie de l'existence*. Paris: Seuil.
Jacob, André. 1998. *L'Homme et le mal*. Paris: Editions du Cerf.
Porée, Jérôme. 1993. *La Philosophie à l'épreuve du mal. Pour une phénoménologie de la souffrance*. Paris: Vrin.
Porée, Jérôme. 2000. *Le Mal, homme coupable, homme souffrant*. Paris: Editions Armand Colin.
Reagan, Charles E. and David Stewart, eds. 1978. *The Philosophy of Paul Ricoeur: An Anthology of His Work*. Boston: Beacon Press.
Ricoeur, Paul. 1948. *Gabriel Marcel et Karl Jaspers. Philosophie du mystère et philosophie du paradoxe*. Paris: Editions du Temps Présent.
Ricoeur, Paul. 1965. *Freedom and Nature*.
Ricoeur, Paul. 1967a. *Husserl: An Analysis of his Phenomenology*. Trans. Edward G. Ballard and Lester Embree. Evanston: Northwestern University Press.
Ricoeur, Paul. 1967b. *The Symbolism of Evil*. Trans. Emerson Buchanan. Boston: Beacon Press.
Ricoeur, Paul. 1984. *Time and Narrative, vol. 1*. Trans. Kathleen McLaughlin and David Pellauer. Chicago : The University of Chicago Press.
Ricoeur, Paul. 1988. Le Scandale du Mal. *Esprit*, no. 140–141 (Juillet-Août): 57–63.
Ricoeur, Paul. 1992a. La souffrance n'est pas la douleur. *Psychiatrie française* (Juin).
Ricoeur, Paul. 1992b. *Oneself as Another*. Trans. Kathleen Blamey. Chicago: The University of Chicago Press.
Ricoeur, Paul. Intellectual Autobiography. In *The Philosophy of Paul Ricoeur*. Ed. Lewis E. Hahn. Chicago: Open Court, 3–53.
Ricoeur, Paul. 1995. Evil: A Challenge to Philosophy and Theology. In *Figuring the Sacred*. Trans. David Pellauer. Minneapolis: Fortress Press, 249–261.
Ricoeur, Paul. 2004. *Memory, History, Forgetting*. Trans. Kathleen Blamey and David Pellauer. Chicago: The University of Chicago Press.
Ricoeur, Paul. 2007. *Reflections on the Just*. Trans. David Pellauer. Chicago: The University of Chicago Press.
Ricoeur, Paul. 2009. *Living up to Death*. Chicago: The University of Chicago Press.

Index

Amalric, Jean Luc:
 Affirmation originaire, attestation, reconnaissance, 163;
 L'Imagination poético-pratique dans l'identité narrative, 103;
 Paul Ricoeur, l'imagination vive, 98n5, 199n9
Aristotle, 13, 56, 90–91, 94, 148–49, 153, 168, 198n1;
 Eudaimonia, 160n4;
 Nicomachean Ethics, 168
Ascárate, Luz:
 L'utopie: du réel au possible, 99
Augustine:
 Confessions, 170

Biran, Maine de, 66, 68, 138
Blundell, Boyd:
 Creative Fidelity, 60n19;
 Paul Ricoeur Between Theology and Philosophy, 60n19
body, 43, 50–51, 60n9, 133–35, 138–40, 142n20, 146, 198n2;
 embodiment, 43, 51, 55, 101, 107, 109, 112, 117, 126, 134, 137–38, 168;
 disembodied, 56;
 images, 119;
 incarnate being, 50, 107;
 incarnation, 50, 167;

language, 116, 134;
 mediation, 51;
 perspective, 136;
 as self, 134;
 sensations, 132.
 See also mystery, of my body
Brentano, Franz, 92, 96–97;
 Psychologie vom empirischen Standpunkte, 90–93
Brunschvicq, Léon, 46
Burgelin, Pierre:
 The Philosophy of Existence of Jean-Jacques Rousseau, 11
Butler, Judith:
 Precarious Life, 80n11

Charon, Rita:
 Narrative Medicine, 140n1
cipher, 4, 20, 137;
 of transcendence, xvii, 21, 36–37
communication, 26–27, 29–34, 39nn24, 25, 40n26, 45;
 concrete, 60n12, 120;
 confession, 4,-6, 8–9, 190.

Dennet, Daniel:
 Consciousness Explained, 140n4
Descartes, 20–21, 44–46, 50, 66, 70–71, 92, 105, 142n18, 146, 189;

Meditations on First Philosophy, 21, 91, 97–98n4
dialectic:
  broken or open, xxii;
  repetition of, 6.
  See freedom, dialectics of necessity; freedom
disproportion, 146–47, 150, 154, 163

enactment, 101–2, 104, 107–12, 114, 116, 119–21, 121, 121n5;
  enactive simulation, 114, 121n1;
  re-enactment, 107, 110, 114
evil, xv, xvii, xx–xxii, 4–9, 13, 15–16, 17n10, 17n18, 60n12, 74–76, 95, 133, 147, 154, 164–66, 172, 181–86, 188, 190, 193, 195–97, 198n2, 199n16;
  enigma of, 190;
  excess of, 65–66;
  and freedom, 7–8, 75–76;
  metaphysical, 185;
  moral, 147, 185, 187;
  origin of, 53, 75, 187, 189;
  physical, 185, 187;
  problem of evil, 51–52, 74, 179, 184;
  problem of suffering, xx–xxii, 38, 52;
  radical, 25;
  reduction of, 186–87;
  reflexive approach to, 75;
  religious experience of, 187;
  theodicy, 187;
  tragic dimension of, 76.
  See also mystery, of evil; suffering; symbolism, of evil; will, corruption of the

faith, 45, 59, 60n12;
  bad, 75
The Fall, xvii, xx, 4, 8–9, 11, 13, 15, 74, 164, 169, 197;
  fallenness, xiii, xvii, 3, 6–7, 15, 17n18, 57, 94, 97, 98n6, 165–67, 171, 173, 175–77;

fallibility, xvi, xx, 25, 43, 49, 51, 53, 95, 136, 146–47, 150, 154–56, 159n2, 163–64, 167, 183, 189;
  fallibility without fault, 95;
falling, 165, 177.
  See also tragedy, lost paradise
fault, ix–x, xv, xviii, xx, 4, 11, 15, 17–18, 38, 60n17, 76, 79, 79n1, 133, 159, 159n1, 170, 182, 185–87, 191–92, 195, 198n4;
  capacity to fail, 147, 163;
  epoche of the fault and transcendence, xx, 179–80, 182–83, 187, 190–91;
  exposed to failure, 147;
  innocence, xix, 10, 14;
  original sin, 25.
  See also The Fall; freedom, and fault; Nabert, Jean; symbol, symbolism of the fault
Ferry, Jean-Marc, 171–72
Fichte, Johann Gottlieb, 46, 71
finitude, xx–xxi, 21, 35–36, 137, 145–46, 184–88, 195;
  finite and infinite, x–xiv, xv, xxi–xxii, 6, 53, 55, 105, 133–34, 137, 142n18, 146, 148, 189;
  sorrow of the finite, 188.
  See also freedom, finite manner of; Pascal, disproportion; transcendence, of finitude
fragility, xiv, xv, 94, 136, 147, 150, 154–55, 158, 189–90
frailty, 74, 163
freedom, 7–8, 22–23, 25–26, 29–30, 33, 45, 49–50, 75–76, 86–87, 148, 170–72, 188, 190, 192, 195, 199n6;
  absolute freedom, 23;
  dialectics of necessity and freedom, 164;
  existential freedom, 23–24, 26–27;
  finite manner of, 148;
  of ideation, 87;
  incarnate, 188;

and necessity, 164, 170;
servile, 181, 183;
See also evil, freedom and; will, freedom of the

Gadamer, Hans-Georg, 33–34
Gallagher, Sean:
  Enactivist Interventions, 101, 108, 113;
  Frontiers in Human Neuroscience, 126;
  "A Pattern Theory of the Self," 140n3
Gilson, Etienne:
  Being and Some Philosophers, 99
Gouhier, Henri, 16n2
guilt, xx–xxi, 4, 8–9, 11, 25, 159, 159n1, 170–71, 179–80, 182–87, 189–93, 195–97;
  constitutive, 187;
  epoche of, 184, 199n5;
  guilty conscience, 190;
  guilty suffering, 191–92;
  philosophical reduction of, 187

happiness, xii, xiii, xix, xx, 13, 145, 147–49, 158m, 160n4, 168;
  happy memory, 156, 159.
  See also Aristotle, *eudaimonia*
Hegel, 59, 60n10:
  Phenomenology of Spirit, 30, 170
Heidegger, xvii, 19, 21, 28–29, 33, 35–36, 39n5, 39nn11, 12, 40n31, 41n39, 138, 185, 187;
  Being and Time, 20, 39n5, 41n38, 41n41, 185;
  Kant and the Problem of Metaphysics, xiv–xv, 189
Helenius, Timo:
  Between Receptivity and Productivity, 89–90
Henry, Michel, 132
hermeneutics, xviii, 3–7, 9–10, 15–16, 16n1, 33, 39n13, 54, 73, 85, 125, 132, 179, 184, 193–94, 196–97;
  hermeneutical circle, 37;

hermeneutical self, 139;
  of suspicion, 54;
  of the symbol, 97, 187, 191
historicity, 19, 25, 32–36, 40n32;
  terror of history, 19
historiography, 155, 160n6
history, 160n6
Honneth, Axel, 171–72
horizon, xii, 20, 30, 35, 40n36, 41n40, 149, 184, 190
humanity, xii–xiii, xv
Husserl, Edmund, xviii, xxii, 5, 13, 15, 28–29, 35, 40n36, 44, 59, 66, 85, 92–93, 96–97, 138–39, 183, 198n2;
  Cartesian Meditations, 138, 183;
  eidetic truths, 86–88, 96;
  epoche, 5, 35, 40n36, 88;
  Ideas I (translated *Ideen I* by Ricoeur), 40n36, 85–88, 96;
  Körper, 138;
  Logical Investigations, 92;
  phenomenological reduction, 5;
  transcendental ego, 46, 93, 183;
  transcendental naivety, 183.
  See also Fault, epoche of the
Hutto, Dan, 141n12:
  "Narrative Self-Shaping: A Modest Proposal," 141n13
Hutto, Dan and E. Myin:
  Narrative and Understanding Persons, 131;
  Evolving Enactivism, 102, 108–10, 115–16

identity, 145;
  idem-identity, 127–33, 140, 140n6, 142n22, 152–53, 166, 196;
  ipse-identity, 127, 129, 132, 140, 140–41n6, 152–53, 160n11, 166, 196;
  phenomenal self, 137–39.
  See also body, as self; hermeneutics, hermeneutical self; narrative, identity

imagination, xviii–xix, 4, 12–14, 89, 95–96, 98n5, 102–3, 105, 107–14, 117–19, 120–21, 121nn2, 3, 4, 198;
of the essential, 173;
of innocence, 9–11, 13, 95–96;
mythical, 15, 198;
philosophical imagination, 14;
of reign, 13–14;
social imaginary, 120–21, 121n5;
transcendental, 89, 93, 96–97, 98n5, 104, 189;
utopian, 14.
See also narrative, imagination

Jaspers, Karl, xvii, 4, 16n2, 19, 21, 30, 38n2, 38n4, 39n15, 39n19, 40n27, 40–41n37, 41n39, 41n45, 45, 62n18, 185, 187;
Introduction à la philosophie, 22, 37, 39n22;
"La Raison et l'existence," 20, 26, 28, 31, 38n3;
Philosophy, 19–28, 33–35, 37, 39n10, 39nn16, 17, 39n23, 40n25, 40n31, 41n38, 41n43;
Vernunft und Existenz, 20–21.
See also ciphers, of transcendence; communication; freedom, existential freedom; historicity; limit situation

Kant, Immanuel, x–xiv, xvi, xviii, xxiin1, 9–13, 22n1, 25, 27, 44–46, 56, 59, 66–68, 74–75, 80n9, 85, 88–89, 93, 104, 147, 149, 158, 172–75;
Anthropology from a Pragmatic Point of View, 172;
Critique of Pure Reason, xi, 77, 90, 90n3, 104, 174;
"Essay on Radical Evil," 8, 12, 73;
Groundwork for the Metaphysics of Morals, 175;
Lectures on Logic, xi;
Religion within the Limits of Reason Alone, 16nn8, 9, 17n10, 74–75.
See also evil, radical; Heidegger, Kant and the Problem of Metaphysics; imagination, transcendental; transcendence, transcendental synthesis

Kearney, Richard:
Thinking the Flesh with Paul Ricoeur, 103
Kierkegaard, 19–20, 22, 36, 170, 186

Lachelier, Jules, 45–46, 66, 80n3
Lagneau, Jules, 45–46, 66–67
Leibniz, Gottfried Wilhelm, 185, 187
Levinas, Emmanuel, 31–32, 44, 80n3
limit situation, 32–36, 38, 40n35, 41n42, 170, 184–85, 199n6

MacIntyre, Alasdair:
After Virtue, 141n9
Marcel, Gabriel, xv, xvii–xviii, 4, 19, 31–32, 41n45, 43–45, 51–53, 57–60, 60n1, 62n18;
Awakenings, 60n3;
Being and Having, 45, 56–57;
"Existence and Objectivity," 45;
Gabriel Marcel's Perspectives on the Broken World, 46–47, 50, 58;
Metaphysical Journal, 45–47, 49–50, 60nn5, 6, 60n8;
"On the Ontological Mystery," 45;
The Philosophy of Existentialism, 60n2;
Tragic Wisdom and Beyond, 45, 48, 60n3, 60n5, 60nn10, 11, 12.
See also reflection, primary and secondary
Marx, Karl, 60n10
Merleau-Ponty, Maurice:
Phenomenology of Perception, 60n5, 181
misery:
pathétique of misery, 55, 59.
See also passion, pathos of misery

Musil, Robert:
  Man Without Qualities, 128
mystery, 20, 43–44, 48–49, 53, 60n6, 60n11;
  of evil, 52–53, 60n11;
  of my body, 50–51;
  mysterious interchange between freedom and gift, 58;
  ontological, 54
myth, x, xiii, xxi, 4, 6, 9–11, 13, 15–16, 96, 98n6, 169–70, 185, 187, 190–91, 193–94, 196–97;
  Adamic, 74, 190, 192, 194, 197;
  concrete mythics, x, 3–4, 7;
  defilement, 191–92;
  demythologize, 185, 196–97;
  mythical consolation, 197;
  transgression, 135.
  See also the Fall; imagination, mythical

Nabert, Jean, xv, xviii, 8–9, 17n12, 46, 49, 65–67, 69–72, 75, 79, 80n9;
  Elements for an Ethic, 65, 67, 69, 71–73, 76, 79, 79n2;
  Essay on Evil, 8, 76, 79n2;
  Inner Experience of Freedom, 79n2, 80n8;
  L'essai sur le mal, 67;
  L'expérience intérieure de la liberté et autresessais de philosophic morale, 67, 80nn4, 5.
  See also reflection, reflexive philosophy
narrative, 5, 9, 14–16, 108, 111, 118, 120, 128–32, 138–39, 142nn22, 23, 145, 149–57, 159, 160nn5, 6, 197, 199n13;
  of action, 152;
  autobiographical narrative, 108;
  character, xix–xx, 145;
  coherence, 129–30;
  historical, 111, 158;
  historical fiction, 160n6;
  idealism, 157;
  identity, xix, 125–26, 128, 129–31, 133–35, 138–40, 140n6, 141n16, 142n18, 142n21, 194;
  imagination, 120;
  narrator, 154;
  performance, 151;
  self, xix, 127, 140, 141n2;
  strong narrativism, 126;
  voice, 155, 158
Nebel, Gerhard, 16n2
Nietzsche, 19–20

Pascal, Blaise, 21, 53, 154;
  Pensees, xxi, 61n16.
  See also disproportion
passion, xiii, xiv, 12–13, 172;
  pathos, 14;
  pathos of misery, xxi–xxii;
  pathos of suffering, 79, 80n10
Percy, Walker, 52–53, 61n15;
  Love in the Ruins, 52–53
person life view, 126–27, 140n5
perspective, xi–xii
Plato, xxi, 17n17, 27–28, 147
Porée, Jérôme:
  La Philosophie à l' épreuve du mal, 197, 199n15
Proust, Marcel, 153

Rawls, John:
  veil of ignorance, 31
Reagan, Charles:
  Paul Ricoeur: His Life and Work, 44
reflection, 67, 69–71, 98n5;
  primary and secondary, 48, 54, 59;
  reflexive philosophy, 66–67, 72–73, 80n4.
  See also evil, reflexive approach to; transcendental, reflection
Revaisson, Félix, 66
Ricoeur, Paul:
  Á l' école de la phénoménologie, 16n6, 94;
  The Conflict of Interpretations, 67, 70–74, 80n6;

The Course of Recognition, 40n27, 40n46, 164–65, 171–72, 174, 176, 180;
Critique and Conviction, 44–45;
Elements for an Ethic, 80n9;
"Evil—A Challenge to Philosophy and Theology," 180, 199n12;
Fallible Man, ix–xi, xiv–xxi, 3, 6–10, 13, 17n17, 39n9, 43–44, 49–53, 55–59, 60n14, 60n17, 65–66, 68–70, 72–73, 76–79, 79n2, 85, 89–91, 93–95, 98n5, 101–11, 116–17, 119, 125–26, 129, 132–33, 135–40, 141n15, 142n21, 145–47, 149–51, 153–54, 156, 158–60, 163–64, 168, 171–77, 180, 182, 187–90, 198n4, 199n9;
Finitude and Guilt, ix, x, xx, 5, 7, 156, 159nn1, 2, 179;
Freedom and Nature, ix–x, xv, xviii, xx, 6, 8, 21, 25–26, 36, 39n6, 39n21, 43, 49–51, 54, 56, 59, 62nn20, 21, 79n2, 95, 101, 107, 110–11, 137, 146–47, 153–54, 158, 160n3, 164–65, 167–68, 170–71, 176, 179–80, 182, 186–89, 191, 198n4;
Freud and Philosophy, 195;
From Text to Action, 16n4, 66, 103, 105, 109, 118–19, 157, 165, 168;
Gabriel Marcel and Karl Jaspers, 21, 31, 45, 186;
Gabriel Marcel and Phenomenology, 59;
"The Hermeneutics of Symbols," 74;
Histoire de la philosphie allemande, Appendix, 94;
History and Truth, 16n2, 78, 173, 175–76;
"Intellectual Autobiograpy," 19, 54, 80n4, 154, 160n5, 195, 197;
The Just, 180, 196;
Karl Jaspers et la philosophie de l'existence, 19, 24, 28–29, 36, 38, 38n2, 39n10, 40n32;
La marque du passé, 159;
La mémoire, l'histoire, l'oubli, 158;
La significatino de l' action se détache de l'événement de l'action, 151;
"*L'attestation: entre phénoménology et ontologie,*" 157;
Lectures on Ideology and Utopia, 97n1;
The Lectures on Imagination, 97n1;
L'essai sur le mal de Jean Nabert, 17n12;
L'homme et son mystère, 53, 56;
"Life in Quest of Narrative," 142n23, 152;
Living up to Death, 199n16;
Memory, History, Forgetting, 33, 36, 38, 146, 156, 158, 160nn11, 12, 176, 184;
Méthod réflexive appliqué au problème de Dieu chez Lachelier et Lagneau, 80n3;
Methods and tasks of a phenomenology of will, 198n3, 199n10;
Oneself as Another, xix, xxiin1, 17n14, 32, 101–3, 105, 111, 118, 125, 129–32, 138–39, 140n2, 142nn20, 21, 142n23, 146, 153, 160n11, 164–65, 167, 176–77, 180, 185, 195–96, 199n8;
Parcours de la reconnaissance, 156, 158;
Philosophie de la volonté, 98n5;
Philosophy as a Rigorous Science, 198n2;
The Philosophy of the Will, 3, 43, 49, 53–54, 85, 179–81, 183–84, 190, 193–96, 198n2, 199n4;
Poetics of the Will, 49;
Reflections on the Just, 180;
"The Scandal of Evil," 180;
"Suffering is not Pain," 180, 199n13;
Symbolism of Evil, ix–x, xv, xvii, xx, 3, 5–6, 9–11, 15, xvin2, 49,

74, 79nn1, 2, 80n10, 96, 159n1, 168, 179, 187, 191–94, 196, 198, 199n4;
Temps et recit, 3, 157;
Time and Narrative, 132, 146, 150, 155–56, 160n5, 198;
"Tragic Guilt and Biblical Guilt," 5;
"What is a Text? Explanation and Understanding," 61n15
Rousseau, Jean-Jacques, xv, xvi–xvii, 10–13, 17n13, 57, 74

Sartre, Jean-Paul, 44–45, 60n1, 78, 132, 141n15, 148.
See also faith, bad
Schechtman, Marya, 140n4, 140n6, 141n9, 141n11;
The Constitution of Selves, 126, 128–29, 140n6;
Staying Alive, 126–27, 130, 140n5, 141n16;
Stories, Lives, and Basic Survival, 130–31.
See also person life view
Scheler, Max, 94
Schelling, Frederick Wilhelm Joseph, 49
Spinoza, Baruch, 49, 69, 71, 80n7, 80n9
Strawson, Galen:
"Against Narrativity," 130, 141n10
Suarez, Francisco, 92
suffering, 77–78, 154–55, 179–81, 185–86, 190–93, 195–97, 199n6, 199n13;
innocent, 193, 195–96;
suffering of, 65–66, 77, 79;
suffering of the fault, 79, 195.
See also guilt, guilty suffering; passion, pathos of suffering
symbol, xiv, 4–5, 37, 98n5, 109, 112, 114, 120–21, 121n5, 160n6, 190, 193–94, 196–97;
crisis of symbolization, 196, 199n14;
deciphering, 4–5, 20–21, 37, 51, 134;
gives rise to thought, 7;
starting from the, 7;
symbolics, 151;
symbolism of evil, 6–10;
symbolism of the fault, 79n2.
See also cipher; hermeneutics, of the symbol

Tolston, Jay:
Pilgrim in the Ruins, 61n15
tragedy, 5, xviii2, 32, 76, 182, 191–93, 197, 198n2;
Book of Job, 191–93, 195, 197;
drama of divided human being, 168;
lost paradise, 168, 170;
See also evil, tragic dimension of
transcendence, 3, 20, 29–32, 36–38, 39n5, 40n33, 41n40, 43–45, 49, 58, 111, 135, 137, 149, 179–80, 182–83, 189, 192, 199n4
of finitude, 21;
the holy, 168;
and language, 142n18;
transcendental argumentation, 59;
transcendental conditions, 171;
transcendentalism, 106;
transcendental reflection, 55, 62n19, 98n5;
transcendental synthesis, 104, 106–7.
See also cipher, of transcendence; imagination, transcendental; fault, epoche of fault and transcendence; Husserl, transcendental ego; Jaspers, ciphers of transcendence

Varela, Francisco J., 107, 123

Wahl, Jean, 44
Weil, Eric, 38n4
will, xxiii, 6, 101, 107, 149, 169, 181, 183, 188;
bad will, 147, 156, 181;
corruption of, 74;
and desire, 168, 181;
eidetics of, ix, 3, 15, 182–83;
empirics of, ix, 7, 147;

freedom of the, ix, 8–9, 23, 75, 181;
involuntary, ix–x, 25, 85, 146–47, 150, 153, 167, 188;
phenomenology of, 158;
philosophy of, 146, 152;
Poetics of, 3, 199n4;
servile, 7–9;
voluntary, ix–x, 85, 146, 150, 167, 188;
weakness of, 74.
See also evil, and freedom

Zahavi, Dan, 136–37, 139;
Self & Other, 131, 132, 133, 139, 140n1, 141–42n16;

About the Contributors

Jean-Luc Amalric is Agrégé and Doctor of Philosophy from the University of Paris 1, Panthéon-Sorbonne. He is a Professor of Philosophy of Art and Design in Nîmes (CPGE) and Associate Researcher at the EHESS, Paris (Ecole des Hautes Etudes en Sciences Sociales–C.R.A.L: Centre de recherches sur les Arts et le Langage). Together with Farhang Erfani, he is the general editor of *Etudes Ricœuriennes/Ricœur Studies*. A member of the Scientific Board of Advisors (*Conseil Scientifique*) of the Ricœur Archives (*Paris*), he is currently editing and translating, in collaboration with George Taylor, the "Lectures on Imagination" (a course taught by Paul Ricœur at the University of Chicago in 1975). He is the author of *Ricœur, Derrida. L'enjeu de la métaphore* (P.U.F., 2006) and *Paul Ricœur, l'imagination vive: Une genèse de la philosophie ricœurienne de l'imagination* (Hermann, 2013).

Luz Ascárate holds a doctorate in Philosophy and Social Sciences (EHESS-PUCP). She belongs to the Peruvian Circle of Phenomenology and Hermeneutics (PUCP), to the Center of Research on Arts and Language (EHESS), to the Digital Ricoeur Project, and is an intern at the Fonds Ricoeur. A specialist in Paul Ricœur's phenomenological philosophy, she has published several articles and book chapters devoted to the confluence of phenomenology and hermeneutics.

Scott Davidson is Professor of Philosophy at West Virginia University. His work focuses primarily on French phenomenology (Levinas, Henry, Ricoeur, Marion). In addition to many articles and chapters on Ricoeur, he has edited three other books on Ricoeur: *A Companion to Ricoeur's Freedom and Nature* (Lexington, 2018), (with Marc-Antoine Vallée) *Hermeneutics and Phenomenology in Paul Ricoeur* (Springer, 2016), and *Ricoeur Across the*

Disciplines (Continuum, 2010). He currently serves as an editor of the *Journal of French and Francophone Philosophy* (www.jffp.org).

Geoffrey Dierckxsens currently works as a Post-Doctoral Researcher in the Institute of Philosophy of the Czech Academy of Sciences (CAS) in Prague. He specializes in French phenomenology and hermeneutics, and in contemporary analytical philosophy (moral theory and philosophy of mind). His publications include *The Animal Inside. Essays at the Intersection of Philosophical Anthropology and Animal Studies* (Rowman and Littlefield, 2017) and *Paul Ricœur's Moral Anthropology: Singularity, Responsibility and Justice* (Lexington Books, 2017), which situates Ricœur's moral anthropology in relation to contemporary moral theories in analytical philosophy.

Daniel Frey is Professor of Philosophy and of the Psychology of Religion in the Faculté de Théologie Protestante at the Université de Strasbourg. In addition to numerous articles on Ricoeur's thought, he is the editor of the following books: *La jeunesse d'une pensée. Paul Ricœur à l'Université de Strasbourg (1948–1956)*, (Presses universitaires de Strasbourg, 2015); Paul Ricœur, *Écrits et conférences 2. Herméneutique. Textes rassemblés et annotés par Daniel Frey et Nicola Stricker. Présentation par Daniel Frey* (Seuil 2010); P. Bühler and D. Frey (dir.), *Paul Ricœur: un philosophe lit la Bible. À l'entrecroisement des herméneutiques philosophique et biblique* (Labor et fides, 2011); Paul Ricœur, *Herméneutique. Cours professé à l'Institut Supérieur de Philosophie de l'Université Catholique de Louvain (1971–1972). Édition électronique établie par Daniel Frey et Marc-Antoine Vallée* (Fonds Ricœur, 2014); and *L'interprétation et la lecture chez Ricœur et Gadamer* (Presses universitaires de France, 2008).

Brian Gregor is Associate Professor of Philosophy at California State University, Dominguez Hills. He has published numerous articles on religion, ethics, and esthetics, and is the author of two books: *A Philosophical Anthropology of the Cross: The Cruciform Self* (Indiana University Press, 2013) and *Ricoeur's Hermeneutics of Religion: Rebirth of the Capable Self* (Lexington Books, 2019).

Annemie Halsema is Assistant Professor of Philosophy at Vrije Universiteit Amsterdam (The Netherlands). Her research interests are in the fields of phenomenology, hermeneutics, and feminist philosophy. She has published some articles on Ricoeur's notions of the self and the body, is the author of two books on Luce Irigaray (1998 and 2010) and edited several volumes, including *Feminist Explorations of Paul Ricoeur's Philosophy* (with Fernanda Henriques, Lexington 2016).

About the Contributors

Timo Helenius received his PhD in philosophy from Boston College in 2013 and has been a Visiting Scholar at the Department of Religious Studies at Brown University since 2016. Helenius has taught philosophy and ethics at Boston College, Mount Ida College, and—most recently—at the University of New Brunswick Saint John as a Visiting Assistant Professor of Philosophy. Helenius's research and publications have focused on contemporary Continental philosophy in general and on Paul Ricoeur in particular. His work, *Ricoeur, Culture, and Recognition: A Hermeneutic of Cultural Subjectivity*, was published by Lexington Books (Rowman & Littlefield) in 2016.

Jérôme Porée is Professor in the UFR de philosophie at the Université de Rennes I. A specialist on Paul Ricoeur, he is the author of a dozen books, including most recently *L'existence vive* (Strasbourg 2017) and *Phénoménologie de l'aveu* (Hermann, 2018).

Pol Vandevelde is Professor of Philosophy at Marquette University. He specializes in contemporary French and German philosophy, theory of interpretation, critical theory. He is the author of *Être et Discours: La question du langage dans l'itinéraire de Heidegger (1927-1938)* (Académie Royale de Belgique, 1994); *The Task of the Interpreter: Text, Meaning, and Negotiation* (University of Pittsburgh Press, 2005); and *Heidegger and the Romantics: The Literary Invention of Meaning* (Routledge, 2012), among other books. He is the coeditor of the bilingual journal *Études phénoménologiques—Phenomenological Studies*.

www.ingramcontent.com/pod-product-compliance
Lightning Source LLC
Chambersburg PA
CBHW021547020526
44115CB00038B/867